THE EVOLUTION OF COMPUTATION IN ARCHITECTURE

This book is the first comprehensive overview of the pioneering works, events, and people that contributed to the paradigm shift defined by computation in architecture.

Only recently has computation fostered profound new ways of designing, fabricating, constructing, and thinking about architecture. While the profession sits at the end of the beginning of this historically transformative shift, it is now possible to look back upon the rapidly maturing landscape of projects, influencers, and tools that have finally begun to catch up with the visionary thinking of the past. Readers are guided through the fascinating and fast-paced historical timeline of the development of computation in architecture. Beginning with an account of the pioneering futuristic thinkers, the authors then guide the reader through the birth of computation, the appropriation of tools and the impact of experimentation on the profession, leading into the legitimacy of research and how paradigms have been expanded. The examples and influences are presented in a way that they can be understood and built upon.

This book is a must-read for students of computation in architecture as well as researchers and practicing architects thinking about how the tools we use and the ways we design our buildings and environments with them can truly impact our lives.

Michael Fox received his Master of Science in Architecture degree with honors from MIT and his undergraduate professional degree in Architecture from the University of Oregon. He has been elected twice as the President of ACADIA (Association for Computer Aided Design in Architecture). Fox founded a research group at MIT to investigate interactive and behavioral architecture, which he directed for 3 years. He has taught at Art Center College of Design, USC, MIT, HKPU, and SCIARC and is a Full Professor at

Cal Poly Pomona. Fox's work has been featured in numerous international periodicals and books and has been exhibited worldwide. He is the author of two previous books on architectural computation. He is a practicing registered architect and directs the office of FoxLin Architects.

Brad Bell received his Master of Science in Architecture degree from Columbia University Graduate School of Architecture Planning & Preservation and a Bachelor of Environmental Design from Texas A&M. Brad is the former Director of the School of Architecture (2016–2023) and an Associate Professor at The University of Texas at Arlington. He currently directs the Digital Architecture Research Consortium (DARC) at UT Arlington and was a founding member of TEX-FAB (2008–2017). In 2020 Brad was honored by the Texas Society of Architects with the Award for Outstanding Educational Contribution in Honor of Edward J. Romieniec FAIA. He has previously taught at Tulane University and the University of Colorado. His research focuses on innovative material applications and computational fabrication within the architectural design process.

THE EVOLUTION OF COMPUTATION IN ARCHITECTURE

Michael Fox and Brad Bell

With Forewords from Mario Carpo, Jenny Sabin, and Branko Kolarevic

Routledge
Taylor & Francis Group
LONDON AND NEW YORK

Designed cover image: Axel Schmitzberger.

First published 2025
by Routledge
4 Park Square, Milton Park, Abingdon, Oxon OX14 4RN

and by Routledge
605 Third Avenue, New York, NY 10158

Routledge is an imprint of the Taylor & Francis Group, an informa business

British Library Cataloguing-in-Publication Data
A catalogue record for this book is available from the British Library

Library of Congress Cataloging-in-Publication Data
Names: Fox, Michael, 1967 August 22- author. | Bell, Bradley, author.
Title: The evolution of computation in architecture / Michael Fox and Bradley Bell.
Description: Abingdon, Oxon : Routledge, 2025. | Includes index. |
Identifiers: LCCN 2024020912 | ISBN 9781032670836 (hardback) |
ISBN 9781032670713 (paperback) | ISBN 9781032671208 (ebook)
Subjects: LCSH: Architectural design--Data processing--History. |
Architecture--Technological innovations.
Classification: LCC NA2728 .F72 2025 | DDC 720/.4--dc23/eng/20240722
LC record available at https://lccn.loc.gov/2024020912

ISBN: 978-1-032-67083-6 (hbk)
ISBN: 978-1-032-67071-3 (pbk)
ISBN: 978-1-032-67120-8 (ebk)

DOI: 10.4324/9781032671208

Typeset in Optima
by Taylor & Francis Books

CONTENTS

ACKNOWLEDGEMENTS AND DEDICATIONS

This book was in the making for a very long time and such a book would not have been possible without the contributions of many fantastic pioneers. Thanks especially to those who generously contributed images of their work. Thanks to the many people who read various parts of this book and provided invaluable feedback including Axel Kilian, Mario Carpo, Branko Kolarevic, Jenny Sabin, Sasha Ortenberg, Aron Cayer, and Chris Lasch. Thanks to Axel Schmitzberger for the cover design. Thanks to my amazing wife Juintow Lin for putting up with one more project and to Juneau, Ori and, Io who just like to see their names in books. Thanks to Brad for the amazing partnership. Last, although he will likely cringe when he reads this: *This book is dedicated to the selfless and brilliant Axel Kilian.*

Michael

* * * *

Many have provided inspiration, focus, and encouragement along the journey of this project. Through it all, I am reminded we never really do anything in a vacuum. Events of our past, if not remembered, fail to shape our future. Reliving some of my own memories through the writing of this book has made me excited again for what lies ahead. I am also reminded of how inspired I am by the community of people this book is about.

Our deepest gratitude goes to Axel Kilian, Mario Carpo, Branko Kolarevic, Jenny Sabin, Sasha Ortenberg, Aron Cayer, Chris Lasch, Andrew March, and Axel Schmitzberger for the cover art. A special thanks to Michael, a friend who became a writing partner and then an even better friend.

However, my dedication truly goes to Julie, who has made life a ride I am always up for taking – her joy is forever contagious. To Witt, Bliss, and Iris, who have made smiling easy most days. And to Vera June, who has always believed there are stories that are worth telling.

Brad

FOREWORD

Mario Carpo

Where is the divide between chronicle and history? Or, to make things easier, where do we stop writing chronicles, and start writing histories? As I am not a professional historian, I try to keep to a simple rule of thumb. When I write about the deeds of someone I met at dinner last night, or has been my colleague at school for the last ten years, I know I can't be writing history. Stories about people we know or have known in person tend to be anecdotic, in the etymological sense of the term: derived from, or influenced by, unpublished sources. History, on the contrary, is primarily ecdotic: Based on published sources – or, more generally, on written documents, even if unpublished. So, when – some 25 years ago – I started writing on computational design, I always assumed I was writing something akin to a running commentary; even if my books included at times historiographical digressions, I was always aware that I was not writing history, last but not least because the story I was telling did not have a conclusion, and the last chapter in each book covered ongoing developments which I expected to get back to in my next book – and I often did.

For me, as for Michael Fox and Brad Bell, this state of mind, so to speak, changed with the onset of the COVID pandemic. Even if I have not discussed with them their motivations for writing this book, I sensed reading their pages that for them, as for me, the pause imposed by the pandemic brought about a different view of the recent history of computational design. On the one hand, the pandemic factually vindicated – albeit in a tragic context – many assumptions and principles of digital design theory. When the industrial-mechanical world was shut down by the contagion, the Internet stepped in and kept the global economy functioning, thus proving that digital technologies of mass customization and electronic telepresence are a valid alternative to the mechanical technologies of mass production and mass transportation we inherited from the industrial revolution (and, incidentally, also validating the environmental credentials of digital tools in general: A zoom call has a lower carbon footprint than transatlantic air travel, even if many authoritative sources keep claiming the opposite). At the same time, even though I cannot speak here for Michael and Brad, I had the feeling, back then, that when the pandemic unexpectedly speeded up the delivery and adoption of digital technologies, an entire cycle of digital theories had more or less come to its natural conclusion; that the conceptual framework of our forthcoming computational universe had, by that time, been entirely marked out, and most future technical implementations would thenceforth align with already established ideas and views of computation. Evidently, this also suggested a new approach to the historiography of the digital turn in architecture – one that, for the first time in a generation, would not be shooting at a moving target.

This is how a few years ago I thought I could start writing a general history of the use of electronic computation in architecture – not an entirely straightforward idea, it turned out, as computers and architecture, if we look at them not as design professionals, but from the vantage point of the general public, belong to quite different phenomenological realms. And, indeed, some of my first attempts at such a quixotic, comprehensive project were well underway – a couple of them even published – when the AI tsunami struck, and the ball started rolling again. I wouldn't go so far as to call Generative AI a party crasher, as Michael and Brad do, but I share their mixed feelings on such a matter. For the time being, Generative AI is little more than a power-guzzling image processing tool, and we already have plenty of that in our schools, and in the profession. On the other hand, Generative AI is a brand-new technology, unrelated to vintage artificial intelligence – a failed project of the 1950s and 1960s that is now mostly relegated to the dustbin of technical history. The technical logic of Generative AI is fascinating, and it has vast epistemological, critical, and even practical implications; imitation learning applied to robotic automation could be a game changer, for example.

But such developments do not seem imminent, and for the time being it's hard to say if Generative AI will be seen, ten years of now, as a fluke at the end of a long story, or the start of a new storyline. Either way, Michael and Brad's titanic, and truly historiographic effort comes at the right point in time. First of all, this book is indispensable because nothing of the kind exists to date, and the sheer collection of names, dates, people, events, and places that Michael and Brad have managed to put together is a capital scholarly acquisition for all working in the field. And we all know how difficult this data is to find, against all logic and common sense. Particularly in the field of recent technical history – in this instance, the history of hardware and software development, releases, and specifications – this data simply does not exist. Corporate archives do not seem to exist, either, so sometimes our only sources on such matters are Wikipedia entries – which in turn, contrary to the letter but not to the spirit of Wikipedia, do not refer to printed sources but act as aggregators of oral traditions. And we all know that all protagonists of any given event tend to remember, and tell, quite different stories – all equally improbable, i.e., not corroborated by documental evidence.

For all these reasons, and more, this book will offer more than captivating reading to many colleagues and friends, in academia, in the profession, and beyond. It will be a reference book, and a documental milestone for years to come.

Mario Carpo
New York, April 2024

FOREWORD

The Evolution of Computational Cultures in Architecture

Jenny Sabin

The authors of *The Evolution of Computation in Architecture*, Brad Bell and Michael Fox, took on the significant challenge of writing a book on the history of computation in architecture. What they have accomplished is significant and opens the opportunity for our community to address the gaps and hidden or forgotten histories within an expansive, entangled, and international historical archive. Bell and Fox present their point of view on the history of computation in architecture, which bears the great responsibility of being as inclusive as possible, but is never enough. I applaud Bell and Fox for taking this daunting task on and for writing a book that we have all hoped for and wanted to read. I'm sure some of you, like me, may immediately see the gaps, important pioneers, leaders, educators, and emerging visionaries in our field that have not yet found their way into the book. This is not the fault of Bell and Fox, but is due to a faulty historical archive, one that rests on the shoulders of our entire community to fill in the glaring gaps. As I wrote in my article, "Transindividual and Transdisciplinary Design Research: Weaving, AI, Energy Futures, and Bio-Bricks," the gender of computational design has been an elusive and complex topic in the evolution of computation in architecture. On the one hand, the technological spaces that many of us occupy, and the communities that we participate in and learn from (ACADIA, Smart Geometry, SimAUD, SIGGRAPH, FABRICATE, and beyond), have historically been heavily male dominated, western, and white: A condition common in many science and technology fields whose longer histories have yet to be written. On the other, it is precisely the history of computation, digital space, and weaving (see section on Ada Lovelace and First Programming Language) that communicates more expansive and complex gender narratives. "Not only does this history reveal the women who have been erased and barred from being educated and working in these fields, but it positions women at the origins of all three."[1] Bell and Fox offer an opportunity to generate and stitch our own histories into the rich and dynamic scaffold that the authors painstakingly and with care compiled and recompiled and then recompiled again, I'm sure.

Like many of my peers, I was fortunate to study during a transitional period (2002–2005) at the Graduate School of Fine Arts (now Weitzman School of Design) in the Department of Architecture at the University of Pennsylvania where the computer and computational methods, concepts, and thinking were starting to be integrated into the graduate curriculum. The first half of my M.Arch education included traditional methods of architectural notation and hand drawing. I learned the art of ink on mylar, 1, 2, and 3-point perspective, exploded axons, variegated line weights, and beyond. In a full turn pivot, the second half of my education, included studying with my mentor and teacher Cecil Balmond where he introduced me to "Form and Algorithm" and the creative generative design possibilities of the "informal." I was fortunate to study under Cecil, first in a satellite installment of his seminar, Form and Algorithm, at the Advanced Geometry Unit, Arup, while I was studying at the Architectural Association with Homa Farjadi and Theo Spyropoulos in London and then through an advanced research studio, during which I established algorithmic methods for digitally weaving large dynamic datasets on Jacquard machines through an early project, BodyBlanket. The late Detlef Mertins was Chair of the Department of Architecture at UPenn at that time. Detlef fostered and created an intellectually stimulating and transformative environment in the department centered around a critical approach to the digital in architecture. It was during this time that I co-taught with Cecil, taught my own studios and seminars at the intersection of design, emerging technologies, and the sciences, and honed my teaching skills as a young teacher alongside launching the Sabin +Jones LabStudio. In looking back to this time, I don't think any of us quite knew how special and impactful this period was as an important moment in computational design in architecture. Whether it was Robert Aish announcing that he had a new build of Generative Components ready to share via USB at an early Smart Geometry conference in Cambridge, the UK (2006) or groundbreaking exhibitions curated by Marie-Ange Brayer and Frédéric Migayrou such as the 9th ArchiLab, Naturalizing Architecture (2013), at heart, the evolution of computational culture has been about the people and the community. The technology and a new computational approach to design brought us together. Schools of thought where immanence, morphogenetic processes, generative design, and constructivist theories thrive influenced and partially shaped my design process and thinking. These include Gilles Deleuze's infinite folds, Detlef Mertins's bioconstructivisms, Manuel DeLanda's meshworks, Anni Albers's pliable plane, Bernard Cache's objectile, and Cecil Balmond's informal.[2] In the sciences, my work is influenced by epigenesis and the science of the extracellular matrix.[3] In many ways, we turned to science to try and make sense of what we were generating and seeing on the screen. It is hard to believe that it took nearly 20 years of navel gazing with our heads down tinkering with scripts and digital fabrication experiments to try and make sense of the tools and how they were impacting the making and building of architecture before taking on pressing critical questions.

As intricately outlined and thoroughly represented in this book, the evolution of computation in architecture is rich and touches many fields, but it is also entangled. At the threshold of the millennium and moving into the early 2000s, new developments in digital fabrication, parametric design, digital data and simulations, and generative design allowed for emergent and bottom-up design processes. These new methods framed conversations around controlled indeterminacy, responsive architecture, technologies that hybridize physical and cyberspaces, as well as questions around access and the availability of computers in the design studio. For example, the ACADIA 2004 conference, co-chaired by Philip Beesley, Nancy Cheng, and Shane Williamson, examined the digital practice of architecture through fabrication where cutting-edge built projects such as the SmartWrap Pavilion by Kieran Timberlake, the Bahai Temple/Temple of Light by Hariri Hariri Architects, and the innovations in digital fabrication in construction processes on the Sagrada Familia set the stage.[4] In 2008, Silicon+Skin: Biological Processes and Computation, co-chaired by Andrew Kudless, Neri Oxman, and Marc Swackhamer, brought biology to design computation to explore new forms of making in collaborative contexts.[5] In their opening introduction, the editors write,

> It is curious that in order to define a discipline one must describe its boundaries. This delineation is especially problematic in the field of design computation as it encounters an expanding constellation of related domains. It has become rhizomatic, spreading horizontally across the various disciplinary landscapes, creating a multiplicity of creative nodes.[6]

Over the last decade, with the integration of materials and making, and more recently robotic fabrication, we see innovative developments that embed ecological design thinking, concepts of responsiveness, smart geometry, digital craft, embodied fabrication, responsive and social expression in architecture, synthetic landscapes, pervasive and ubiquitous computing, feedback, interactive and sensing technologies, and adaptation to unearth new reciprocal models for engagement and entanglements between architecture, humans, machines, and the environment.[7] Over the last two years, critical dialogue has also framed the rapidly expanding and changing frontier of Generative AI and AI in architecture research and practice.[8]

The 2020–2023 Association for Computer Aided Design in Architecture (ACADIA) conferences marked an important shift in the conference topics and critical discourse. In 2020, a critical, thought-provoking, and inspiring conference appropriately titled *Distributed Proximities*, challenged us all to deepen our thinking around creative practices and engagement with ecology and ethics; access and bias as it pertains to algorithms and big data; automation, agency, labor, and practice; computational design and issues of health and wellness; and new forms of collaboration. The mission was to identify next steps and to, in the conference chairs' words, highlight and reflect upon the "…resilience and ingenuity of the computational design community in the face of crisis."[9] Indeed, the COVID-19 crisis forced a reconsideration of workspaces, residences, and other occupied structures while also revealing ongoing systemic racism and persistent issues impacting diversity, equity, and inclusion. The 2021 conference marked the 40th anniversary of the ACADIA organization. ACADIA was founded in 1981 by some of the pioneers in the field of design computation mentioned in this book including Bill Mitchell, Chuck Eastman, and Chris Yessios. Board members and now President Shelby Doyle and Melissa Goldman initiated the ACADIA Cultural History project to reflect upon and celebrate the 40+ years of ACADIA's history, which included taking on the daunting task of amassing the entire archive of ACADIA proceedings and making them free and accessible to all on the ACADIA website. The project includes a series called Voices of ACADIA, which captures the stories of the community that have made the organization what it is today. Similar initiatives need to take place in other venues and peer groups to ensure that our collective histories are preserved and important gaps identified to build a much more inclusive archive. I hope that now that we've opened the doors to these important questions and topics that these conversations persist, grow, and continue to contribute to the richness and diversity of our community.

It is an important time to reflect, celebrate, and critically assess our histories and where we are headed as a field and community in the future. Bell and Fox took on the challenge of stitching together a dynamic and rich history. Now, it is up to our entire community to fix the archive to impart a more inclusive and comprehensive evolution of computational cultures in architecture. In looking back, I'd like to bring attention to one computational design pioneer that has not received due credit for her seminal contribution to our field, Anne Tyng. An architect and professor, Tyng taught in the Department of Architecture at the University of Pennsylvania for over 30 years while also collaborating with Louis Kahn in his practice based in Philadelphia for 29 years. Tyng presented the first major installation of her work based on her conceptual approach to geometry in 1964. Presented 60 years ago in the lobby of Meyerson Hall at UPenn, Tyng's first installation was titled "Divine Proportion in the Platonic Solids Exhibition." It featured a gallery-scale construction, along with drawings, photographs, and text panels presenting Tyng's research. In researching Tyng's work and contribution to teaching in preparation for an essay that I wrote in the catalogue for her second retrospective, "Anne Tyng: Inhabiting Geometry," curated by the late Srdjan Jovanoviç Weiss at the Institute for Contemporary Art in Philadelphia, I discovered a treasure trove of artifacts documenting her pioneering teaching in computational design.

> From Tyng's papers, now in the collection of Penn's Architectural Archives, we learn that she sought out early computing through a short course in Fortran at the University of Pennsylvania during the spring of 1967.[10] Fortran, an early programming language developed by IBM, founded basic computational logic, manifesting it in series of punch cards. Her course notes show extensive work on the fundamentals of programming, including exercises based on averaging, sorting and function-based algorithms, complex calculations, graph functions and optimization methods for a variety of narratives and data sets. There is no evidence indicating that she applied this knowledge directly to her generative work on geometry. It may be inferred, however, that this exposure to computation influenced her enough to impact her methodological approach especially in geometric series such as the Fibonacci sequence. This was also exemplified in her geometry courses during the early 1980s at the Graduate School of Fine Arts at Penn. Arguably at the very beginning of what has now completely transformed the making and building of architecture through digital design and fabrication, Tyng was limited to using computation as a digital and analog tool acting only as a labor-intensive calculation assistant rather than being fully integrated within her creative process, something that is possible today.[11]

As a frequently forgotten computational designer and pioneer in our field, I'm sure that Tyng would have also stated, "You have no idea how difficult things used to be." This is one story that needs to be told and recorded, there are many. Our community has come a long way through the hard work of many individuals, including Bell and Fox, to reach gender parity in our organizations and build pathways to create a more inclusive and diverse environment. As a community, we have a commitment to evolve and at the same time maintain a foundation of rigor and excellence. The diverse, experimental, pioneering, and innovative array of contributions in this book articulate a robust tapestry of computational cultures in architecture. Our work is not done. We need to continue to dissolve binary conditions and inherent hierarchies in our history to record forgotten and overlooked contributions by women and people of color who have significantly shaped our culture and technological innovations. Filling in the gaps within the evolution of computational culture in architecture will inform how we embrace new modes of practice and research. This is the only way that we can build upon a robust and diverse foundation to respond with informed intention to a rapidly changing context and new technological paradigm for computational design in our community, the field, and built environment.

Jenny E. Sabin

Notes

1 See Sabin, J. (2024). "Trans-individual and Disciplinary Design Research: Weaving Artificial Intelligence, Energy Futures, and Bio-Bricks and Tiles," in *Bio/Matter/Techno/Synthetics: Design Futures for the More than Human*, edited by F. Trubiano, S. Kolber, M. Llor, M.J. Fuente, and A. Farrow. Barcelona: Actar.

2 See Deleuze, G. (1993). *The Fold: Leibniz and the Baroque*. Minneapolis: University of Minnesota Press. Mertins, D. (2004). "Bioconstructivisms," in L. Spuybroek (ed.), *NOX: Machining Architecture*. London: Thames & Hudson, pp. 360–369. DeLanda, M. (1977). *A Thousand Years of Nonlinear History*. New York, NY: Zone Books. Albers, A. (1993). *On Weaving*. Middletown, CT: Wesleyan University Press. Cache, B. (1995). "Décrochement," in *Earth Moves: The Furnishing of Territories*, trans. A. Boyman, ed. M. Speaks. Cambridge, MA: MIT Press. Balmond, C. (2007). *Informal*. London: Prestel.

3 Lloyd Jones, P. (2007). "Context Messaging: Modeling Biological Form," in *Models*, ed. E. Abruzzo, E. Ellingsen, and J.D. Solomon. New York: 306090, Inc., pp. 31–38.

4 See Beesley, P., Yen-Wen Cheng, N. and Williamson, R.S. (eds.) (2004). *Fabrication: Examining the Digital Practice of Architecture*. Toronto: University of Waterloo School of Architecture Press.

5 See Kudless, A., Oxman, N. and Swackhamer, M. (eds.) (2008). *Silicon+Skin: Biological Processes and Computation*. Minneapolis: The Association for Computer-Aided Design in Architecture.

6 Ibid., p. 15.

7 See ACADIA Proceedings 2012–2019.

8 See my foreword as President of ACADIA in the 2021 Conference Proceedings. *ACADIA 2021: Realignments: Toward Critical Computation. Proceedings of the 41st Annual Conference of the Association for Computer Aided Design in Architecture (ACADIA)*, edited by Kathrin Dörfler, Stefana Parascho, Jane Scott, Biayna Bogosian, Behnaz Farahi, June Grant, Jose Luis García del Castillo y López, and Vernelle A. A. Noel, ACADIA, 2021. See my foreword as President of ACADIA in the 2022 Conference Proceedings. *ACADIA 2022: Hybrids & Haecceities. Proceedings of the 42nd Annual Conference of the Association for Computer Aided Design in Architecture (ACADIA)*, edited by Dorit Aviv, Masoud Akbarzadeh, Hina Jamelle, and Robert Stuart-Smith, ACADIA, 2022.

9 *ACADIA 2020: Distributed Proximities / Volume I: Technical Papers. Proceedings of the 40th Annual Conference of the Association of Computer Aided Design in Architecture (ACADIA)*, edited by B. Slocum, V. Ago, A. Marcus, et al., ACADIA, 2020.

10 From Tyng's course notes and punch cards, Architectural Archives, University of Pennsylvania. Thank you to William Whitaker for bringing this to my attention.

11 Excerpt from Sabin, J. (2012). "Geometry in Transformation: Computing Mind and Matter," in *Anne Tyng: Inhabiting Geometry*, edited by I. Schaffner, S. Jovanoviç Weiss, and A. Imperiale. Philadelphia, PA: Institute of Contemporary Art, University of Pennsylvania, pp. 80–95.

FOREWORD

Looking Forward to the Next Episode

Branko Kolarevic

The historical context of computational technologies in architecture is rarely fully explored. What has been published so far often focuses on very specific applications, such as digital fabrication or performance simulation, or on some key individuals. This book by Michael Fox and Bradley Bell addresses this gap in literature related to the history, i.e., the evolution of computing in architecture. It offers a comprehensive overview of key developments, events, and important figures and does so convincingly and succinctly.

I was already familiar with the book's contents before I was approached by Michael and Brad to write a foreword. The publisher (Routledge) asked me to review their proposal and I supported wholeheartedly its publication. The proposal was very well written, with a broad coverage of various topics. This was to be expected as both Brad and Michael are "old hands" when it comes to digital design and production and have decades of experience in teaching and research (and professional practice) and numerous publications that made them well known among their peers.

The book is certainly a monumental endeavor as the topic is huge. Brad admitted as much in one of his emails: "Writing this has been a bit like watching fungus grow in a petri dish. A controlled experiment – yes, but from one day to the next, everything seems to multiply... getting bigger and bigger." I think that this "fungus" analogy is perfect for the kind of endeavor that Brad and Michael have embarked on. The book could have easily become too unwieldy to write as there were many disparate, unconnected yet related developments, often unreported in conference papers or journal articles, that had to be properly researched. The authors acted as real historians, patiently combing through early books and papers, trying to connect ideas and people, and then present the results of this painstaking research in accessible fashion, without getting lost in unnecessary details or elaborate descriptions of key concepts.

Needless to say, this book is very well written. The history of design computing is presented as a set of chronological "episodes" that focus on key developments during the distinct time periods identified by the authors. I won't summarize what the "episodes" are about as that can be easily surmised from the table of contents but would agree with the authors that the episodes offer an appropriate way to bracket the key ideas, developments, events, people, over the past few decades.

I lived much of the history described in this remarkable book, starting with Episode 2 (1981–1991). I came across computer aided design in the mid-1980s as an undergraduate student at the Faculty of Architecture at the University of Belgrade. I remember an exhibition in 1984 in Faculty's hallways that featured plotted, rudimentary wireframe perspectives of a digital 3D model of some building. I don't remember who created them, but I was mesmerized by the drawings and the apparent ease with which they were produced (having spent hours drawing perspectives by hand). The real "clincher," however, was a set of shaded renderings – with shadows! – of a house presented at an event in 1986 hosted by my future employer, Energoproject, created using an in-house developed modeling and rendering program running on the company's IBM 360 mainframe and state-of-the-art 32-bit Tektronix workstations. Discovering the HATCH command in AutoCAD version 2.08 (running on an IBM AT) was the next best thing – and a clogged pen in the plotter the new source of frustration…

When I went to Harvard GSD in 1988 for my master's and later doctorate degree under Bill Mitchell's mentorship, I had read already his seminal "Computer Aided Architectural Design" book published in 1977. Bill, who moved to Harvard in 1987 from UCLA, attracted an amazing group of students who had access to state-of-the-art software (ComputerVision, Artisan, SOM's AES, etc.) and hardware (Sun Microsystems and Silicon Graphics workstations, scanners, recorders, plotters, etc.). Back then, ALL architecture students at the GSD had to take "Fundamentals of Computer Aided Design" that Bill co-taught with Malcolm McCullough (now at the University of Michigan) and Stephen Ervin – and had to learn how to program in Pascal. Bill also taught "Introduction to Geometric Modeling" as an elective course – and more importantly – he (and Malcolm) also taught an "electronic" design studio.

These early curricular breakthroughs at top schools in the second half of the 1980s, such as the introduction of required CAD courses, and innovative pedagogic initiatives, such as the "electronic" or "digital" design studios in the late 1980s, deserve special mention as they set the course for the rest to follow. There was a seminal CAAD Futures conference that took place at Harvard GSD and MIT in 1989 under the theme of "The Electronic Design

Studio" and its purpose was to signal that CAD has gotten into that last curricular bastion – the design studio – but it was still very early days. There were too many who were deeply skeptical of the design potential of computer technologies.

With the spread of the Internet, virtual design studios emerged in the mid- and late 1990s enabling schools and firms to operate more or less seamlessly around the globe, which was unprecedented. In 1997, a group of us located at three different schools around the world, roughly eight hours apart, ran a first non-stop 24-hour global virtual design studio ("Multiplying Time: 3 x 8 = 24") over the course of one week. The idea for the studio was Gerhard Schmitt's; I then brought Brian Johnson onboard, and we developed collectively the details of that experimental design charrette, with much of the technological backend technology provided at ETH by Gerhard's research group. Around the same time, I was elected President of ACADIA and we ran the first Internet-based design competition for "library for the information age" that attracted over 600 entries, far more than we hoped at the time.

Back to Brad's and Michael's book. Did they miss certain things? Maybe. I am sure they had to leave out some developments or events because the text had to fit within a predetermined page count. Their goal was not to produce a door stopper – which could easily have been an outcome – but an accessible yet comprehensive account of design computing history, and in that they have succeeded amply and admirably. The next edition of this historical account, however, is likely to feature an entirely new – and epic – "episode" on Artificial Intelligence (AI) in architecture and design. Generative AI technologies are the most impactful computational development that I have witnessed so far, with profound consequences for all aspects of our lives, let alone architecture as a discipline and profession. My encounter with them is similar to what I experienced 40 years ago when I saw those plotted wireframe perspectives on the walls of the Faculty of Architecture in Belgrade: This is going to change everything.

I hope you will enjoy reading this book as much as I did when it was still in manuscript stage. We finally have a proper historic account of computational design and for that Brad and Michael deserve our collective gratitude.

Branko Kolarevic

INTRODUCTION

Some books write themselves. In the age of AI, this has a new and auspicious meaning. For *The Evolution of Computation in Architecture*, one might think this would be an opportune time to leverage the new technologies to co-author a text, *to set the ball rolling and see where it takes us*. And yet, this book didn't write itself – far from it. It was a tangled web of bibliometrics and research that often felt like quicksand rather than solid ground. One reason is most likely because, not being true historians, we are presenting a particular point of view. A point of view that outlines a rich tapestry of experience, exploration, and even struggles. Also, you cannot recount the narrative of computation in architecture without touching on the development of digital technologies in a broader sense. We also, admittedly acknowledge we offer a western-centric, and even at times North American-centric, perspective to a topic that has a global domain. If others were to write this book, it would inherently contain different content and follow a different path.

This book is also very personal to both of us. We grew up in a world of drafting tables with a real understanding of the analog way of working in architecture. We were in college when computation was still novel and fringe. We also both ended up in academia, deeply entrenched in the evolving world of computation in architecture, constantly struck by the speed of development. Although there are numerous books covering specific trajectories, there is nothing out there that looks at the broad spectrum of development. It was something we wanted to understand a book we wanted to read.

In 2012 at the ACADIA conference in Waterloo, while sitting in the back listening to Philip Beesley introduce a series of young academics and practitioners for an upcoming session, almost as a reflex we instinctually said to one another, "These young kids have no idea how difficult things used to be." Three years later in 2015 while sitting at another ACADIA conference in

DOI: 10.4324/9781032671208-1

Cincinnati, Robert Aish moderated a panel with Don Greenberg, Tom Maver, and Chuck Eastman where they essentially echoed the same sentiment to everyone in the audience, "You all have no idea how difficult things used to be." And so commenced the revelation that nobody really understands the perspective of even their most tangential context, forwards or backwards.

As a result of either our insatiable appetite to make our computational capacity more prolific or to increase fidelity, we often are too quick to discard our past. We typically have nostalgic memories (or hostilities) for the speed, cost, and complexity of how we navigated the digital toolsets a decade or two ago. While simultaneously staring at a diminishing return for Moore's Law and the threshold of quantum computing, we are confronted with the reality that, while seemingly incremental, there have always been large technological advancements that have given flight to our ability to evolve and progress as a civilization. Within the paradigm of architecture and design, this book is fundamentally about how we have chosen to acknowledge, adopt, implement, and advance these technologies.

We began our research with a topical taxonomy across academic CAD organizations. We cross referenced this with notable books, projects, and people. We tried to understand the context of technological advancements, the developing means of dissemination, and even the social, cultural, political, and economic drivers. Frequently a baseline would be established, only to be redrawn so that additional information could be included. The attempt to include early drawing tools and computer history as a precursor to the more direct focus of the text exemplifies the dilemma of widening the scope. The initial outline expanded, as we found another tributary of inquiry, another group of pioneers arduously pursuing their own path which may have been a dead end, and which may have been the seed of an entirely new direction. We wrote and rewrote the detailed table of contents with the sobering realization that it was never inclusive enough. The *mea culpa* is that in a text like this, you will inevitably have glaring omissions, blind spots, and surely things you just couldn't quite figure out how to include.

Yet in the end, we hope it is enough to provide a clear enough picture – or at least a grainy image – to read and provide some perspective. Maybe more importantly, others can take what we have documented and use it to weave a perspective of their own. We embrace the admission that it is possible a more appropriate title for the book would be "A Perspective on the Evolution of Computation in Architecture."

The book is organized into episodes. Each episode gathers activities and occurrences from a particular moment that fold into a larger arc. While the timeframe is not explicit or equal, it became apparent that synergies of *how and why* influence across the field of computation in architecture was taking place. The developmental progress in architectural computation has always been incremental, encapsulating cyclic periods of almost chaotic, open exploration and experimentation that tend to be subsequently followed by periods characterized by consolidation and curation. We attempted to draw these out with examples of texts, events, projects, and benchmarks that illustrated the culmination of thought and direction.

Episode 0 provides a context, one that takes us back several hundreds of years to understand origin stories, traditions, and even radical thought. Starting in Episode 1 we see those who were brave enough to set out as *pioneers* asking questions about possibilities that often had no immediate answer. Episode 2 follows as a time of *translation*, where digital technology is onboarded and implemented, often with mixed results. There is still a widely held attitude of emulating what has already been done. In Episode 3, the questions have evolved, even though the toolsets have not, and some begin to *appropriate* from other sources in order to chart new ways forward. The speed of change accelerates as the means of information dissemination also start to change. By Episode 4 there is a high degree of *experimentation*, with hardware, software, and methodologies resulting in an explosion of trajectories with everyone documenting the short-term accomplishments with as much conviction as they could muster in a world with little reference or precedence. Then in Episode 5, the frenetic exploration gives way to a newfound *legitimacy* coupling research from the field of computational architecture with broader disciplines. There is a coalescing of trajectories, all seemingly intertwined in newfound cultural and ecological awareness, producing a more nuanced and sophisticated built environment. Finally, in Episode 6 *paradigms* of operation are maturing. The peripheral and speculative have started to become more clearly defined. And yet… a new influence appears that has been lurking in the background for 75 years finally making its way to the stage. AI crashes the party with pioneers offering to repeat the entire cycle and provide an entire recalibration of the future of *Computation in Architecture*.

No book really writes itself. However, writing a co-authored book from an idea that started over a decade ago, across multiple time zones, through a pandemic, and the rapidly changing landscape of architectural computation proved to be a circuitous journey. Not too dissimilar to much of the development we tracked in the book. While not a "choose your own adventure" book, I am sure were we to write this again, it might turn out differently. But there are people, events, projects, and texts that unequivocally provide the cornerstones of what all this work has been built upon. In the writing we are ultimately reminded of our friends, colleagues, people, and heroes who have inspired us along the way. The broader community, which is always growing, always *evolving*, is interconnected. Yes, standing on shoulders, but also being inspired by young visionaries. By writing this book and spending time looking for these connections we are thankful to have gained some insight into this network and hope you are as well.

EPISODE 0

PROLOGUE (… 1972)

The central driver for this book is to document and trace significant developments in the short history of computation in architecture, which may, in turn, help enlighten an understanding of future trajectories. The technology, events, people, discoveries, and breakthroughs are loosely categorized into "episodes," providing synergistic connection points to capture developmental periods. The developmental arc of these combined episodes is tied to innovative technologies and new tools. The analog process of working in architecture that led to computational processes deeply rooted in the cyclical nature of the stages outlined in the episodes of this book.

This prologue episode covers a brief history of how architects worked in the past, their role in the building process, and the development of notational systems. It then outlines the birth of computation and the pioneering speculations relative to the profession of architecture that came about very early on, often preceding the actual technological development needed to bring them into reality. The episode concludes with an overview of the very early developmental timeline of the computer as seen through an architectural lens.

The Longstanding Foundations

Notational Pioneering

From a historical perspective, architectural notation has always existed in some form, although the subject is controversial, and the evidence is scant. However, there is evidence of fairly precise architectural construction drawings as far back as the Egyptians.[1] Phillip Bernstein targets a starting point with the statue of Gudea, "the architect with the plan," which has an

DOI: 10.4324/9781032671208-2

architectural plan sitting on his lap as evidence of the notations dating as far back as 2150 BC[2] (Figure 0.1). Then there is the monastic compound Plan of St. Gall, which is the only surviving scaled major architectural drawing from the Roman Empire dating to the 9th century[3] (Figure 0.2). It is debatable what came first in this case, the constructed building or the plan.[4] While there were some notational systems in the form of texts, models, templates, or diagrams,[5] they all implied or required the architect to be on-site to communicate the design intent relative to construction. As early as the 1st century, Vitruvius' De Architectura provides an early outline for what constituted architecture and, by extension, an architect.

By the early 1400s, the Italian architect and engineer Filippo Brunelleschi transcended his lack of any formal training as a builder to apply his innovations in pioneering new construction technologies to design and construct the dome and lantern on the Cathedral of the Santa Maria del Fiore (the Duomo) of Florence.[6] Brunelleschi believed the architect should control all aspects of the building project, which he believed, could not be executed without the architect. While Brunelleschi was also credited for rediscovering the principles of linear perspective, known to the Greeks and Romans, at that time, architecture "was not a notational art at all.[7] At the time of Brunelleschi's accomplishments in design and fabrication, there was no means to draw three-dimensional stone cutting necessary for construction, and even if there was, there was no practice of masons understanding scaled drawings. Most existing drawings conveyed design intent and not any technical aspect related to construction of the actual artisans.

Notation and Authorship

Counter to Brunelleschi's position was Leon Battista Alberti (1404–1472), a Renaissance intellectual who believed architects should be designers, not

FIGURE 0.1 The Seated Gudea, c. 2100 BC, who some consider representing the first "architect with a drawing" based on the temple plan located in the lap of the seated figure.

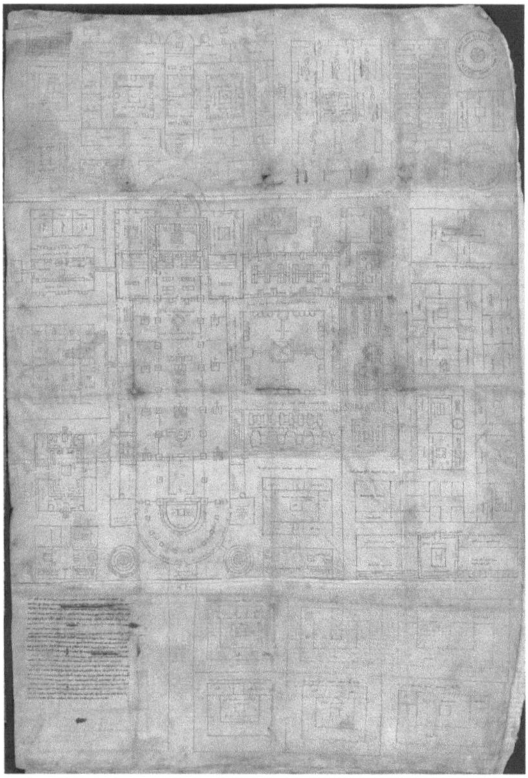

FIGURE 0.2 The Plan of Saint Gall is a medieval architectural drawing of a monastic compound dating from 820–830 AD. It depicts an entire Benedictine monastic compound, including a church, houses, stables, kitchens, workshops, a brewery, and an infirmary.

builders. In *The Craftsman to Draftsman,*[8] Mario Carpo suggests Alberti's position was that architecture should be conceived, documented, and then executed by others. It was in the documentation that Alberti stamped his indelible mark on the future of architecture. Alberti provided his theories on how buildings would be built[9] in his exposition, *On the Art of Building* (*De Re Aedificatoria*),[10] written between 1443 and 1452. He pointed out that architects should use common types of orthographic drawings in plans, elevations, and sections. This unprecedented, notational standardization as a tool for conveying technical information was pivotal to his position on the architect/builder relationship, but also one that would stand the test of time to this day.

Analog Tools for Technical Translation

Many of the earliest drawings dating back to the 16th century were still developed as guides for the builders. Architectural models eventually also grew in sophistication, displaying proportional details serving as an additional guide. Although stone, lead, and graphite were predecessors, ink was the defining medium in most architectural drawings made prior to 1860.[11] With the emergence of the architectural profession, the design and construction functions became increasingly separate, and fewer decisions were left to the builder's discretion. After a drawing was laid out in pencil, the lines were inked in to create a clear and durable image using specialized drafting instruments. Eventually, the tool kit was further defined by the ruling pen, pricker, compass, erasers, and T-squares, which defined a completely different methodology that focused more on design[12] (Figure 0.3). These tools began to describe the standardized ways of working in architecture and have held up with incredible resilience until the birth of the computer.

It is essential to recognize that before the invention of print, individuals made drawings but were prone to mistakes, changes, and omissions in the reproduction process.

In his 2017 book *Architecture in the Age of Printing,*[13] Mario Carpo, again, provides important insight into how these errors changed our cultural artifacts and created a "manual drift." By extension, the modern print format began to affect architectural theory around the 1530s. The invention of print recalibrated the relationship between the text and drawing in that technical information could now be reliably transmitted. Historically, the age of reproducing mass-produced, identical copies "should be seen as an interlude"[14] between the time of the master builder and the age of modern architectural computation (Figure 0.4).

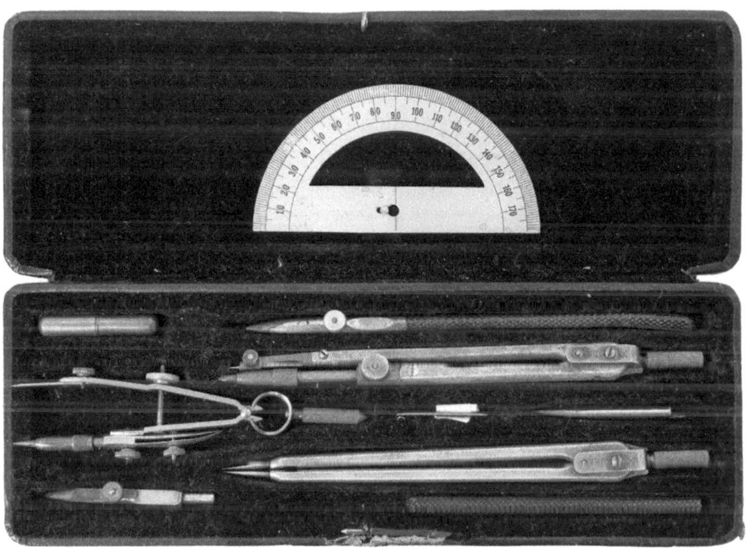

FIGURE 0.3 Antique drafting set showing compass, protractor, stylus, and other tools used for technical drawing.

FIGURE 0.4 The long-standing way of working until the advent of computation in the architecture office involved drafting tables, paper and mylar, pens, pencils, and T-squares.

The automation of the reproduction of architectural documents came about in 1842 when John Herschel discovered the cyanotype process whereby an architectural drawing was made on a semi-transparent paper, then weighted down on top of a sheet of paper or cloth that was coated with a photosensitive chemical mixture of potassium ferricyanide and ferric ammonium citrate. Drafting technicians still copied drawings into the modern period, and various chemical and mechanical processes for reproducing architectural drawings continued development throughout the 19th and 20th centuries.[15]

The Early Paradigm Shift

Recognizing the Early Stages of Computation

The earliest foundational tenets of computation and computer science were built upon analog devices and algorithms that predate the digital computer by hundreds of years. From the abacus to Leibniz's calculator in 1820, early mechanical calculation provided a critical step toward digital calculating. By January of 1947, at the Symposium on Large-Scale Digital Calculating Machinery at the Harvard Computation Laboratory, Professor Samuel H. Caldwell of MIT spoke of the need to organize an association of those interested in computing machinery. Caldwell, along with a small group of computer scientists, physicists, engineers, and military, formed the Association for Computing Machinery (ACM) later in 1947 and counts well over 100,000 members in its organization nearly 75 years later.[16] The ACM, now with over 38 special interest groups (SIGS), forms one of the most comprehensive networks of computation societies in existence today.

Despite all this, as Kevin Kelly stated in 2020,

> we are still at the beginning of the beginning. We have just started to make a technological society. The technological changes in the next 20 years will dwarf those of the last 20 years. It will almost be like nothing at all has happened yet.[17]

Technological developments driven by computation have become the central driver of our cultural development. The cultural influence is heavily tied to the simultaneously evolving ways and means of dissemination influencing the development of architectural computation. Eventually, the permanence of a culture of sharing combined with the willing embrace of allowing data to be tracked has expedited developmental trends. Architecture and computational developments often mirror the larger realm of technological developments. However, incremental improvements are never as provocative as significant breakthroughs but are responsible for most scientific discoveries. Technological change is gradual, and every change often creates as many problems as it solves. As Kevin Kelly again explains,

> Most of the problems we have today are technogenic, meaning that they were created by technology in the past ... Technology is a means of producing new problems. It's a means of producing new solutions, but the fact that we have a choice between those two is what tips the balance very, very slightly in the favor of the good for the long term.[18]

Although technological development often focuses on the intangible, architecture often embraces the tangible. Trajectories of fabrication, materiality, and building performance will eventually come to have a significant effect on our built environment itself.

Computation Recognized by the Profession (Emulating Processes)

Several early developments paved the way for general processes that still exist today and have profoundly influenced architecture. Two important software examples were PRONTO (1957), which became the precursor to CADD/CAM, and Sketchpad (1963) (Figure 0.5), which paved the way for computer drafting. PRONTO (Program for Numerical Tooling Operations),

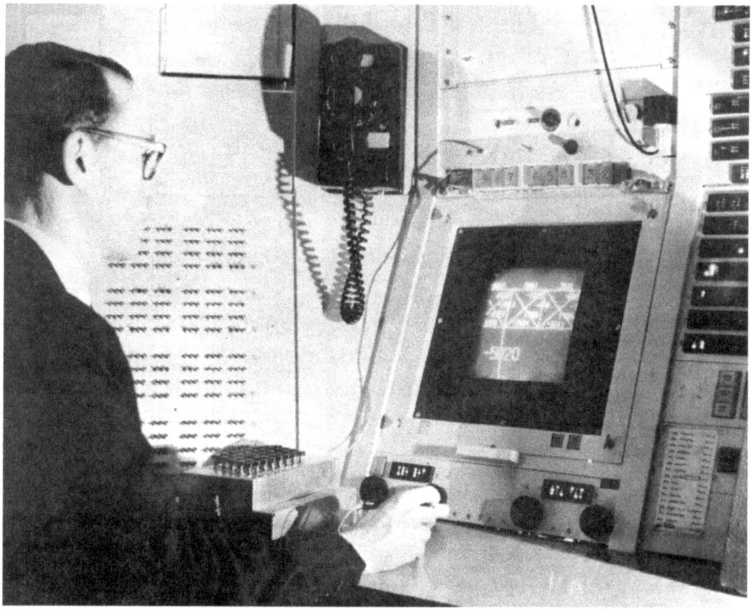

FIGURE 0.5 Sketchpad, developed by Ivan Sutherland in 1962, is considered the first computer drawing application.

developed in 1957 by Patrick Hanratty while at GE, became a predecessor to CAD and essentially was the first CNC programming system. Sketchpad was invented by Ivan Sutherland in 1962 while at MIT for his Ph.D.[19] and is recognized as essentially the first computer drawing program and the derivative of the graphical user interface (GUI). It was an innovative program that influenced alternative forms of interaction with computers. Sketchpad accepted constraints and specified relationships among segments and arcs, including the diameter of arcs. It could draw horizontal and vertical lines and combine them into figures and shapes; figures could be copied, moved, rotated, or resized, retaining their basic properties. Sketchpad also had the first window-drawing program and clipping algorithm, which allowed zooming. It is regarded as the parent of contemporary computer-aided design (CAD) tools and an important achievement in general computer graphics development, having pioneered the human-computer interface (HCI). It is often viewed as a "breakthrough" in computer graphics.[20]

A very short time later, another vital component affecting the architecture profession was developed called "X-Y Position Indicator for a Display System," in simpler terms: The computer mouse. Douglas Engelbart, along with Bill English, both at SRI International, were exploring the interactions between humans and computers and built the first computer mouse prototype in 1964. Designs with multiple buttons soon followed. The design was a single wheel used to translate the motion of the mouse into cursor movement on the screen. Engelbart was named the inventor of the basic patent filed in 1967 and issued in 1970. This simple tool has remained almost unchanged and is indispensable for architects interfacing with computers to this day.

The rest of the 1960s brought additional architecture-related developments, including the initial production of an interactive graphics manufacturing system and the first digitizer. However, a decade later, in the 1970s, a growing list of companies were founded to commercialize their initial CAD program designs, including luminaries such as M&S Computing, Applicon, Computervision, and SDRC. As we will see in the next episode, the rest of the 1970s saw research begin to transition from 2D to 3D, which included several major breakthroughs ranging from solid modeling to the invention of NURBS (Non-Uniform Rational Basis Splines) geometry, which allowed for mathematically precise models.

Computer technology as applied to architecture, or as it would become known as "Computer Aided Architecture Design" (CAAD), started with the Design Methods movement in the 1960s in London. Computer scientists were interested in the design process, while designers were increasingly interested in digitizing analog tools. For the most part, however, these conferences and academic footholds had no apparent organization or broader trajectory.[21] Regardless of the pioneering feel of this early stage, what came out of these initial developments for the architecture profession were mostly pragmatic outcomes that emulated the heuristics and processes already rooted in analog ways of doing things. There was the persistent recognition we could do better with the use of computation. The use of computation in architecture began with a rather banal history of emulating those traditional methods. We will see technological advances in computation eventually cause some professions to cease to exist and some professions to transform completely. The introduction of computation into the production of architecture was not necessarily a seamless or simple transition. Like many other fields, efficiency guided initial adoption in the early stages, ultimately, the transformation of operational models and relinquishing of existing methodologies did not happen easily or overnight.

Speculations and Possibilities

The Beginnings of Virtual Realities

Prior to computer technologies becoming accessible to the general public and outside of the realm of pragmatic advancements, there were a number of pioneering developments in computation that would eventually foster tools for the profession. One such example is the birth and early history of VR, which would ultimately impact architecture. The history of VR/AR and tangent technologies is broad and encompasses a wide array of modalities and steps for bringing the viewer into an altered reality by introducing a viewing device. Charles Wheatstone demonstrated that the brain processes the different two-dimensional images from each eye into a single object of three dimensions. These developments laid the foundation for the seeds of modern-day technological advancements in the middle of the 20th century. In 1929, Edward Link developed the "Link Trainer," which was probably the first example of an entirely electromechanical commercial flight simulator. The development then picked up with the American cinematographer and inventor Morton Heilig, who described his vision of a multi-sensory theater in a 1955 paper entitled "The Cinema of the Future."[22] In 1962, he built a prototype of the immersive, multi-sensory, mechanical multimodal theater called the Sensorama. The Sensorama is considered one of the earliest virtual reality (VR) systems to interface users with automated systems in both input and output[23] (Figures 0.6 and 0.7).

Helig would go on to create and patent the first mobile VR headset in 1961 called the Telesphere Mask,[24] followed by important contributions by Ivan Sutherland in 1965 on the "Ultimate Display theory" and then in 1968 by building the first VR headset mounted to a computer called the Sword of Damocles,[25] anecdotally named as such because of the large overhead beam required to support its weight and not any dystopian "Ready Player One" vision of the potential effects of the technology.[26] Yet, as was the case with many early technological visions ensnared in a web of other interwoven developmental histories, it would be more than 60 years before the vision of Helig's VR/AR and MR (Mixed Reality) became a commonplace reality and eventually a part of the profession of architecture in an impactful way. Furthermore, at the time of writing this book, the potential for VR/AR/MR is still very much in its infancy with respect to construction and fabrication.

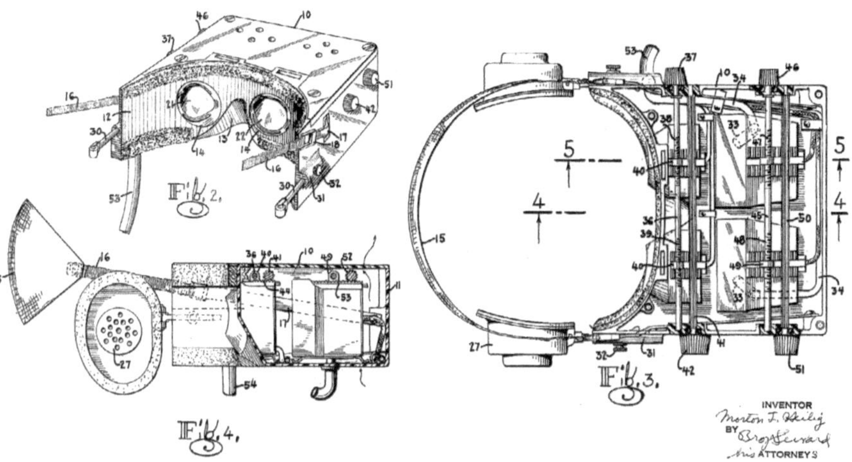

FIGURE 0.6 A detailed illustration of the headset from Morton Heilig's Sensorama patent application. The Sensorama was a precursor to later virtual reality systems.

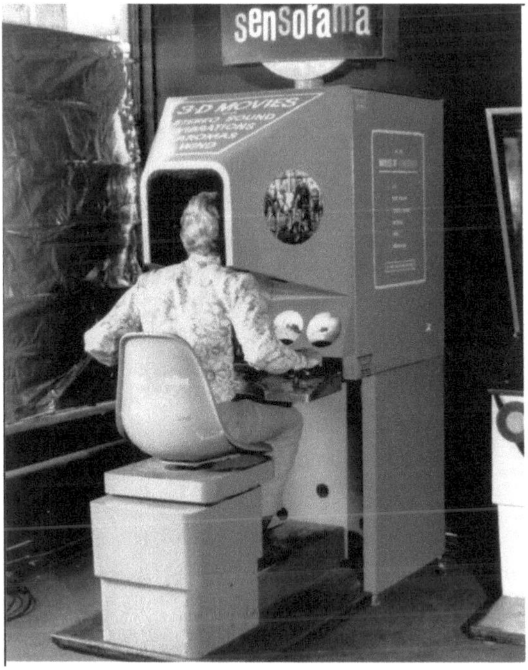

FIGURE 0.7 The Sensorama was introduced as a concept by Morton Helig in 1955. He later developed a full-scale prototype in 1962. His design is considered one of the earliest virtual reality (VR) systems to interface users with automated systems in both input and output.

Understanding Human-Computer Interactions

Similar to the development of the computer mouse, understanding how computers and humans interacted with each other was a central driver for several other early developments in computation. "Media Technology" is a term coined by Nicholas Negroponte and Andrew Lipman. Together, they co-founded the Architecture Machine Group at MIT in 1968 as a test bed for interactive computers, sensors, and programs that sought to change how these interactions occurred. The group's work often preceded the technology that existed at the time. Although actual computers were yet to arrive in any practical way, there was a promise of technology that would allow architects to do things in different ways. Negroponte published the seminal book *The Architecture Machine*[27] in 1970, forecasting a future man-machine dialogue. The Architecture Machine Group eventually folded into the Media Lab in 1985, as discussed in Episode 2. The term: "Media Technology," now encompasses all the technical inventions through which people communicate meaning and feeling using sight, sound, and imagery of the mind.[28] Negroponte envisioned a world where everybody would live in immersive, intelligent environments.

Cybernetics and Anticipatory Architecture

A few individuals were thinking specifically about architecture and technology, and were committed to going beyond the obvious commercial and pragmatic concerns. The futuristic thinking leapfrogged the actual technology that existed at the time for reasons we will see explained in the next episode, and we will see that many of these visions did not win out to the initial pragmatic computational development. However, the early speculations were not lost and eventually fostered developments that would become a reality but with a longer fermentation period. Much of this early theoretical work in architecture and computation was done by people working in cybernetics in the 1960s. The common definition of cybernetics is the science of communications and automatic control systems in machines and living things. As Norbert Wiener puts it, "It combines under one heading what is known in the human context as 'thinking' and what in engineering is known as control and communication."[29] Wiener and Gordon Pask laid much of the groundwork in interactive and adaptive architecture, a concept in line with those of Negroponte and the MIT Architecture Machine group mentioned above.

At this time, Pask and Wiener made advancements toward understanding and identifying the field of interactive or adaptive architecture by formulating their theories on the topic. Pask's "Conversation Theory," highlighted in his book "An Approach to Cybernetics," published in 1961, served as the basis of much of the architectural development in interactive architecture at the time.[30] Although Pask was "rediscovered" by the architectural community in the 1970s, he faded away for quite some time. These early ideas rooted in cybernetics were picked up by a few architects who solidly translated them into architecture. However, at the time, the problem was that computational means had not evolved enough for concepts in cybernetics to provide a strong enough foothold.

Cedric Price was perhaps the most influential of the early architects to adopt the preliminary theoretical work in cybernetics and extend it to an architectural concept of "anticipatory architecture." Many of his unbuilt projects, such as the Fun Palace in 1961, influenced an architecture of process that was indeterminate, flexible, and responsive to the changing needs of users and their times (Figure 0.8).

Price would go on to have an influential four-decade career, with his 1978 *Generator* project counting as a significant and early contribution to artificially intelligent architecture. Richard Rogers and Renzo Piano would cite his work as one of the key influences for their 1972 design of the Centre Georges Pompidou in Paris, which embodied Price's cybernetic theories.

Influential Foundations

The foundations in the field of computer science are considered mainly to have been laid in the 1950s and 1960s with the early computer theoretical

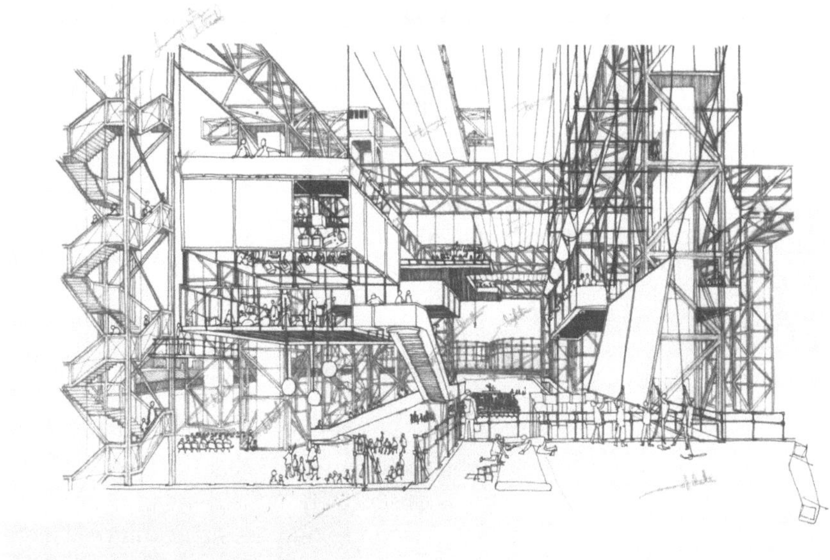

FIGURE 0.8 Cedric Price, in 1961, was perhaps the most influential of the early architects to adopt the theoretical work in cybernetics and extend it to an architectural concept of "anticipatory architecture."

frameworks, programming languages (FORTRAN, LISP, COBOL), integrated circuit development, and preliminary groundwork in AI. It was not until the 1980s and 1990s that an explosion of development occurred within the field of computer science with the creation of the Internet of Things (IoT) and Embedded Computation (IE). These early developments hinged on a few important theories of logic at the time. Ivan Sutherland, the recurring pioneer responsible for the "Ultimate Display," was among the first to voice an understanding of logical relationships in his 1963 Ph.D. thesis when he included parametric change in his Sketchpad system through topological connections. "If the user moves one vertex of a polygon, both adjacent sides will be moved. If the user moves a symbol, all lines attached to that symbol will automatically move to stay connected to it."[31] Sutherland would go on to receive the Turing Award in 1988.

Within the field of applied mathematics and architecture, many credited the Italian Luigi Moretti as the one who originally coined the term "parametric architecture." Moretti's association as one of the first to use the term is largely for his introduction of an eight-point definition of "parametric architecture" in his article published in *Moebius* in 1971.[32] In the article, he defined this term as an architecture governed by mathematical logic underpinned by computer techniques and analytical decision making. It should be noted that before his published parametric manifesto, he worked for years on the underlying concepts. In 1957, he founded the Institute for Operations Research and Applied Mathematics Urbanism (IRMOU) to continue studying "parametric" architecture. Moretti established a critical framework for systems thinking and components-to-whole relationships, contrasting with the contemporary design process of that time. Several at this time built upon the early foundations defined by Moretti, whereby architecture was governed by mathematical logic underpinned by computer techniques and analytical decision-making methods. Beyond Moretti's theoretical framework, many would step further back and point to Antonio Gaudi and Frei Otto's early string and weighted models as having a "propagation-based" parametric form-finding aspect to their design methods. As software advanced, there was an expected intersection with Moretti's theory and the early maquettes like those of Gaudi and Otto.

The Artificial Intelligence pioneer Marvin Minsky and the linguistics pioneer Noam Chomsky would formulate the early tenets of what became known as Shape Grammars. The logical foundations resided in the overlap of computer science (AI) and cognitive linguistics. Marvin Minsky was a cognitive scientist and co-founder of MIT's AI laboratory in 1959 with John McCarthy. Minsky was a proponent of connectionist models of cognition, which emphasized the role of interconnected neural networks in language processing, which he saw as more in line with the complexities of human language and cognition. On the other hand, Chomsky was specifically focused on formal rule-based grammatical structures.[33] The work of Minsky and Chomsky went on to be highly influential on a young James Gips and George Stiny, who became the leading authority on Shape Grammars and defined the field for decades. Giving rise to the theories, Stiny and Gips initiated their legacy with seminal texts in the early seventies that would influence generations of researchers in several fields beyond strictly architecture.

The Influence of the Computer Timeline

Ultimately, many of the computational developments relevant to the architecture profession began with a pioneering idea, often even a prototype, and then a massive time lag before they became practically influential. This is because digital technology needed to be accessible, affordable, and powerful enough for the pioneering ideas to become reality. We will see in subsequent episodes how even profound future trends, such as the internet and ubiquitous computing, manifested out of these simple principles related to development.

Beyond these principles, several patterns have also proven to strongly influence the development trajectory of computation. The first two patterns are identified as Moore's Law and Metcalfe's Law. Moore's Law (1975) states the number of transistors that can fit on a chip will continue to double approximately every two years, and computer memory will cost half as much while taking up half as much space. The impact of Moore's Law on the advancements in microprocessor technology has driven digital electronic development such that it is now a clear metric for productivity and economic growth. Metcalfe's Law (1980) states the network benefit increases as a square of the number of users. George Metcalfe was correct in communicating the value of a network grows faster than its size measured in linear terms. This theory paved the way for the assumption that networks of sensors, actuators, and code will become part of our everyday environments. A third pattern more specifically relevant to architecture is that of recontextualizing the chemistry term of autocatalytic processes.[34] The autocatalytic process is defined as the catalysis of a reaction by one of its products. In the context here, such processes describe how the pace of change accelerates because digital technology reinforces the development of innovative products. This pattern will gain increased traction when coupled with communication modalities that synthesize products with communication and awareness. From publications for buildings and research to conferences and social media, autocatalytic acceleration of applied digital technology helps to fortify developmental trends discussed in subsequent episodes.

While we cannot cover the history of the computer in the scope of this book, it is necessary to understand a very brief overview of computing. By definition, a computer is a device, typically electronic, that follows a set of instructions known as a program to execute sequences of logical operations or arithmetic functions. A digital computer differs only in that it typically stores information and performs operations at a much higher rate of speed. The first use of the word "computer" suggests a 17th-century origin related to arithmetic and humans doing calculations of many different types. This application lasted even through the mid-20th century and analog computer development when it was necessary for manual information input. In the 20th century, women were often hired for this role due to the disparity in higher pay rates of their male counterparts. By the start of the 1940s, the majority of "human" computers were women due to the war and the pay rate – a social factor often overlooked.[35]

The study of the history of the computer itself is now an academic enterprise often rewritten as seen through the lens of changing cultural perspectives. The book *Computer: A History of the Information Machine*[36] recognizes this advancement in its later editions by now including chapters on topics such as the globalization of information technology, the rise of social media, and new regulatory frameworks. The extended computer history grew out of technologies made over centuries devised to calculate and precisely account for information objectively. As speed, power sources, calculation complexity, and information storage informed the technological innovation, so did the sophistication of the computing devices and, ultimately, their subsequent impact on the broader cultural application.

Analog Computing

Computational devices date as far back as the abacus (2400 BC), the Antikythera mechanism from Ancient Greece (150 BC), and even the English slide rule (1620). Wilhelm Schickard and Blaise Pascal (Figures 0.9 and 0.10) independently designed, prototyped, and constructed the first calculators from the 1620s to 1640s.[37] It is not hard to see the progression of the Jacquard Loom (1804) that facilitated weaving patterns taken from paper tape to the invention of the punch card by Herman Hollerith in the 1880s used for data storage, to the application of the punch card by IBM to administrate everything from social security to local library card catalogs.[38] Other advances like Giovanni Piana's Perpetual Calendar (1835) and Leonardo Torres Quevedo's analog machines (1890) provided essential advancements toward the first analog computer.

As early as the 1820s and 1830s, Charles Babbage designed the groundbreaking proposals for what are widely considered the first mechanical computers. The Difference Engine was a special-purpose digital computing machine for automatically producing mathematical tables. It operated on discrete decimal digits rather than binary and

FIGURE 0.9 Schickard's "calculating machine" is based on the 1623 letter from William Schickard to astronomer Johannes Kepler. Schickard's calculator could perform functions up to six digits.

FIGURE 0.10 Pascal's calculator was invented in 1642 and was one of the first mechanical calculators. Pascal's calculator, like Schickard's, was able to perform functions up to six digits.

consisted entirely of mechanical components of gear wheels, rods, ratchets, and pinions. Babbage never completed the full-scale machine but did complete several fragments, including a small working model, in 1822.[39] Over a decade later, in 1833, Babbage proposed The Analytical Engine (Figure 0.11), which secured the first significant step toward modern computers. Although it was never built, its design embodied the major characteristics of modern computers. The Analytical Engine included memory, a central processing unit, and the ability for input and output. Ada Lovelace worked with Charles Babbage to design the analytical engine, and just a few years later, in 1843, she developed the first-ever computer algorithm. It was Ada Lovelace[40] who foresaw the possibility of using the Analytical Engine for non-numeric computation beyond its use for calculation. Encapsulated in her notes of an article that she translated on the Analytical Engine are what many consider to be the first computer program.[41]

It was not until 1936 that Alan Turing, the mathematician, computer scientist, and philosopher who pushed the limits of what a computer could do so profoundly that it would put him on a trajectory to become one of the most influential figures from the first half of the 20th century in terms of modern computing – both in theory and practical application.[42] His impacts were so inclusive that many consider him the father of

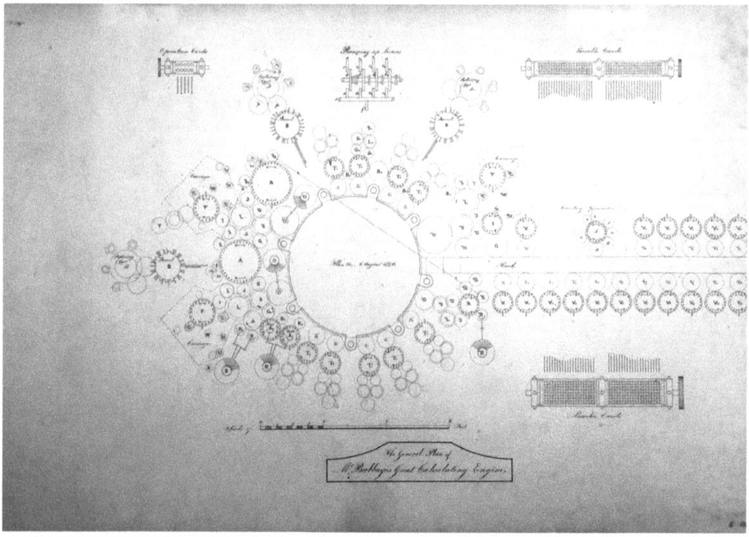

FIGURE 0.11 The Analytical Engine by Charles Babbage was first described in 1837 as a successor to his Difference Engine from the 1820s. It was proposed as a digital mechanical general-purpose computer.

computer science theory and artificial intelligence. His "Turing Machine" – or computing machine – consisted of a tape divided by squares containing single binary digits. For many in the computer science field, the Turing Machine represented the main theoretical model of the modern computer using a processor, programs, and memory – also known as the von Neumann computer architecture.[43] The Turing Test, developed in 1950 and built upon Turing's theories of artificial intelligence, is a series of behavioral tests used to detect thought or intelligence.[44] While variations of the Turing Test now exist, aligning with present-day definitions of AI, the general framework of Turing's original test remains to this day.[45]

Computing and War Machines

The acceleration of computational development by the early 1940s is inextricably linked to the global context of WWII. Yet, computing already had a long history with military efforts, specifically using programming information for precise calculation. For instance, Charles Babbage's Difference Engine originated by producing astronomical and actuarial tables for battle.[46] However, it would be Turing's ideas about universal computing – the ability to compute any type of information, that would lead to a seismic shift in computing development by the time WWII arrived. The move from mechanical to electromechanical and electric computing in the 1940s and

1950s meant the number of calculations and processing speed accelerated. From 1939 through 1940, Alan Turing, Gordon Welchman, and Harold Keen developed the "Bombe," which was an electromechanical encryption device used to decipher the German Enigma machine's daily settings. This early computing accomplishment was critical in turning the war efforts for Allied forces. By 1943, Tommy Flowers developed the Mark I Colossus, also a part of Turing's Bletchley Park British deciphering team. The Colossus was an electronic computer that proved essential in the war efforts all the way through D-Day.

Two additional early developments in computer technology taking place at this time were the Z3 and the ABC. In the case of Z3, Konrad Zuse created the first fully programmable automatic electromechanical computer in Berlin in 1941. The other important electromechanical contribution was the Atanasoff-Berry Computer (the ABC). John Vincent Atanasoff and Clifford Berry developed their arithmetic logic unit using vacuum tubes to solve linear equations in 1942. While the Z3 and the ABC had little to no direct effect on the war efforts other than demonstrating capabilities, they both laid the groundwork for significant technological advancements critical to hardware and software taking place at that time and tied into broader computer efforts taking place in subsequent years, namely the ENIAC.

By 1946, John Mauchly and Presper Eckert developed the ENIAC (Electronic Numerical Integrator and Computer). The ENIAC was a massive machine with more than 17,000 vacuum tubes, 70,000 resistors, and 10,000 capacitors, filling a 30′ × 50′ room and weighing around 60,000 pounds (Figure 0.12). Developed by the US Military at the University of Pennsylvania, the ENIAC was engineered to "compute the values of artillery range tables."[47] The ENIAC was technically the first general-purpose digital computer, and while it could complete extensive calculations, it had no programmable capacity or memory. Given this limitation, the ENIAC required data input for each new calculation. A team of women known as the ENIAC Six (Kathleen Antonelli, Jean Bartik, Frances "Betty" Holberton, Marlyn Meltzer, Frances Spence, and Ruth Teitelbaum) were the driving force in working out the daily programming and notation of the ENIAC for it to function.[48] This group, who was not recognized until the 1990s for their important role, is in no small way a direct connection to the earlier programming work of Ada Lovelace and her work with Charles Babbage and also echoes the residual latency of women getting just credit within the computer science field at that time.

Pushing Computation into the Broader Marketplace

After the ENIAC came the UNIVAC (Universal Automatic Computer) in 1951 as the first general-purpose commercially available computer. The UNIVAC was also very large, weighing 16,000 lbs. and utilizing over 5,000 vacuum tubes. However, it was able to make its way into corporate research labs and

FIGURE 0.12 The ENIAC was the first general-purpose digital computer. When replacing bad tubes, the technician needed to go through each of the 19,000 possibilities to identify which one needed to be replaced.

university basements to begin the digital computing revolution (Figure 0.13). The UNIVAC and other first-generation computers were replaced by transistor computers of the late 1950s, like the IBM 608 and the Philco-Transac S-1000, which were smaller, used less power, and could perform nearly a thousand times more operations per second. These were, in turn, supplanted by the innovative development of the integrated circuit in 1958 by Jack Kilby and Robert Noyce. While the vacuum tube and the transistor were advances in computing in how they reduced size and processing speed, they still required many parts and were expensive. The Integrated Circuit System (ICS) was constructed out of a single material, small and inexpensive to build by comparison. This, in turn, started the rapid development of reducing the size and increasing the capacity of computing power.[49] By the 1950s, the "interconnections problem" or "the numbers barrier" stood as the most important unsolved problem in electronics.[50] That problem would gradually be solved by Jack Kilby and Robert Noyce, which would eventually make possible the silicon microchip, ultimately earning Kilby the Nobel Prize for physics in 2000 for working out the early ideas.

Getting beyond the primary trajectory of this episode but relevant in understanding many of the non-linear developmental lags, we see one of the most important developments coming in 1971 with the Intel 4004 Microprocessor as the first general-purpose programmable processor on the market

FIGURE 0.13 The UNIVAC I (Universal Automatic Computer I) was the first general-purpose electronic digital computer design for business applications produced in the United States. It was designed principally by J. Presper Eckert and John Mauchly, the inventors of the ENIAC and made available starting in 1951.

(Figure 0.14). The microprocessor was a "building block" that engineers could purchase and customize with software to perform different functions in various electronic devices. It was the first commercially produced microprocessor and the first in a long line of Intel CPUs.

It was Marcian Hoff who is credited for initially developing the concept and was then joined by Stan Mazor. Still, it was not without two critical technical innovations by Federico Faggin that Hoff's concept could be realized in a single chip.[51] The move to the microprocessor proved critical in the transition of moving the large, room-sized computers of the time into the hands of individuals and businesses to revolutionize many social and cultural frameworks.[52] The single innovation provoked a sense that now was the time for democratizing access and exploration.

FIGURE 0.14 The Intel C4004 Processor utilized silicon gate technology (SGT), developed by Federico Faggin, Ted Hoff, and Stan Mazor in 1971. The 4004 provided twice the number of transistors with five times the operating speed.

Conclusion

Many of the theoretical foundations relevant to computational developments in the profession of architecture have been around for quite some time, preceding any actual development in many areas. The point is related strongly to the concept of autocatalysis mentioned previously, where we find a relatively linear incremental progression of computational development in general while, at the same time, much of the development related explicitly to architecture had a good deal of very early pioneering development, which lay dormant until the technology was sufficiently developed to demonstrate technologically feasible practical application. As we will see throughout the following episodes, architecture often usurps what it can best implement and use. This phenomenon certainly extends into the recent history of computational technologies and how architects have marshaled, adapted, and even pioneered toward a specific intention. This sentiment will be explored over time through oscillating roles of toolmaking from within the profession. If architects are to play a role in directing the technological development affecting design and the built environment, then they may be better served to reframe the thinking to ask what is architectural about computation, not the inverse.

Notes

1 Kostof, S. (1977). "The Practice of Architecture in the Ancient World: Egypt and Greece," in S. Kostof (ed.), *The Architect: Chapters in the History of the Profession*. New York: Oxford University Press.
2 Bernstein, P. (2022). *Machine Learning: Architecture in the Age of Artificial Intelligence*. London: RIBA Publishing.
3 Gerbino, A. and Johnston, S. (2009). *Compass and Rule: Architecture as Mathematical Practice in England, 1500–1750*. London: Yale University Press.
4 Nadali, D. (2011). "2013 When Ritual Meets Art. Rituals in the Visual Arts versus the Visual Arts in Rituals: The Case of Ancient Mesopotamia," in C. Ambos and L. Verderame (eds.), *Approaching Rituals in Ancient Cultures. Proceedings of the Conference*, November 28–30, 2011, Rome (Supplemento n. 2 alla Rivista Degli Studi Orientali Nuova Seria), pp. 209–226. RIVISTA DEGLI STUDI ORIENTALI LXXXVI. Approaching Rituals in Ancient Cultures.
5 Carpo, M. (2011). *The Alphabet and the Algorithm*, pp. 16–17. Ukraine: MIT Press.
6 Vittorio, P., Attilio P., and Sigrid A. (2020). "Statics of Self-Balancing Masonry Domes Constructed with a Cross-Herringbone Spiraling Pattern." *Engineering Structures*, 215. doi:10.1016/j.engstruct.2020.
7 Carpo, M. (2013). "Craftsman to Draftsman: The Albertian Paradigm and the Modern Invention of Construction Drawings," in *The Working Drawing*, edited by A. Spiro and D. Ganzoni, pp. 278–281. Zurich: Park Books.
8 Ibid.
9 Rykwert, J. (1988). "Introduction," In *Alberti, Leon Battista. On the Art of Building in Ten Books*. Cambridge, MA: MIT Press.
10 Note, for details on the dates associated with the bulk of the authorship see the following account: Grayson, C., in *Kunstkronik, 213* (1960), and *Münchener Jahrbuch der Bildenden Kunst, 11* (1960).
11 Gerbino, A. and Johnston, S. (2009). *Compass and Rule: Architecture as Mathematical Practice in England, 1500–1750*. London: Yale University Press.
12 Ibid.
13 Carpo, M. (2017). *Architecture in the Age of Printing: Orality, Writing, Typography, and Printed Images in the History of Architectural Theory*. Cambridge, MA: The MIT Press.
14 Ibid.
15 Syravong, P. (2020, February 11). *Top Construction Inventions That Have Shaped Our Modern World*. Digital Builder. See https://blog.plangrid.com/2016/04/the-history-of-blueprints/
16 "ACM History." *Association for Computing Machinery*. Available at: http://www.acm.org
17 *The Technium*. Edge.org. Available at: https://www.edge.org/conversation/kevin_kelly-the-technium [accessed February 6, 2023].
18 Ibid.
19 "Ivan Sutherland," A.M. Turing Award Laureate. Available at: https://amturing.acm.org/award_winners/sutherland_3467412.cfm [accessed February 8, 2023].
20 Ross, H. (2021, January 4). *The History of the Sketchpad Computer Program – A Complete Guide*. History-Computer. See https://history-computer.com/sketchpad-guide/
21 Celani, G. and Veloso, P. (2015). "CAAD Conferences: A Brief History." *Conference: The Next City – New Technologies and the Future of the Built Environment:16th International Conference CAAD Futures 2015* at São Paulo, pp. 47–58.
22 *The Sensorama: One of the First Functioning Efforts in Virtual Reality: History of Information*. Available at: https://www.historyofinformation.com/detail.php?id=2785 [accessed February 8, 2023].

23 Stivers, T. and Sidnell, J. (2005). "Introduction: Multimodal Interaction." *Semiotica, 156*(1/4), 1–20.
24 *The Evolution of Virtual Reality* (2016, August 16). SYR-UMT. See https://onlinegrad.syracuse.edu/blog/virtual-reality-infographic-accessible/
25 Van Krevelen, D. W. F. and Poelman, R. (2010). "A Survey of Augmented Reality Technologies, Applications and Limitations." *International Journal of Virtual Reality, 9*(2), 1–20. doi:10.20870/ijvr.2010.9.2.2767.
26 Cline, E. (2011). *Ready Player One*. New York: Random House Publishing Group.
27 Negroponte, N. (2021). *The Architecture Machine*. Cambridge, MA: The MIT Press. See https://mitp-arch.mitpress.mit.edu/the-architecture-machine
28 *The Architecture Machine Group at MIT Produces the Videodisc "Discursions": History of Information*. Available at: https://www.historyofinformation.com/detail.php?id=5418 [accessed February 9, 2023].
29 Wiener, N. (1948). "Cybernetics." *Scientific American, 179*(5), 14–19. doi:10.1038/scientificamerican1148-14.
30 Pask, G. (1969). "Architectural Relevance of Cybernetics." *Architectural Design*, September 1969, 494–496. Available at: https://compscicentral.com/history-of-computers/
31 Sutherland, I. E. (1980), *Sketchpad: A Man-Machine Graphical Communication System*. New York: Garland Publishers.
32 Moretti, L. (1971). "Ricerca Matematica in Architettura e Urbanistica." *Moebius, 4* (1), 20–53.
33 Beaugrande, R. D. (2014). *Linguistic Theory: The Discourse of Fundamental Works*. Oxford: Taylor & Francis.
34 Kumar, S. and Bentley, P. (2003) *On Growth, Form and Computers*. Amsterdam: Elsevier Science.
35 Smith, E. E. (2013). "Recognizing a Collective Inheritance through the History of Women in Computing." *CLCWeb: Comparative Literature and Culture*, 15(1). doi:10.7771/1481-4374.1972.
36 Campbell-Kelly, M., Aspray, W. F., Yost, J. R., Tinn, H., and Con Díaz, G. (2023). *Computer: A History of the Information Machine*. Oxford: Taylor & Francis.
37 "Calculator" (1998, July 20). *Encyclopedia Britannica*. Available at: https://www.britannica.com/technology/calculator [accessed February 10, 2023].
38 "The Punched Card." *IBM*. Available at: https://www.ibm.com/history/punched-card
39 Copeland, B. J. (2000). *The Modern History of Computing*. Available at: https://plato.stanford.edu/entries/computing-history/#analog [accessed February 10, 2023].
40 Campbell-Kelly, M., Aspray, W.F., Yost, J.R., Tinn, H., and Con Díaz, G. (2023). *Computer: A History of the Information Machine*. Oxford: Taylor & Francis.
41 Essinger, J. (2014). *Ada's Algorithm: How Lord Byron's Daughter Ada Lovelace Launched the Digital Age*. London: Melville House.
42 Cooper, S. B. and van Leeuwen, J. (2013). *Alan Turing: His Work and Impact*. Amsterdam: Elsevier.
43 Mol, D. *Turing Machines*. Available at: https://seop.illc.uva.nl/entries/turing-machine/#AlteHistModeComp [accessed February 10, 2023].
44 Copeland, B. J. (2004). *The Essential Turing*. Oxford: Clarendon Press.
45 George, B. St. and Gillis, A. S. (2023, April 25). "Turing Test." *TechTarget*. Available at: https://www.techtarget.com/searchenterpriseai/definition/Turing-test
46 "Computer History: All about the ENIAC." *HP Canada*. Available at: https://www.hp.com/ca-en/shop/offer.aspx?p=computer-history-all-about-the-eniac [accessed February 10, 2023].
47 Ibid.
48 "The World's First General Purpose Computer Turns 75." *Penn Today*. Available at: https://penntoday.upenn.edu/news/worlds-first-general-purpose-computer-turns-75 [accessed February 10, 2023].

49 Reid, T. R. (2007). *The Chip: How two Americans Invented the Microchip and Launched a Revolution*. London: Random House, pp. 3–23.
50 Ibid.
51 Faggin, F., Hoff, M. E., Mazor, S. and Shima, M. (1996). "The History of the 4004." *IEEE Micro, 16*(6), 10–20. doi:10.1109/40.546561.
52 Note, for an accounting of early university labs and marketplace development in the 20th century see Metropolis, N. (2014). *History of Computing in the Twentieth Century*. Amsterdam: Elsevier. Information provided on locations in the US, UK, Western and Eastern Europe, and Japan.

EPISODE 1

PIONEERING (1973–1981)

This episode marks a time when the futuristic speculations of the past finally begin to be matched by the present technological advancements. The prologue covered a history of the architect's analog working methods, the birth of computers, and the pioneering architectural speculations ahead of their "digital" time. In this episode, we see that although computers were still extremely exclusive and challenging to operate, the computer moved out of the hands of a few and into the hands of many, allowing several pioneers to develop actual proof-of-concept work in architecture.

In general, it did not take long for the computer to move from the basements of university buildings, onto office desktops, and into our houses. As far back as 1973, Robert Metcalf introduced one of the most profound early-stage digital communication building blocks with his preliminary work on the Ethernet, and in 1977, the desktop "Trinity" became available to the general public. The Apple II, the TRS-80, and the Commodore PET were released as some of the world's first highly successful mass-produced microcomputer products. These commercially available computers were introduced at the first West Coast Computer Fair in San Francisco in 1977, showcasing a broader subcultural phenomenon for personal computing that would unfold over the next decade. Broader social interest in computer technology was spurred on by these developments, and the general proliferation of personal computing was on the rise.

The previous decade saw visions cast by bold voices regarding a daring future, although often preceding any technological means to bring them to reality. Nevertheless, we find several pioneers who developed significant foundational work in solid modeling and visualization. Most of the work in architectural computation at this time was at the level of university research without commercially available software. It was led by notable pioneers, including Chuck Eastman, George Stiny, and William Mitchell, among

DOI: 10.4324/9781032671208-3

others, who covered vast areas of development that served as the foundational work that defined areas such as BIM, design cognition, solid and parametric modeling, cybernetics, and even digital/human interaction.

The Future Is Now

This episode also opens against a backdrop of significant social and technological changes. It was a time when the pendulum of national identity and global/spatial responsibility was starting to emerge. In the United States, the Apollo Space Mission had concluded a year earlier, in 1972, and wrapped up four years of feverish lunar exploration. The technology used to capture a sense of extraplanetary adventure and computational prowess was large, expensive, and tethered to specific corporate, military, or academic institutions regarding use and application.

In the previous decade, architecture was equally bold and outwardly projective in how it envisioned a future. From the TWA terminal to the Olympiastadion in Munich and from Buckminster Fuller to Oscar Niemeyer, a heroic ambition characterized the cross-pollination of architecture and engineering. By the time 1973 arrived, the appetite for large expressive technological goals gave way to a sense that now was the time for the democratization of access and exploration. Less governed by any political position, the stops and starts of capitalist instincts and new forms of information sharing would characterize this phenomenon for the next ten years. The symbols, speeches, and iconic moments of the previous years were exchanged for the transition of moving the large room-sized computers out of the basements and secure locations of labs and universities and into the hands of individuals and businesses to revolutionize all social and cultural frameworks.[1] Design professions benefitted from this as much as any industry. The ability to ultimately develop a toolset (hardware/software) that heightened precision, efficiency, communication, and innovation was profound. The future was no longer an eventuality; it was here and now. While the process was slow to emerge, and with predictable miscues and dead ends, the proliferation of digital technology into the hands of innovators, visionaries, entrepreneurs, and a creative class that would revolutionize the introduction of mobile computer technology defined this moment.

A strategic number of companies and universities recognized the potential of expanding their hardware and software infrastructure as the 1970s began. Decades before, we can point to the RCA Lab at Princeton (1942), developed by John von Neumann, inventor of the MANIAC,[2] or Howard Aiken's early work with the Mark 1 for the US Navy (1945–1955) as early precedents of computer science labs and government partnerships joining forces for military technology R&D.[3] However, by the time the 1970s arrive there were new motivations and emerging players. IBM dominated the mainframe business during the 1960s and 1970s, but their business model transitioned to provide consulting and a research mandate for many institutions in subsequent decades.[4] Similarly, Project MAC at MIT bridged a new model of computing (including Marvin Minsky's work in AI) with Bell Labs and General Electric.[5] Subsequent groups and labs would go on to be developed and lay the groundwork for multiple decades of development in digital technology. Even if these labs did not initially generate commercially viable market-ready outcomes, the critical advancement of their work was essential for how it would later become the technology that now proliferates our lives today. Within the architecture design context, this period represented the foundational building blocks on which many of the earliest promises of hardware and software were delivered and when the early seeds of CAD/CAM were spread.

Bringing the Questions Forward

Certainly, as digital toolsets were being developed for architecture, this brought a new series of questions into focus that had been percolating for some time. No single design voice correlated the ambitions of the early 1960s with the social and political awakening of the early 1970s. Some architects and designers, like the Eames, questioned broader manufacturing processes, as well as social identity and responsibility.[6] More specific to computation, the research initiated by Leslie Martin and Lionel March at the University of Cambridge and out of the LUBFS (Land Use and Built Form Studies), was seminal in opening the debate about the usefulness of applying new quantitative methods and theories to planning and architecture. The LUBFS was founded in 1967 with several research groups impacting the recognition of the theoretical importance of mathematics in design, particularly regarding computation. Dean Hawkes and Richard Stibbs were one of the first to bridge the theoretical in developing a computer program for building envelopes and energy performance.[7] March was particularly interested in understanding how geometrical form could be described symbolically and represent a correct relation to its surrounding environment. João Rocha outlines the fascinating early connections in his Ph.D. thesis at MIT,[8] where he explained how March welcomed the new paradigm that "shape grammars" represented for design as relevant to his own work.

Others, like Nigel Cross, presented caution in the promises being made through emerging technologies as an early treatise questioning the role of the computer in the design process. Nigel Cross's book *Automated Architects*[9] (1977) suggested that relegating tasks, specifically design functions, would not produce superior outcomes. Based on his research, he believed the computer was not a tool capable of playing a role in the design process. Others, discussed later in this episode, disagreed with his premise, and yet inherently, Cross's questions brought about specificity in the desired role of computer technology in the design process. While Cross's position on the capacity for computational tools to function in the design process would evolve,[10] his research for nearly three decades laid the groundwork for both design theories on cognitive and human behavior and questions related to the emergence of AI in design. As computational capacity increased and levels of interaction became more sophisticated, Cross continued to transform his thinking about the role of computational tools, always keeping an eye on the digital/human balance. Cross would ultimately arrive at a more causal position relative to technology, searching for an understanding of how designers think, "For me, the value of asking the question 'Can a machine design?' is that it begs the corollary question, 'How do people design?'"[11]

By the early 1970s, many academics and theorist from computer science, engineering and mathematics, architecture and design, information technology, cognitive science, and human behavior were exploring the intersection of their various fields. New digital toolsets were making opportunities available

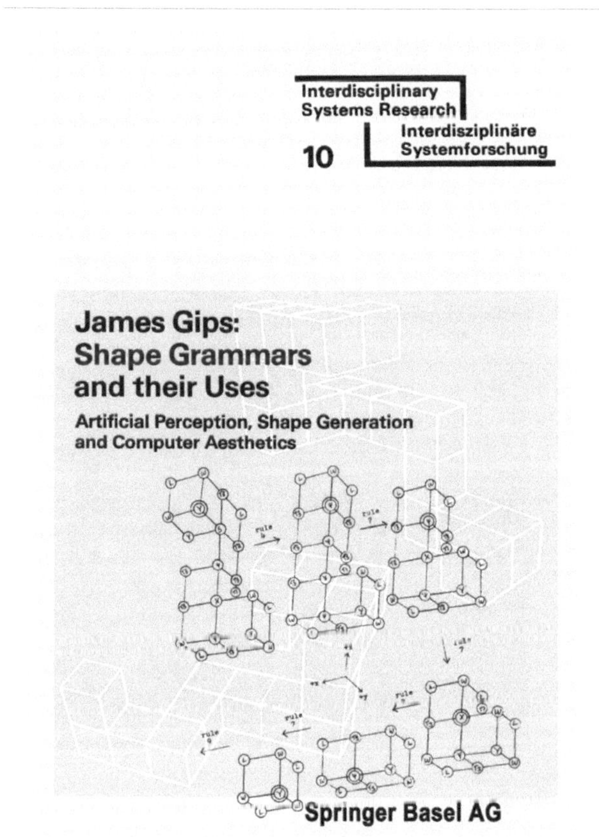

FIGURE 1.1 1975 cover of James Gips's *Shape Grammars and their Uses: Artificial Perception, Shape Generation and Computer Aesthetics.*

for experimentation and exploration. Building on the foundations of Minsky and Chomsky, mentioned previously, as well as the parametric thinking of Moretti, James Gips went on to write his doctoral thesis on Artificial Intelligence (AI) while at Stanford, which ultimately led to its publication by Birkhäuser of *Shape Grammars and their Uses: Artificial Perception, Shape Generation and Computer Aesthetics*[12] in 1975 (Figure 1.1), while George Stiny would attend UCLA and formulate similar thoughts while writing his doctoral dissertation in the Systems Science Department. His three-volume edition entitled *Pictorial and Formal Aspects of Shape and Shape Grammars: On Computer Generation of Aesthetic Objects*[13] would also come out simultaneously as Gips's treatise in 1975 (Figure 1.2).

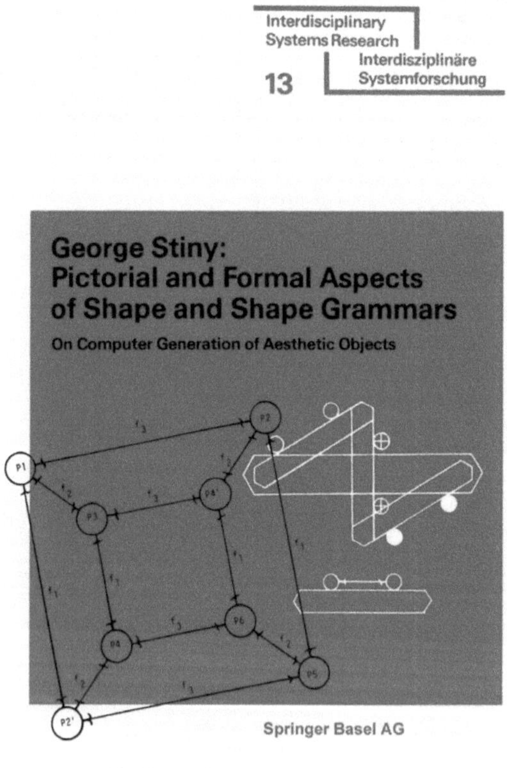

FIGURE 1.2 1975 cover of George Stiny's *Pictorial and Formal Aspects of Shape and Shape Grammars: On Computer Generation of Aesthetic Objects*.

What Stiny and Gips established in their work, and others would take up with them over the next several decades, was the way shapes or geometries provided the language for procedural operations based on chosen rules represented a wholly new approach. As a rule-based system used to generate design, the visual language of initial 2D and eventually 3D geometry provided a clear link to design methodology.[14] The ultimate link to procedural modeling and work was done by William Mitchell and Robyn Liggett at UCLA, which started a more direct integration of shape grammar into design applications when Stiny joined the faculty in 1979. Terry Knight would significantly contribute to the direct integration of design procedures beginning in the 1980s.[15]

Additional scholars like Jose Duarte, Jose Beirao, and Jonathan Cagan would work with, and ultimately go on to expand on, the potential of Stiny and Gips's early work. There would be a broad exploration into many fields, such as urban design, architecture, landscape design, craft, painting, product design, and mechanical design. Most recently, Denis Sheldon and Larry Sass (discussed in later episodes) found computational software design and parametric applications for shape grammars, showing the enduring legacy of this pioneering work.[16]

Directed Research | Bridging Architecture

One of the salient developments leading to the critical research and dissemination of new knowledge in computer hardware and software at the start of the 1970s was the role directed research organizations played in bridging the academic and professional context. Existing labs focused on technology integration, and new emerging labs with this focus on digital technology provided a fertile environment for entrepreneurial exploration and innovation. These labs, many of which implemented public/private funding or academic/governmental funding, served as a precursor to a broader expansion of research groups, labs, and centers that led to important computational design purposes mentioned in later episodes.

Bell Labs was one of the oldest and most diverse research labs in the United States. Its origins date back to Alexander Graham Bell and his patent for the telephone in 1876, but subsequently, it has never been a singular focus research entity. Peripheral technological advancements throughout the early to middle 20th century provided undeniably critical parts of the framework needed to advance the toolsets in use today, such as advancements in acoustics (1925), advanced radar (1941), information theory (1948), laser creation (1958), and UNIX OS (1968).[17] In 1972, Dennis Ritchie developed the C programming language that led to Bjarne Stroustrup initiating the development and release 11 years later in 1983 of C++.[18] Additional inventions and patents came out of Bell Labs continuing to pioneer in parallel fields such as the creation of HDTV technology (1988), Self-Organizing Networks (2010), and Quantum Computing (2010).[19]

In 1970, the Xerox Corporation created the multi-disciplinary Palo Alto Research Center (PARC). Early success in developing laser printing and object-oriented programming laid the groundwork for one of the most important developments ever to come out of PARC, the ALTO personal computer, in 1972. Attribute as the first personal computer (PC) (Figure 1.3). Xerox never made the ALTO commercially available. However, the development of technology foreshadowed the wave of change that was to take place in the computing world. This machine's physical and virtual foundation would launch a generation of PCs that inspired the commercial success of many companies and would translate the technology exhibited in the ALTO into a global success. Of note was the involvement of Alan Kay, considered one of the fathers of personal computing, who helped guide the ALTO's operational development. Alan had introduced the progenitor to the tablet computer called the Dynabook (1972), and while it was not a direct

FIGURE 1.3 The Xerox PARC Alto Computer features 128KB of memory, a 2.5 MB removable cartridge hard drive, a 5.8 MHz CPU, a 64-key keyboard and a 5-finger key set, bit-mapped black and white display sized 606 × 808, and a three-button mouse.

success, the Dynabook laid the ground for the windowing graphic user interface (GUI) and the early work for the development of the Object-Oriented programming language that would go on to produce SmallTalk-80 in the ALTO (Figure 1.4). In 1978, Xerox PARC placed ALTOs in four locations: The White House, the US House of Representatives, the Atlantic Richfield Company, and its own sales division in Santa Clara. In addition to these governmental and commercial testing grounds, Xerox PARC donated 50 systems to universities throughout the United States, such as MIT, Stanford, and Carnegie Mellon. The ALTO served as an early distributed technology advantage for these institutions that would help seed the next round of computational innovation.

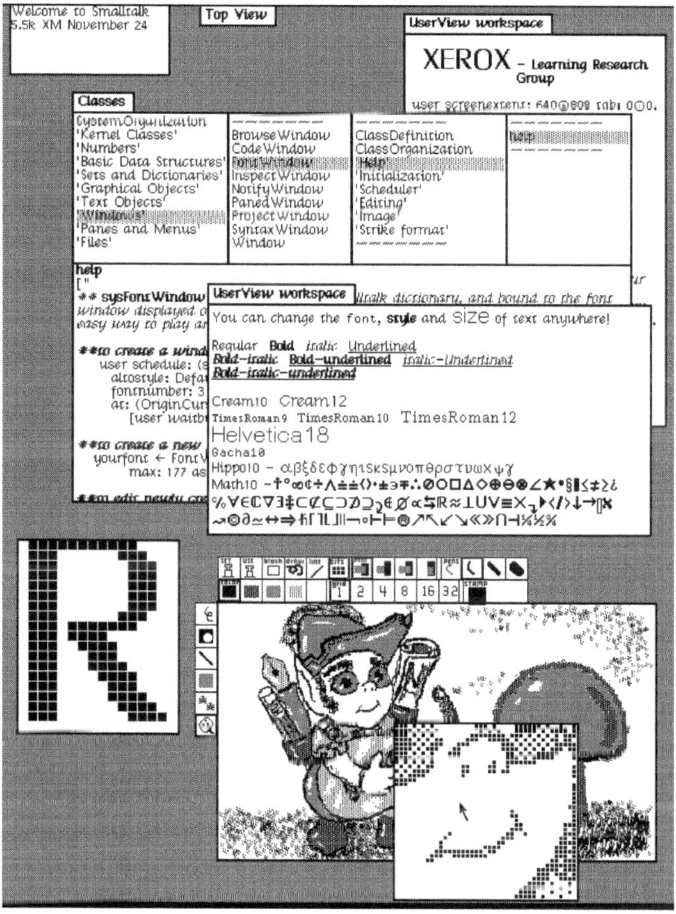

FIGURE 1.4 Graphic User Interface for SmallTalk-80 developed by Alan Kay and as part of the standard ALTO OS. The object-oriented programming language and direct influence on the Lisa and Macintosh computers designed by Apple.

At the same time, another innovation originating from the brain trust of PARC was the ethernet, the origins of which are credited to Robert Metcalf's Ph.D. dissertation.[20] However, it would be the more gradual work of Metcalf, David Boggs, Butler Lampson, and Chuck Thacker working to link the hundreds of computers at Xerox PARC while also running the fast laser printers being developed there that brought the ethernet into reality in 1973. By linking the computers to a larger system, the PARC scientist achieved a higher speed of communication in a networked manner than what existed at the time. Standardization took place in the early 1980s through the Institute of Electrical and Electronics Engineers (IEEE), which formalized the 802.3 standard, thus making it possible for a more unified expansion and adoption of the technology.[21] Ethernet formed the groundwork for network systems, both local area network (LAN) and wide area network (WAN), which eventually became a global system by the late 1980s and early 1990s and one of the primary vehicles of the internet.

The ethernet (1973), WYSIWYG (1973), SuperPaint Frame Buffer (1974), Graphic User Interface – GUI (1975), and Very-Large-Scale-Integration – VLSI Circuit Design (1977) were all key to many CAD tools that would go on to be developed.[22] Michael A. Hiltzik's account of PARC's unparalleled impact on the future of digital and popular culture suggests that we wouldn't have a mouse interface, Gothic font, infrared link to laser printers, ATM touch screens, or local internet networks without PARC. To put a finer point on it, he writes that PARC's technology is so pervasive that "When Apple sued Microsoft in 1988 for stealing the 'look and feel' of its Macintosh graphical display to use in Windows, Bill Gate's defense was essentially that *both* companies had stolen it from Xerox."[23]

The Architecture Machine Group (AMG) at MIT, as mentioned in Episode 0, was formed by Nicholas Negroponte and Leon Groisser in 1967. The AMG, most succinctly, explored the relationship between the human and machine dynamic. Negroponte's treatise on this subject, *The Architecture Machine: Toward a More Human Environment,*[24] published in 1970 by MIT Press, outlines the forward-looking potential for how digital technology and humans had entered a new and profound moment of symbiosis where the mutualism of our dialogue would carry us toward new vernaculars. The book's conceptual framework was especially poignant for translation into the design process, on which Negroponte focused his research.[25] The URBAN5 Software was the first significant research project undertaken by AMG and exemplified the theories outlined in Negroponte's Architecture Machine text (Figure 1.5). Interaction and a dual language interface allowed for contextual development and a non-hierarchical user interface. There are also seeds of evolutionary and intelligent systems in the earliest stages of URBAN5. Negroponte would articulate in his follow-up book *Soft Architectures* (1975)[26] that the space between man and machine would close quickly moving forward, and the need for a professional mediator in the design process might flatten or

FIGURE 1.5 Developed in 1968, URBAN5 was an urban design software programmed in FORTRAN. Nicholas Negroponte and Leon Groisser, sought to test language input and the democratization of the design process.

even disappear. In this regard, the argument for intelligence or Artificial Intelligence mapped out from the previous two decades of pioneering thinkers like Minsky, Turing, Pask, and Feldman was important to Negroponte's own work for this text.[27] The compression of space between the computer and designer (machine and man) foreshadowed the implications of Artificial Intelligence, language interface, and cybernetics almost five decades later.

By the time the AMG had run its course in the early 1980s, the building blocks for the MIT Media Lab were already well established. As mentioned, Negroponte and other research collaborators at MIT ensured demonstrating technological advancements was secure in the new pedagogical and research framework. One of the early examples, The *Aspen Movie Map*, a now seemingly innocuous immersive technology, was a multimedia program placed in Aspen, Colorado's topographic and urban environment. Partially funded by the Department of Defense, the prototype was thought to have the potential for advanced urban warfare tactics.[28] The broader impact of this project would be the clear precursor for the development of Google Maps, interactive shooter games, and video simulation training.[29]

Negroponte would leverage his position at MIT to expand the academic and public reach to rapidly create a network of engagement with some of the most impactful thought leaders in the earliest moments of computational design development. The AMG and subsequent Media Lab established a collaborative prototype for other digital design academics around the world to model. The proliferation of similar models took time, and as research, funding, and scholarly networks expanded, variations on this early AMG model were set in place by other institutions and labs.

Birth of the Personal Computer

In 1974, the philosopher and sociologist Ted Nelson self-published *Computer Lib/Dream Machines*[30] (Figures 1.6) as a manifesto on communication theory predicting many of the philosophical trajectories that would shape the next decade of personal computing. A decade later, Steve Levy, in his essential book on hacker culture in the mid-1980s, would reference Nelson's book as the starting point for him – "the epic of the computer revolution, the bible of the hacker dream."[31] What Nelson argued for was the liberation of communication. He coined the terms "hypertext" and "hypermedia" and was instrumental in giving vision to the idea that computers could be more than scientific instruments. He saw the computer as an instrument for creation, communication, and a tool for everyone – liberating the masses.

In this regard, his text foreshadows the personal computer and serves as a guidepost for the rapid development of a networked system spreading affordable machines throughout society.

FIGURE 1.6 Originally self-published in 1974, the two-front cover of Computer Lib/ Dream Machines by Ted Nelson is considered the first book about the personal computer. The book could be read from either direction, and introduced new words into the digital lexicon such as "intertwingled."

Nelson would go on to envision a reworking of the hierarchical computation system. The computer offered access and freedom to everyone, and with it came agency to explore and implement commercial and non-commercial outcomes, and the design community took full advantage of this newfound freedom. Many in the design community found the computer to be a tool not only for organization but also for creative exploration. As Ted Nelson argues:

> My special concern, all too tightly framed here, is the use of computers to help people write, think and show. But I think presentation by computers is a branch of showbiz and writing, not of psychology, engineering, or pedagogy. (…) I have not mentioned the emotions. Movies and books, music and even architecture have for all of us been part of important emotional moments. The same is going to happen with the new media. To work at a highly responsive computer display screen, for instance, can be deeply exciting, like flying an airplane through a canyon, or talking to someone brilliant.[32]

The PC Arrives

On April 16th of 1977, in San Francisco, what had only been the backroom rumblings of smaller cohorts of enthusiasts and individuals spilled out into the mainstream with 12,000 people gathering for the multi-day event called the West Coast Computer Faire. The event brought together the young Steve Jobs, Steve Wozniak, Bill Gates, and Paul Allen – along with many more early trailblazers. It synchronized the inventors and entrepreneurs of the personal computer world with a growing and eager audience. As the West Coast Faire and other events would catalyze over the next several years, the fast proliferation of inventors, companies, enthusiasts, and investors was spreading faster than anyone could keep up with. One of the Faire's most impactful marks was the introduction of what would later be called the "1977 Trinity" of personal computers: the Commodore PET, the Apple II, and Tandy Corporation's TRS-80 (Figure 1.7).

The Commodore PET 2001 was the first PC system introduced to the public at the Consumer Electronics Show in January 1977. The PET worked similarly to its competition, offering 8K of RAM with a built-in monochrome monitor and cassette drive for information storage. Due to the manufacturing capabilities of Commodore International, the company could keep the price low at $795, which offered a competitive advantage. The PET was powerful enough to do what programmers needed but still within reach of most people's budgets.[33] The PET laid the foundation for what would go on to become the highly successful Commodore 64.[34]

Apple Computers emerged out of the Job's family garage on the heels of the Apple-I experiment with what would serve as a catalyst toward a

FIGURE 1.7 The 1977 "Trinity" personal computer trio as described in *BYTE* Magazine in 1995 for how it launched a PC revolution. Shown from left to right: Commodore Pet 2001, Apple II with monitor, and the TRS-80.

personal computing revolution in the Apple II. The company marketed the Apple II with the tagline: "Simplicity is the ultimate sophistication."[35] This mantra would capture the spirit of Wozniak's brilliance in computing design, which he had been refining while at Hewlett Packard and perfecting as a side hustle with Jobs on projects for Atari. With the Apple II, the user had the agency to customize the computer in a way that was not previously possible by allowing simultaneous flexibility and expandability. The first Apple II's initial RAM was similar to its competitors. 4K of RAM priced the system at $1,298 and pegged the unit well above the Commodore PET 2001 and the TRS-80. The fully expanded Apple II with 48k of RAM was well over double that price tag and came in at $2,638. Despite these initial costs and some early manufacturing challenges, the cost of memory quickly came down, and thus, by 1980, the price of almost every system was cut in half.

Tandy Leather and Radio Shack formed Tandy Radio Shack (TRS) in 1963. In doing so, the company created a market niche for many different types of electronic products. Nearly 15 years later, the company took a calculated risk, moving into the new PC market using the Z-80 processor, from which it derived its name, and offering 4k of RAM. The monochrome monitor used block graphics and cassette tape for data and program storage combined with the hardware box to retail for $599.95. The TRS-80 was a success in both home and business applications almost immediately.[36] With over 3,000 retail locations across the country, RadioShack had a built-in distribution network and brand recognition that made early marketing an easier on-ramp to the public. The low entry level to ownership, the use of BASIC programming, and the no-frills approach to component-based design made it an accessible selection for many looking to get a foothold in the PC world. As the prices came down on RAM and other amenities became selling features like color monitors and advanced GUI, the TRS series had to evolve with subsequent iterations. Later models would include these features and keep sales strong into the early 1980s. However, the TRS impact was most profoundly felt in the earliest days of the PC launch, spreading to many households and businesses across the United States.

The Rise of the Graphic Workstation (1980)

If the 1977 Trinity represented inroads with the home user, by 1980, the development of software, specifically graphic software, liberated many design professions to adopt more affordable machines that could now take on numerous existing and new tasks that introduced networked computer systems into the professional context. These machines were not available at the same price as the growing personal computer market. Still, they were essential to distributing the CAD and eventual 3D modeling technology that would become more popularized over the 1980s and 1990s.

The Apollo Computer was launched by William Poduska in 1980 and headquartered in Boston. Apollo Computer Inc. epitomized the East Coast regional development trajectory of early-stage personal computers. A highly successful, early-to-market, proprietary approach for key technology that relied on the regional supply chain to seek a market advantage.[37] The corporate self-sufficiency mold would lead to early success and openings for market competition due to a more regional market configuration. The Apollo systems' unique power and graphic capabilities appealed to the scientific and professional AEC communities. The CAD/CAM software industry was on the rise, and as the Dataquest Report of 1983 pointed out, the advantages of a superior operating system, high-speed graphics, and the use of virtual memory distributed over a network made the Apollo computer an industry favorite. The competitive advantage remained even as competition grew tighter into the middle part of the 1980s. The industry fought to target the needs of technical professionals and, by 1987, included a clear message about how it approached the market:

> The Apollo system represents a unique architecture supporting a new way of using computers and offering substantial performance for a relatively low price. These products directly address the needs of technical professionals who require high-performance, low-cost graphic systems that can share information among various users.[38]

Apollo Computers' success in the early 1980s to mid-1980s made it a prime target for corporate restructuring and takeover in the latter half of the decade.

When Hewlett Packard bought Apollo in 1989, much of the core CAD/CAM industry was already changing.

The earliest seeds of the Sun Workstation computer rose out of the Stanford Computer Science Department with Professor Forrest Baskett, along with leading students Andreas Bechtolsheim, Vinod Khosla, Scott McNealy, and Bill Joy. Stemming from the earlier mentioned ALTOs donated to Stanford from PARC, the team combined unique networking capabilities with UNIX and the commonly used Motorola 68000 for the CPU.

While prototyped and prepared for the market throughout 1981, the workstation was launched early in 1982. The four students would ultimately take the Sun Workstation and form Sun Microsystems (Figure 1.9). Sun Workstation produced a personal computer system focused on the combination of "graphics and networking capabilities with powerful local processing."[39] Capitalizing on the adaptive integration of technology and the agile market integration, Sun quickly found a market foothold. Unlike the Apollo computer, the Sun machines came from a research-based institution funded partly by DARPA and connected to Xerox PARC. As one of the companies to join the Silicon Valley technological revolution in the 1970s and 1980s, Sun embodied the open system approach of many of these entrepreneurial start-ups and thrived on a different view for R&D and marketing of their machine. While similar in the desire to create a system that competitively offered a powerful graphic user interface, the open system and more agnostic manufacturing approach allowed Sun to surpass Apollo by the mid-1980s. However, like many of the early success stories of the hardware companies of the early 1980s, Sun was acquired by Oracle in 2009 for its ability to bring substantial hardware products to the existing company portfolio.

Early Digital Design Pioneers

In this episode, it is important to identify several individuals, many of whom worked in overlapping circles, creating the foundation upon which the architectural computation world developed over the next five decades. If much of the previous text in Episode 0 and Episode 1 represents the "root system" of the computational architecture tree, then these early pioneers helped establish the early formation of the "tree trunk," with their trajectories still informing what is taking place today. Many of these people started, and even in some instances remain, in academic positions. Still, their reach was felt through innovations bridging far into the public, professional, and organizations of our computational design infrastructure.

We have already mentioned Nicholas Negroponte and his work at MIT with the formation of the AMG and later the MIT Media Lab, as well as Stiny and Gips for their contributions to symbolic geometry and Shape Grammars in the 1970s. Beyond these are the important contributions of computer scientists like Don Greenberg and Patrick Hanratty and architects and technologists like Charles "Chuck" Eastman, William "Bill" Mitchell, and Tom Maver. We will see in subsequent episodes that the names of important contributors often reappear throughout the book. This is because so many of these pioneers were cutting new paths through uncharted territory by inventing or using emerging computational toolsets toward new processes or even entirely new fields, and their discoveries and advancements rarely fit within just one period.

In the field of Computer Graphics and Visualization, Donald Greenberg has been one of the most influential thinkers and educators over the past five decades. His work and research have set much of the foundation upon which the modern film and computer visualization industries reside.[40] This work in animation would open the eyes of a broad community to gain awareness of what was on the horizon for visualization and the direction of computer-aided design. So much so that a still of the animation was featured on the cover of *Scientific American* in May of 1974 (Figure 1.8). In 1973,

FIGURE 1.8 A still from the "Cornell in Perspective" animation developed and would go on to become the cover of the May 1974 *Scientific American* was developed by Greenberg and his student team at the General Electric Visual Simulation Laboratory. The animation of I.M. Pei's Johnson Museum of Art helped shape early consciousness of computer rendering and animation.

FIGURE 1.9 The Cornell Box establishes the benchmark for rendering accuracy in computer graphics software. The first publication of this demonstration was in 1984 without objects. Future developments create versions to test various lighting conditions, rendering types, material properties, and geometry.

Greenberg's interest in computer graphics did not easily conform to any specific academic department. The architecture department thought it was too technical, the engineering department thought it was too superficial, and computer science thought it was too much in applied research. Cornell University, as an institution, had the good sense to support the research as an interdisciplinary center and matched funding to start one of the first and longest-recognized research initiatives into the role of computer visualization in the design process. Later, in the mid-1980s, Greenberg and his colleagues at the Program for Computer Graphics established the "Cornell Box" as the benchmark for verifying accuracy in rendering software. One determined accuracy by selecting parameters for comparing a rendering with the actual photograph of the same scene, thus making it possible to test 3D modeling lighting accuracy (Figures 1.9). Much of what now constitutes accurate lighting in commercial software can be traced back to Greenberg's Program for Computer Graphics at Cornell.[41]

His influence in the architecture and animation fields related to how we think of visualizing space and form has been profound, with an ongoing specialization in real-time/realistic image generation, color science, and computer-aided architectural design. Greenberg's recent course at Cornell on Digital Twinning reflects five decades of work on visual communication in architectural representation. His legacy is defined by rigorous and groundbreaking nationally-funded research and a list of nearly 20 former students who have won technical Oscars for their accomplishments in the field of computer animation.[42] Greenberg, while at a retrospective panel discussion with Robert Aish, Chuck Eastman, and Tom Maver, highlighted a prevailing sentiment for the group regarding architects taking control over the development of their tools: "I spent my life as a toolmaker. The architecture field is much to blame because they never put their creative input into what they want. That's why you're stuck with what you have now."[43] The underlying sentiment is that if architects are to play a role in directing the development of the technology that affects architecture, they ought to ask what is architectural about computation, not the inverse.

Most consider Patrick J. Hanratty to be the "Father of CAD/CAM" technology. Hanratty, it is suggested, provided the starting point for 70% of 3D mechanical CAD systems in use today.[44] After returning from the Korean War, Hanratty was hired by General Electric (GE). He accomplished several important projects in the late 1950s, leading to his early formation of a lifelong investment in CAD/CAM work. One of the earliest projects Hanratty was assigned while at GE was the development of the PRONTO numerical control software package. PRONTO (Program for Numerical Tooling Operations) translated machining instructions from the machining specialist provided from code sheets into punch cards and then processed these into digital instructions for the operations of the tool and pathway. At that time, this operated on a 2½ axis contouring operation and could machine parts at different Z levels but not machine complex 3D surfaces. By the 1960s, Hanratty was working for General Motors (GM) and was implementing his knowledge of CAM and numerically controlled software. By 1970, Hanratty started ICS (Integrated Computer Systems). ICS presented the first fully closed CAD/CAM operation using the software they created called INTERAPT. While this was a benchmark accomplishment, it also came with marketing challenges and proved too much to overcome, with most businesses needing greater flexibility at the time. However, this technical and financial failure would lay the groundwork for the ultimate triumph of Hanratty's career in creating MCS (Manufacturing and Consulting Services). MCS was pivotal in how CAD/CAM technology intersected with broader public and manufacturing awareness. Hanratty and MCS first developed ADAM and eventually AD-2000 as the CAD/CAM software standard.

In the 1980s, MCS would expand its market share further from mechanical, manufacturing, and nuclear to broader markets by releasing the ANVIL series software. During the 1980s, other companies provided competing

CAD/CAM products like SolidWORKS and Pro/ENGINEER. The ANVIL series remained superior for 5-AXIS milling capabilities and a manufacturing industry standard for several decades. However, as the CAD/CAM field diversified and generated more competitive price points, MCS could not remain competitive by the early 2000s. Hanratty did not set out to initiate CAD/CAM as a computational design tool for the academic or professional architecture context. By all accounts, his energies were primarily focused on the aeronautics, aerospace, and automotive industries. However, his pioneering work, like many of his contemporaries, laid the foundation upon which those in later episodes will pick up the inspiration and build the new toolsets used in universities, industry, and professional practices operate to this day.

The enduring title of the Father of Building Information Modelling (BIM) goes to Charles "Chuck" Eastman, who was best known as an early pioneer for the use and implementation of CAD in the fields of architecture, engineering, and construction.[45] While at Carnegie Mellon University in 1975, he first published his peliminary thinking on BIM in the article "The Use of Computers Instead of Drawing in Building Design."[46] In this article, he covered the possibilities of building description systems to facilitate a more fully descriptive 2D and 3D geometry within a digital environment. In 1977, Eastman began developing many of the primary features of what would go on to be known as BIM. His title for the new modeling program was GLIDE (Graphical Language for Interactive Design). Out of this development, he founded his own software company called Formtek (Formative Technology) in 1982, which operated for five years until it was sold to Lockheed Martin in 1987. During this highly influential time of creating GLIDE and launching Formtek, Eastman also recognized the importance and role of the academic organization in disseminating cutting-edge methods regarding digital toolsets. As a founding member and first president of the Association for Computer-Aided Design in Architecture (ACADIA) in 1981, he established the first of an eventual series of global networks of organizations to disseminate formal computational research discussed in the next episode.

It was at Georgia Tech that Eastman led the Digital Building Lab (DBL) until his retirement and also author his widely disseminated books, *Building Product Models: Computer Environments, Supporting Design and Construction* (1999) and then nearly 20 years later with *BIM Handbook: A Guide to Building Information Modeling for Owners, Designers, Engineers, Contractors, and Facility Managers* (2018). Eastman, like so many forging a new path would see his full vision develop and grow several decades after his original concepts were introduced. His research invented software that has revolutionized the way we practice today in the AECO (Architecture-Engineering-Construction-Operation) industry, and he influenced multiple generations of students with whom he worked and taught.

Another lifelong academic who has made a profound impact within the fields of information technology applied to architecture and building design is Tom Maver. Maver started as a research fellow at the University of Glasgow from 1961 to 1965, followed by the University of Strathclyde from 1967 to 1970. This second appointment was where he would establish his academic roots and one of the most crucial research initiatives for the next three decades. At the very earliest moments in the exploration of computer-aided design, Maver founded ABACUS (Architecture and Building Aids Computer Unit, Strathclyde), a research group within the Department of Architecture and Building Science at the University of Strathclyde. Early research projects for the ABACUS group centered on economics, building performance, and early visualization of 2D plotting technology for what would become the first "virtual prototype." By the 1980s, the group advanced to more sophisticated 3D modeling that ultimately helped push advanced energy behaviors, cultural heritage, and research related to large-scale urban modeling, virtual reality, rapid manufacture, and shape-grabbing technologies.

In 1982, Maver would go on to be instrumental in founding two highly influential organizations that disseminated research on the emerging field of computer-aided design. First, in 1982, Maver helped establish *Education and Research in Computer-Aided Architectural Design in Europe* (eCAADe) with Rik Schijf, Marijka Molleart, and Hendrijka Buelinckx. Later, in 1985, Tom Maver, Rik Schijf, and Harry Wagter established CAAD Futures. Both organizations worked together collaboratively and were vehicles for advancing issues related to computer-aided architectural design in Europe and abroad, functioning through international conferences and publications. These are discussed in greater detail in the next episode and within the context of other formal organizations established around the same time period.

Although not a technology specialist like the others, a long-lasting influential academic voice was that of the technology futurist William "Bill" Mitchell, who could connect computation's present and future implications. His prolific publications included pioneering research in information technologies integration into urban and architectural design. After a highly influential time as a student at Yale, he quickly started to shape his broader thinking on the physical and urban context, first as a professor and then as chair of the UCLA Architecture Department (1970–1986). At UCLA, he started to encounter the emergence of early digital technology and the influence of other fields that would shape a later appropriation of methodology, such as aeronautics animation and automotive. After UCLA, he went on to teach at the Harvard Graduate School (1986–1992) and then at MIT as Dean (1992–2003), where he cemented a legacy of almost prescient awareness of where technology and the built environment were moving. His salient understanding of the coming influence of issues related to digital technologies and how they would transform the field of architecture allowed him to research, publish, and mobilize some of the most forward-thinking aspects of where the field and our future design fields would head.

Some of his most influential texts are a roadmap for thinking about how the built environment will transform based on new technology. *The New York Times* credited his 1977 book *Computer-Aided Architectural Design*[47] and his 1990 work *The Logic of Architecture: Design, Computation, and Cognition*[48] as having "profoundly changed the way architects approached building design."[49] Later, Mitchell would continue his forward speculations into such areas as Smart Cities, digital networks, transportation mobility systems for a future city, and a sustainable future.

With these early pioneers, an unwavering boldness transcended the unknown to provide confidence to generations after them. Often, they had no pre-existing evidence to support the direction they were pursuing. However, the throughline with all these examples suggests that if we can gain anything from their stories so far, they looked at the evidence of the development of the cultural and technological advancements of that moment and applied it to the experiences of their lives to make a poignant and clarifying voice for where the digital toolsets would evolve over the next 50 years.

Conclusion

In this episode, we see that although computers were still extremely exclusive and challenging to operate, they did begin to become both technically and economically accessible to many.

The ability to develop a toolset (hardware/software) that heightened precision, efficiency, communication, and innovation was to serve as a profound catalyst. The moment was defined by the proliferation of digital technology getting into the hands of innovators, visionaries, entrepreneurs, and a creative class. Although most of the work in architectural computation was at the level of university research without commercially available software, it still produced foundational work that defined areas such as BIM, design cognition, solid and parametric modeling, cybernetics, and even digital/human interaction.

Notes

1 Note, for an account of early university labs and marketplace development in the 20th century see: Metropolis, N. (2014). *History of Computing in the Twentieth Century*. Amsterdam: Elsevier. Information provided on locations in the US, UK, Western and Eastern Europe, and Japan.

2 ETHW. (2017, April 12). "RCA Laboratories at Princeton, New Jersey – Engineering and Technology History wiki." ETHW. Available at: https://ethw.org/RCA_Laboratories_at_Princeton,_New_Jersey

3 Eckert, J. P., Jr. (2014) "The ENIAC," in *History of Computing in the Twentieth Century*, edited by N. Metropolis. Amsterdam: Elsevier, pp. 525–550.

4 Cortada, J. W. (2018). "Change and Continuity at IBM: Key Themes in Histories of IBM." *Business History Review, 92*(1), 117–148. doi:10.1017/s0007680518000041

5 "The History of Computing: Project MAC and Multics." Available at: https://thehistoryofcomputing.net/project-mac-and-multics [Accessed August 28, 2023]. See also https://multicians.org/project-mac.html [Accessed August 16, 2023].

6 Note, Charles and Ray Eames exemplified a salient design voice capitalizing on the new ethos to ask larger questions that cut across many disciplines. In their introduction to the Powers of Ten at the Norton Lecture Series at Harvard on

October 26, 1970, Charles Eames situated the core meaning of the earliest version of the film to be philosophically environmental. The scientific facade exploring scales of microbiology to astrophysics concealed the more coded message related to ecological issues. In this regard, the Eames were crafting a parallel vision for the next generation of innovators, designers, and scientific minds that would ask how we would see ourselves aligning with larger principals that required a recalibration of what defined success from the past decade or more.

7 Stibbs, R. J. (1968). "A Computer Aided Design Analysis System." Dissertation, Cambridge University Mathematical Laboratory. See also, Stibbs, R and Steadman, P. "A Computer Aided System for Architectural Design and Analysis." *Cambridge Research, 2*(1), 18–22.

8 Rocha, A. J. M. (2004). "Architecture Theory, 1960–1980: Emergence of a Computational Perspective." Universidade de Évora.

9 Cross, N. (1977). *The Automated Architect.* London: Methuen.

10 Cross, N. (2001). "Can a Machine Design?" *Design Issues, 17*(4), 44–50. doi:10.1162/07479360152681083

11 Ibid., p. 54.

12 Gips, J. (1975). *Shape Grammars and Their Uses: Artificial Perception, Shape Generation and Computer Aesthetics* (1st ed.). Basel: Birkhäuser.

13 See https://medium.com/@isohale/shape-grammars-1989ddcdeef7 [Accessed August 29, 2023].

14 Knight, T. and Stiny, G. (2015). "Making Grammars: From Computing with Shapes to Computing with Things." *Design Studies, 41*, Elsevier Ltd. 8–28.

15 Knight, T. (2015). "Shapes and Other Things." *Nexus Network Journal, 17*(3), 963–980. doi:10.1007/s00004-015-0267-3

16 Tepavcevic, B. and Stojakovic, V. (2012). "Shape Grammar in Contemporary Architectural Theory and Design." *Facta Universitatis – Series: Architecture and Civil Engineering, 10*(2), 169–178. doi:10.2298/fuace1202169t.

17 See https://www.bell-labs.com/timeline [Accessed August 17, 2023].

18 Bhave, M. and Patekar, S. (2012). *Object Oriented Programming with C++.* Chennai: Pearson Education India.

19 See https://www.bell-labs.com/timeline [Accessed August 17, 2023].

20 Brock, G. W. (2003, September 25). *The Second Information Revolution.* Harvard University Press.

21 Hill, S. (2023). "Everything You Need to Know About Ethernet." *Wired*, April 20. Available at: https://www.wired.com/story/what-is-ethernet/ [Accessed August 18, 2023].

22 "PARC History – A Legacy of Innovation and Inventing the Future" (2018, June 20). PARC – The Future Concepts Division of SRI. Available at: https://www.parc.com/about-parc/parc-history/ [Accessed August 18, 2023].

23 Ibid., p. 21.

24 Negroponte, N. (1970). *The Architecture Machine: Toward a More Human Environment*. Cambridge, MA: MIT Press.

25 Ibid., p. 9.

26 Negroponte, N. (1975). *Soft Architecture Machines*. Cambridge, MA: MIT Press.

27 Ibid., pp. 7–8.

28 Beck, M. (ed.) (2012). *The Aspen Complex*. London: Sternberg Press, pp. 138–157.

29 Halpern, O. (2019, November 21). "A History of the MIT Media Lab Shows Why the Recent Epstein Scandal Is No Surprise." *ARTnews.com*. Available at: https://www.artnews.com/art-in-america/columns/mit-media-lab-jeffrey-epstein-joi-ito-nicholas-negroponte-1202668520/ [Accessed August 10, 2023].

30 Nelson, T. H. (1975). *Computer Lib/Dream Machines*. Self-published (1st ed.) Tempus Books/Microsoft Press (2nd ed., 1987).

31 Levy, S. (1984). *Hackers: Heroes of the Computer Revolution*. New York: Doubleday, p. 143.

32 Nelson, T. H. (1975). *Computer Lib/Dream Machines* Self-published (1st ed.) Tempus Books/Microsoft Press (2nd ed., 1987), p. 127.
33 Pitre, B.G. and Loguidice, B. (2013). *CoCo: The Colorful History of Tandy's Underdog Computer.* Boca Raton, FL: CRC Press, pp. 13–15.
34 Lunduke, B. (2022, April 7). "Ground Zero for the Personal Computer Industry: 1977s West Coast Computer Faire." *The Lunduke Journal of Technology.* Available at: https://lunduke.substack.com/p/ground-zero-for-the-personal-computer [Accessed August 19, 2023].
35 See https://www.apple2history.org/museum-a-l/ads/ [Accessed August 19, 2023].
36 *BYTE* (1995, September 9), *20*(9), 99.
37 Saxenian, A. L. "The Limits of Autarky: Regional Networks and Industrial Adaptation in Silicon Valley and Route 128," by the Department of City and Regional Planning; University of California at Berkeley.
38 CAD/CAM Industry Service Company Profiles Prepared (1987, September 9) by Dataquest, p. 165.
39 Bechtotsheim, A., Baskett, F., and Pratt, V. (1982). *The Sun Workstation Architecture,* Technical Report No. 229, March 1982, Computer System Laboratory Department of Electrical Engineering and Computer Science, Stanford University.
40 Handler, P. and Handler, M. *True Big Red: Professor Don Greenberg '55.* https://ecommons.cornell.edu/handle/1813/3462 [Accessed February 15, 2024].
41 Carlson, W. E. (2017, June 20). *5.1 Cornell and NYIT.* Columbus, OH: The Ohio State University. https://ohiostate.pressbooks.pub/graphicshistory/chapter/5-1-cornell-and-nyit/ [Accessed August 27, 2023].
42 Fleishman, T. (2022). "At 88, Greenberg Still on Cutting Edge with New Course." *Cornell Chronicle,* October 19, 2022. Available at: https://news.cornell.edu/stories/2022/10/88-greenberg-still-cutting-edge-new-course
43 Modelo. (2015, October 30). "Pioneers in Computational Design." *Medium,* October 30. Available at: https://medium.com/@Modelo/pioneers-in-computational-design-bb1c0f8a8234 [Accessed August 28, 2023].
44 Waurzyniak, P. (2010). *Masters of Manufacturing: Patrick J. Hanratty.* Available at: https://www.sme.org/technologies/articles/2010/masters-of-manufacturing-patrick-j.-hanratty/ [Accessed August 28, 2023].
45 Eastman, C. (1999). *Building Product Models: Computer Environments Supporting Design and Construction.* Boca Raton, FL: CRC Press.
46 Eastman, C. (1975). "The Use of Computers instead of Drawings." *AIA Journal,* March, 46.
47 Mitchell, W. J. (1979). *Computer-Aided Architectural Design.* New York: Van Nostrand Reinhold Company.
48 Mitchell, W. J. (1990). *The Logic of Architecture: Design, Computation, and Cognition.* Cambridge, MA: MIT Press.
49 Grimes, W. (2010). "William J. Mitchell, Architect and Urban Visionary, Dies at 65." *The New York Times,* June 15, 2010. Available at: https://www.nytimes.com/2010/06/16/us/16mitchell.html [Accessed August 28, 2023].

EPISODE 2

TRANSLATION (1982–1991)

This episode marks a prolific period of development in architecture and computation. In a dramatically short period of time, the personal PC became widely available, and no less than seven major architecturally specific software were released to the public, all vying for users in a profession that was clearly on the brink of being digitized. The newfound computer accessibility and discipline-specific software created a space for rapid expansion and exploration. Arriving almost simultaneously with the proliferation of computer and software access were newly formed academic and professional organizations created to initiate a more rigorous discourse on computer-aided design.

The Scramble

There was a mass scramble in the early 1980s to understand the impact and usefulness of computation in a world that had previously relied on analog procedures. This episode is simultaneously characterized by the architecture profession's rather pragmatic efforts to transition its methods and identity into digital means while simultaneously connecting several speculative and ambitious outposts of exploration that would stretch the "what if" thinking about where trajectories would head over the next decade. Mark Weiser may have been as prescient as anyone. His time at XeroxPARC in the mid-1980s to mid-1990s was definitive for his vision of how pervasive computing could become "everywhere, all the time." Weiser coined the term "ubiquitous computing,"[1] forecasting that computing would occur using any device, in any location, and in any format. He also went on to forecast theories of "calm technology" and "portable computing."[2] These predictions initially projected questions on the future potential of the value of data, energy, access, and agency but

DOI: 10.4324/9781032671208-4

ultimately projected a digital future that is all but a reality today. By 1983, and as a cultural harbinger, *Time Magazine* announced the PC would be the Person/Machine of the Year – beating out a disgruntled Steve Jobs.[3]

On the more speculative side and fueled by Weiser's theories of ubiquitous computing, there continued to be several developments in VR and haptic interfaces along with Mixed Reality (MR) in general. As established in Episode 0, Virtual Reality (VR) has a long history, with early traces built upon an analog foundation and then later Helig's Sensorama. However, by the mid-1980s, Jaron Lanier and Thomas Zimmerman founded *VPL Research*[4] to become the first company to sell virtual reality peripherals like goggles working off technology that we more closely associate with VR today (Figure 2.1). Like most bleeding edge technology, the market entry point was steep, making the accessibility point challenging for the average household to obtain

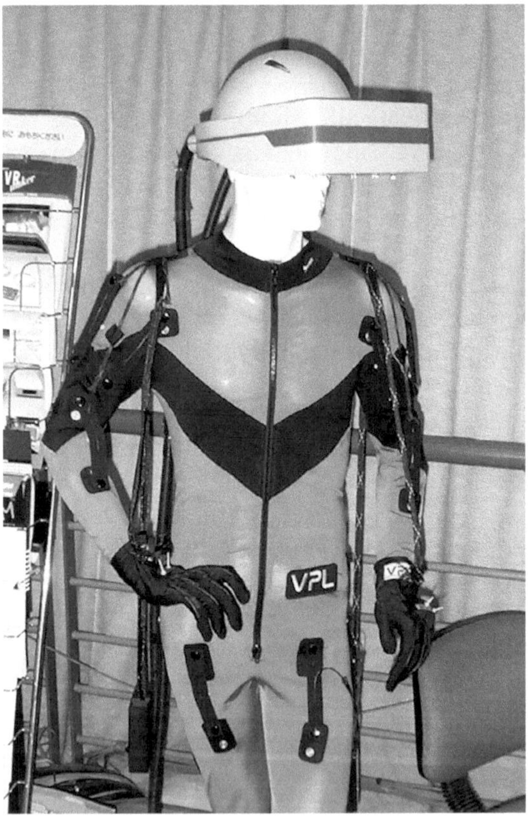

FIGURE 2.1 A VPL Research DataSuit, shown in 1989, includes a full-body outfit with sensors for measuring the movement of arms, legs, and trunk. The suite also includes the fully integrated peripheral Eyephone Goggles and Dataglove.

(EyePhone 1 $9,400; EyePhone HRX $49,000, and gloves $9,000).[5] Undeterred by slow market adoption, by 1987, VPL had universalized the term *Virtual Reality* and thus helped to start a unifying movement toward a growing field for many disciplines interested in exploring the newly available *mixed realities* made possible by the software and digitally tethered devices. By the decade's end, some took up the VR call to explore spatial design in urban and social spaces. "The Legible City" virtual reality installation of cityscapes by Jeffrey Shaw and Dirk Groeneveld (1989) at the World Design Exposition, Nagoya, Japan, showed pioneering navigation of urban context in VR space[6] (Figure 2.2 and Figure 2.3). This haptic bridge for architects and designers would take several years to fully register in terms of potential and implementation, but undoubtedly, this moment foreshadows one of the largest waves coming in future design impacts in subsequent generations.

Speculation on what it would mean to operate in the future of a digital world was in full bloom in the literary world. In his groundbreaking novel about our digital future, *Neuromancer*[7] (1984), cyberpunk pioneer William Gibson created alternate visions of digitized space that stretched social, technological, and even reality boundaries. Steven Levy's *Hackers: Heroes of the Computer Revolution* (1984)[8] traced how the proliferation of computer knowledge placed power into the hands of the users. With this power, these

FIGURE 2.2 Jeffrey Shaw and Dirk Groeneveld's "Legible City" VR installation at the 1989 Nagoya, Japan World Design Exposition. The bicycle allowed the viewer to navigate through different parts of a city animation, providing self-determination and customization of the user experience.

FIGURE 2.3 The Legible City was comprised of streets using the street plans of Manhattan, Amsterdam, and Karlsruhe to define the space for navigation. Riding through the city created various "storylines" for the rider.

new users crafted a new ethic and interface, creating a symbiotic balance between the hacker and the computer. For decades to come, the cinematic world would try and interpret what the science fiction world of Gibson, Bruce Sterling, Orson Scott Card, Philip K Dick, Arthur Clarke, Isaac Asimov, Michael Crichton, and others were inventing as bold new worlds. In the early 1990s, *Cyberspace: First Steps,*[9] edited by Michael Benedikt collected a more pointed application of these forays into technology, social structure, and reality and directly injected architectural consequences into the mix. Important essays, such as "Liquid Architecture,"[10] by Marcus Novak and "Mind is a Leaking Rainbow,"[11] by Nicole Stenger, hypothesized spatial consequences with physical/metaphysical constructs.

Michel Feher and Sanford Kwinter also curated a vision of the future through the edited volume of *The Contemporary City* (1986),[12] which took a multi-pronged approach to the physical, political, and perceptual transformations redefining the contemporary city. This book was a particularly compelling collection as it included academics and several critical practicing architects of the time recognizing and reconciling the urban transformations taking place, such as Christopher Alexander, Peter Eisenman, and Rem Koolhaas. These writings helped stretch the audience and speculation of where a new computational technological world would lead, as well as a vehicle for what role designers would play in helping to shape this world.

Understanding Impacts

The Rise of CAD Software

While concentrated activity dealt with how analog ways of doing things could be digitized, the progression was neither linear nor systematic. The initial steps were not so much of reconceptualizing a digital methodology but of recreating analog methodologies in digital space. Once the design software companies started to gain a foothold and companies understood the potential benefits of efficiency, accuracy, and scale, widespread adoption spread rapidly. While information manipulation in the math, science, and even word processing fields provided easy on-ramps for software development, the visual integration of the design disciplines proved to be an entirely different set of challenges. 2D and eventually 3D software capabilities expanded through representational and design processing power, presenting entirely new possibilities. The affordability of software followed a similar trajectory to hardware, making the computing approach a ubiquitous utilitarian tool. The proliferation of use and experimentation was possible where, previously, the lack of accessibility and affordability made hardware and software only attainable for large companies and specialized purposes. What would play out through the 1980s would be another tug-o-war for market share. The tension would continue between operating systems of PC, Mac, and Unix but now also include the cost of entry and products built for generalization or specialization.

Autodesk, maker of AutoCAD, would grow into the ubiquitous 800 lb. CAD gorilla but not before a much more inconspicuous start, emerging from earlier programs named InteractCAD and MicroCAD in the late 1970s. With a 1.0 release in 1982, the company presented a modest 2D CAD drafting program that brought digital drawing capabilities to the architecture and drafting community to replace analog toolsets (Figure 2.4). John Walker founded the company after acquiring the software from inventor Michael Riddle for $10 million dollars. Early success allowed the company to go public in the mid-1980s. Due to unique features for material and quantity take-offs, the software was widely adopted in the architecture, engineering, and construction fields. By the end of the 1980s, the company had cash and securities of over $100 million and owned 60% of the market.[13]

An additional CAD program developed by Lockheed Martin and running on IBM computers made strong inroads in the marketplace from the late 1960s through the late 1980s. Lockheed's CADAM Software was widely adopted within the engineering community because it completed tasks in "hours instead of days."[14] Up until 1986, CADAM was only available on a mainframe, making it a sizable investment for hardware and software licensing, ranging from $50k to $67k per system.[15] The CAD industry was a growing business by the mid-1980s,[16] and as Autodesk, IBM, and Lockheed

FIGURE 2.4 The 1987 newspaper advertisement shows an architect using an early version of AutoCAD on a PowerPak 286 IBM PC computer workstation. Combined with the digitizer, plotter, and scanner, drawings were developed using a range of digital modalities.

were joined by CATIA (discussed in a later section), the market started to differentiate based on smaller systems but also on 3D modeling capabilities, particularly surface modeling.

Early-Stage BIM

CAD in the 1980s can be understood as 2D capabilities becoming 3D, and to that end, architects, engineers, and computer scientists would find increasing synergistic ground. In some instances, individuals would emerge with the capacity to unite all three. As mentioned in Episode 1, Chuck Eastman is considered the "Father of BIM." His early writing on the Building Description System (BDS)[17] in 1975 foreshadowed a single integrated database for visual and quantitative analysis.[18] BDS was modeled after theoretical research by a young Ian Braid and Charles Lang at the University of Cambridge's Computer Laboratory. Their groundbreaking work in Boolean operations and 3D modeling, coupled with Eastman's previous educational experiences and interests in wicked problems, human behavior, and Artificial Intelligence,[19] coalesced around a vision for what became an integrated 3D graphic language modeler he called GLIDE in 1983.[20] After creating a parametric modeling start-up called Formteck in that same year and selling it to Lockheed Martin in 1987, he would spend the next thirty years in the academic context pioneering topics such as solid parametric modeling, interoperability, product models, and design cognition. In the case of Dr. Jonathan Ingram, his training as an engineer and a computer scientist led him to a computer-centric architecture practice in the UK in the early

1980s.[21] Here, the firm's limited 2D drafting capabilities led him to create his own 3D modeling software, which he called RUCAPS. Ingram's success with creating this software led him to form his own company and create SONATA in 1985. As Ingram describes many years later in his extensive history of BIM software, *Understanding BIM: The Past, Present & Future*[22] (2016), Autodesk passing on acquiring the SONATA software in 1987 was fortuitous because, ultimately, this would lead to the creation of REFLEX in 1992. These three programs were some of the earliest building blocks and precursors for modern-day BIM software. As we will see in later episodes, Ingram's influence didn't end in the early 1990s, as he would go on to be an active player in helping to develop the core features of what eventually became REVIT, which is now synonymous with BIM.

3D Possibilities and the OS Wars

During the 1980s, operating systems and software programs were uniquely compatible and reinforced operational configuration. As a result, this alignment developed produced distinct user factions. However, more than brand loyalty, the software and OS started to create initial tendencies based on the characteristics of the software and hardware employed. The OS wars had added tension within the architectural computing communities driven by the programs that were used. It was a time when several architecturally specific software were brought to the market, often ensnared in the OS they depended upon.

Vectorworks, created initially as MiniCAD in 1985 by the Diehl Graphsoft company, offered an alternative to PC-based operating systems. This software was used by architecture firms for construction document production and had widespread adoption for Mac OS users initially in specific global markets such as Europe. Vectorworks was an early adopter of 3D modeling and was one of the first software to introduce BIM capabilities well before it became a widespread industry standard.[23] Like Vectorworks, ArchiCAD was another privately developed software using the Mac OS. Originating out of Hungary and targeting the architecture community, ArchiCAD launched in 1987 after a five-year transition from complex terrain modeling origins. This background of surface modeling complexity made the push to BIM modeling a quick and initial characteristic of the software from its very early releases.

Beyond the operating system split highlighting the architecture CAD development in the mid-1980s, many iterative developments grew out of parallel fields outside architecture with profound impact. From software development in civil engineering and aerospace to animation, these all provided continued opportunities for parallel expansion in architecture and appropriation toward alternative design approaches altogether.

Silicon Graphics launched in the early part of the decade, providing a high-powered hardware/software combination that initially ran on a Unix-based OS (Figure 2.5). The power of the machine was matched initially by a

FIGURE 2.5 In 1991, Silicon Graphics, Inc. (SGI) introduced the IRIS Indigo workstation computer. One of the most advanced graphics workstations at the time, the hardware contained a 32-bit MIPS R3000A microprocessor and proprietary memory slots that supported up to 96 MB of RAM.

high price that made implementation challenging for many. Performance, however, was unmatched at the time. As other companies caught up to speed and undercut the performance/cost ratio, SGI, as it was later renamed, was challenged for where it could reside within the ecosystem of the architectural design community.[24] A back-and-forth between computing power, price, and targeted output proceeded for the next two decades. Within most architecture professional offices, networked and integrated systems of operation mattered the most. By contrast, experimentation and appropriation were prioritized in academic and research labs to explore new opportunities.

Bentley Systems was founded in 1984 and was initially offered to run on a Unix-based operating system before switching to a DOS-based OS with MicroStation in 1985. This market foray was noteworthy for building off the Intergrpah's IGDS CAD software that quickly led to the founding of Micro-Control Systems and the founding of the first 3D wire-frame CAD software for PCs called CADKEY.[25] Similarly, in 1981, CATIA (Computer-Aided Three-Dimensional Interactive Application) was initially created as a proprietary software for Avions Marcel Dassault company to design the Mirage fighter jet. The software was eventually spun off to provide CAD/CAM/CAE services to the aerospace and defense industries. The software ran on Unix mainly through the 1980s and 1990s but later became supported by Windows OS. Within the architecture and design communities, the software was popularized by Frank Gehry's office, who appropriated the software early on to design some of his most expressive work, such as the Guggenheim Museum in Bilbao (1991) and Disney Concert Hall in Los Angeles (1994).[26]

Filmmaker Gary Yost and his team released 3D Studio Max in 1990, which became the flagship product within the Kinetix group inside Autodesk.[27] The software revolutionized graphics and specifically animation software due to new approaches to materials and geometry and was an instant hit with the gaming and film community.[28] The design community appropriated the software for what it could offer as a means to explore new ideas regarding materials and geometry and how animation would now begin to unlock an entirely different dimension of the discourse. Around the same time as 3D Studio was emerging, FormZ also came to market initially as a Macintosh-based alternative to cartesian-driven software. FormZ was adopted similarly to 3D Studio as a tool for those interested in modeling complex shapes and surfaces not easily achieved by the standard CAD tools of the time. Chris Yessios and former student David Kropp founded AutoDesSys, Inc. in 1990 and released FormZ the following year. As a Professor at Ohio State, Yessios was responsible for many pioneering works in software development, 3D modeling, and building information modeling. His persistent marketing of FormZ pushed the design world into 3D modeling from the iron-clad initial embrace of 2D drafting.

Two agendas rose to the forefront at this relatively early stage of software creation. There was software developed to extend the capabilities and methods of the professional design process, and by contrast, there was software appropriated to disrupt the capabilities and methods of the design process. This duality was an extension of the professional/academic differences pre-dating digital technology arriving at this time. The distinctions, however, were not entirely mutually exclusive. There were firms experimenting with technology, and academic institutions were also simultaneously training digital literacy for the workforce of the future. As an indication of where the discussion sat midway through this episode, the North American and European conferences focusing on CAAD issues[29] held robust gatherings to debate the future of education, research, *and* practice brought on by the emerging digital toolsets. Regardless of the agenda, there was a case to be made that ultimately, both the academy and the profession followed Everett Rogers's Diffusion of Innovation Theory, where a small percentage of *"innovators"* and *"early adopters"* grew into an *"early majority,"* poised to make substantive changes heading into the end of the 20th century.

The Birth of Dissemination

This episode also begins an entirely new means of disseminating information, testing, researching, and hypothesizing about the future. Conferences that introduced the use and application of computer technology dated all the way back to the 1960s with the Design Methods movement in London, mentioned in Episode 0. At that time, computer scientists were interested in the design process, while designers were increasingly interested in digitizing analog tools. For the most part, however, these conferences and academic footholds had no clear organization or broader trajectory.[30] That changed in the early 1980s when several of the major educational CAAD (Computer Aided Architectural Design) organizations in North America and Europe were founded during this brief period, which today still serve as the primary outlets for research in computation and architecture. These organizations started as a collection of pioneers coming together to share ideas and methodology from their various regions. The earliest gatherings were titled workshops, highlighting the simple emphasis on exchanging information. However, it didn't take long for the formation, mission, and direction of these organizations to accelerate into vehicles for critical information exchange and dissemination. These organizations were led by innovators and pioneers who had been working, in some cases, for well over a decade in architectural computation from within their respective silos. The gatherings were a means to understand the intersection of architecture and digital technology, and diligently worked to quickly progress the structure and reach of their respective groups.

The Association of Computer-Aided Design in Architecture (ACADIA) was established in 1981 by CAD pioneers Bill Mitchell, Chuck Eastman, and Chris Yessios. Three years later, they are joined by Yehuda Kalay and nineteen[31] other founding members to establish bylaws for the organization, which focuses on establishing a platform for exchanging information used in computer usage in architecture design, planning, and the building sciences. From its earliest days, the organization saw its mission to explore technology related to the creative process and to enhance the physical and built environment instead of simply concentrating on production.

Shortly after ACADIA was established in North America, *Education and Research in Computer Aided Architectural Design in Europe* (eCAADe) was founded in 1983 by Tom Maver, Rik Schijf, Marijka Molleart, and Hendrijka Buelinckx. eCAADE was comprised of institutions and individuals with a common interest in promoting good practice and sharing information about the application of computational technologies in research and education for architecture and related professions across Europe. These two organizations comprised what would become known as the first of the "sister organizations," eventually forming a global alliance once additional groups joined them in the 1990s. The organizations collectively focused on strengthening the discourse and research framework on computational architecture and its many topics.

By 1985, individuals, organizations, and institutions were forging several different directions in response to how computational architecture would unfold. The conversation was simultaneously hyper-specific and localized, creating an ever-increasing larger venue for discourse and globalized participation and involvement. CAAD Futures was established in 1985 as a broad-based organization engaged in advancing topics of computer-aided design, unlike the two proceeding organizations, CAAD Futures has always remained geographically nomadic, anchored to whichever institution hosted the conference for that two-year cycle (Figure 2.6). Also founded by Tom

FIGURE 2.6 Cover for the proceedings from the first CAAD Futures conference taking place at the Department of Architecture, Technical University of Delft. The proceedings divided content into four sections: 1) systematic design, 2) drawing and visualization, 3) Artificial Intelligence, and 4) implications for design practice.

Maver and Rik Schijf along with Harry Wagter, this conference very early on established an important benchmark for publication quality, one that had not yet been established for the growing field of CAD and CAAD conferences but had a clear foothold within other areas of design and engineering disciplines. A truly seminal CAAD Futures conference took place at the GSD and MIT in 1989: "The Electronic Design Studio" and its purpose was to signal that CAD had entered the last curricular bastion of the design studio. Similarly, the International Building Performance Simulation Association[32] launched its first conference in 1987, and hosting conferences called the Building Simulation Conference every two years in various locations around the globe. These conferences focused primarily on research on the quantifiable aspects of building performance using computer-based modeling and folded in a different cross-section of the computational community, including those invested in the construction, maintenance, and operation of buildings.

John Gero's more topically concentrated and geographically anchored conferences served as a counterpoint to those that moved more freely around the globe. The Artificial Intelligence in Design Conference, which started in 1985, was ultimately usurped into Design Cognition and Computing (DCC) almost 20 years later, but not before serving as a critical platform for the early examination of how AI would reconfigure the design process. These conferences, whether content and context-specific or wide-ranging in location and topics, all rapidly expanded the dissemination of how and why people used the now readily available hardware and software. These organizations and their presentations and publications created a pedagogical foundation that would give rise to the rapid and important expansion of the experimentation that would follow.[33]

That same year, in 1985, Nicholas Negroponte and Jerome Wiesner formed the MIT Media Lab. A unique mixture of university-based but privately funded labs dedicated to research and product development involving media. This implementation of digital technology overlaps into the realms of digital/physical environments, Artificial Intelligence, and various modalities of representation and hardware/software development. The Media Lab would serve as an exemplar for public-private collaborations fostering interdisciplinary research that focused on the cutting edge of technology. The Media Lab continued a legacy of art and technology that started in previous decades (Menlo, XeroxPARC, Bell Labs) and, in many ways, would spur a proliferation of labs in schools of architecture around the globe for decades to come.[34] The second half of the 1980s was also a time that served as an entry point to the introduction of CAD into schools of architecture. Often on the fringe of traditional educational pedagogies, there were those who pioneered truly novel curricular paths, including Bill Mitchell at UCLA, Ulrich Flemming at Carnegie Mellon, and then Bill Mitchell again with Malcolm McCullough at the GSD. At that moment, it required vision on the part of academic leadership to recognize the potential of the emerging technology, as well as those who were teaching the courses on CAD, geometric modeling, programming, and design studios. As previously mentioned, conferences like ACADIA, CAAD Futures, and eCAADe became vibrant spaces for pedagogical discourse and exchange. Anton Harfmann,[35] Yehuda Kalay,[36] and Chuck Eastman[37] were also making valuable contributions to the research conversation as well as in the classroom.

While January 1, 1983, is considered the "birthday" of the Internet, the groundwork for what we consider one of the most important technological advancements in global communication accumulated over several decades of innovation. In 1983, however, when with the switch to the Transfer Control Protocol/Internetwork Protocol (TCP/IP), a more universally agreed upon decentralized network to facilitate connection and communication emerged, and the Internet became what we think of it today. This was quickly followed by the Domain Naming System (DNS) adopted in 1984, and this, with TCP/IP, served as the foundational pillar of what would lay the cornerstones of Tim Berners Lee's proposal for the World Wide Web in 1989 (Figure 2.7). By 1990, protocols were finished (HTML, HTTP, and URLs), and the first search engine was completed allowing Tim Berners-Lee to share the first picture via the Internet. By 1991, the first web page was created (Figure 2.8).

While much has been written about the history of tele and digital communications, it is this distinct moment of synthesis where the communities who were invested in computer-aided architectural design found a ready-made vehicle for broader dissemination of ideas. The organizations, conferences, and publications that gained broad-based participation in this episode served to legitimize and structure the communication; however, it was the internet and web that would provide the growing informal platform for more spontaneous and instantaneous dissemination that would deepen the discourse of ideas thus bringing many, many more people to the table to participate in a growing revolution.

Digitizing the Profession

The architecture profession was not exempt from the dynamic landscape of new hardware and software made available during this period. In the earliest days, the profession could see the translation pathway for pedagogical procedures that pre-dated the new technological methods. The initial adoption of the hardware and software was uneven for most firms, and over time, it became clear that some firms were better equipped to navigate the decision making associated with implementation. As noted earlier in this episode, the hardware + software + OS selection is registered directly into the cost and the trained workforce necessary for implementation. Home and office computing were not, at this point, synonymous. The knowledge base of one modality was only transferable to another up to a point. It would take well into the late 1980s to see workforce education gain traction.

CERN DD/OC | Tim Berners-Lee, CERN/DD

Information Management: A Proposal | March 1989

Information Management: A Proposal

Abstract

This proposal concerns the management of general information about accelerators and experiments at CERN. It discusses the problems of loss of information about complex evolving systems and derives a solution based on a distributed hypertext sytstem.

Keywords: Hypertext, Computer conferencing, Document retrieval, Information management, Project control

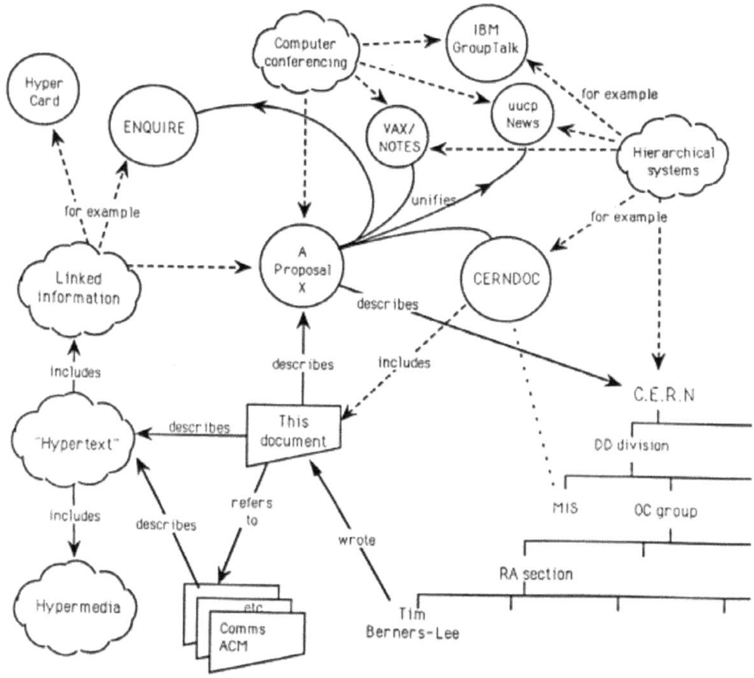

FIGURE 2.7 Tim Berners-Lee diagram in 1989 for the invention of the World Wide Web (WWW), while working at CERN. The web was originally conceived and developed to meet the demand for automated information-sharing between universities and institutes around the world.

World Wide Web

The WorldWideWeb (W3) is a wide-area hypermedia information retrieval initiative aiming to give universal access to a large universe of documents.

Everything there is online about W3 is linked directly or indirectly to this document, including an executive summary of the project, Mailing lists , Policy , November's W3 news , Frequently Asked Questions .

What's out there?
: Pointers to the world's online information, subjects , W3 servers, etc.

Help
: on the browser you are using

Software Products
: A list of W3 project components and their current state. (e.g. Line Mode ,X11 Viola , NeXTStep , Servers , Tools , Mail robot , Library)

Technical
: Details of protocols, formats, program internals etc

Bibliography
: Paper documentation on W3 and references.

People
: A list of some people involved in the project.

History
: A summary of the history of the project.

How can I help ?
: If you would like to support the web..

Getting code
: Getting the code by anonymous FTP , etc.

FIGURE 2.8 By late December 1990, Tim Berners-Lee produced the basic framework for the WWW, including HTML, HTP, and URL. He completed a browser and server software to support the first web page.

The IBM personal computer was released in 1981, shortly after Apple II, the TRS-80, and the Apollo came to market. Within 24 months, The IBM PC would also be joined by the Commodore 64 and the first Macintosh (Figure 2.9 and Figure 2.10). The PC market was crowded, and homes and offices were

FIGURE 2.9 The Commodore 64, with the MPS-801 printer, Vic-modem, 1701 monitor, and 1541 disk drive, entered the market in 1985.

FIGURE 2.10 The first release of the Macintosh in 1984 represented an "all-in-one" design, combining the monitor and CPU. While the GUI, developed by Alan Kay, was compelling, it took some time to find footing in the architecture community.

attempting to understand how to best use the equipment and software quickly becoming available. By the mid-1980s, several software and hardware companies that would go on to be giants in the field were getting their start. AutoCAD, and to a lesser extent, Silicon Graphics and CATIA, started to make an impact within the architecture community. The computers, however, that were needed to run this software required a larger capacity than the home PC market had available, thus necessitating a sizable investment on the part of offices to "digitize" the work process.[38] This, however, would change quickly as prices came down by the end of the decade, and workforce education made staffing an office possible.

Operating systems were ensnared in the hardware and software explosion. The Mac OS System 1 (1984) and the Microsoft Windows 1.01 (1985) were launched in successive years and would evolve into two of the most pervasive user interfaces for the PC market in history. Operating systems that made digital tasks and their organization more accessible were as significant a breakthrough as the PC's processing power and portability/size. In addition to the operating systems, other significant benchmarks for expanding the digitization of the graphic user interface were software like MacPaint (1984), which grew out of Xerox PARC technology. To a lesser-known degree was the release of Thoughtsticker by Gordon Pask and Peter Pangaro in 1983, which became a precursor to the modern-day web browser, which was itself only a few years from making its grand and profound entrance. Paul Coates, along with John and Julie Frazer, considered important figures in early computational design development, founded Autographics in the late 1970s.[39] The company focuses on microcomputer-based computer-aided design and graphics programs, specializing in low-cost, designer-oriented drafting, designing, and modeling programs that are easy to use compared to market competition.[40] Coates and John Frazer would go on to contribute seminal texts over the next several decades, but the early formation of a software company by architects for architects was novel at that time.

Early publications like *Graphic Introduction to Programming for Architects and Engineers*[41] by Yehuda E. Kalay (1987) created roadmaps for navigating the new digital space that was now more widely available. Understanding the tools and how to control them was as essential as the new growing availability and increased capacity they could afford. There were also broader-based works like *Design by Optimization in Architecture, Building, and Construction*[42] by Antony Radford and John S. Gero (1988) that introduced the AEC industry to broader thinking of the digital toolset capabilities while simultaneously foreshadowing a performance optimization capability of the computational capacity that would arrive decades later. Similarly, Gerhard Schmitt started his efforts in 1988 from the ETH Zurich to define the role of simulation, visualization, and interaction more clearly.

Conclusion

As this episode ends, there are profound shifts taking place. The eruption of hardware and software companies would make a lasting impression for decades to come. Even as some fade away and others absorb their competition, it became clear that the hardware/software generation of digital technology had arrived. More specifically, as it applied to architecture, the ability to leverage technological advancements with a digital toolset and to appropriate new toolsets to do new things opened entirely new opportunities. The architecture profession was impacted because of the ability to speculate and consequently represent that speculation within new tableaus and vehicles by which authors and collaborators could communicate. The authors, creating speculations on the future of the built environment, were now free to explore, armed with new ammunition of portable technology that was proliferating and intersecting with many different aspects of the physical world. People were organizing and communicating about these issues and were excited to form groups that could formalize the discourse in a way that was simultaneously accessible and more rigorous. The internet was the wave forming off in the distance that would transform not just the architecture profession but the entire world. By the start of 1990, the pioneering vision of the previous 30 years had become mainstream.

Notes

1 Weiser, M. (1995). "The Computer for the 21st Century," in *Readings in Human–Computer Interaction*. Amsterdam: Elsevier, pp. 933–940. doi:10.1016/b978-0-08-051574-8.50097-2.
2 Weiser, M. and Brown, J. S. (1997). "The Coming Age of Calm Technology," in P. J. Denning and R. M. Metcalfe (eds.), *Beyond Calculation: The Next Fifty Years of Computing*. Berlin: Springer Science & Business Media, pp. 75–85. doi:10.1007/978-1-4612-0685-9_6.
3 Dormehl, L. (2023, December 26). "Today in Apple History: Steve Jobs loses 'Man of the Year' to PC." *Cult of Mac*, December 26. https://www.cultofmac.com/519947/tiah-steve-jobs-man-of-the-year/
4 Virtual Reality Society (2017, June 2). "History of Virtual Reality." Available at: https://www.vrs.org.uk/virtual-reality/history.html [Accessed January 20, 2023].
5 Ibid.
6 Jeffrey Shaw. (n.d.). Jeffrey Shaw Compendium. Available at: https://www.jeffreyshawcompendium.com/portfolio/legible-city/ [Accessed January 20, 2023].
7 Gibson, W. (1984). *Neuromancer*. New York: Ace Books.
8 Levy, S. (1984). *Hackers: Heroes of the Computer Revolution*. London: Anchor Press/Doubleday.
9 Benedikt, M. (1991). *Cyberspace: First Steps*. Cambridge, MA: MIT Press.
10 Novak, M. (1991). "Liquid Architecture in Cyberspace," in M. Benedikt (ed.), *Cyberspace: First Steps*. Cambridge, MA: MIT Press, pp. 225–256.
11 Nicole, S. (1991). "Mind is a Leaking Rainbow," in M. Benedikt (ed.), *Cyberspace: First Steps*. Cambridge, MA: MIT Press. pp. 49–58.
12 Feher, M. and Kwinter, S. (1986). *Zone 1/2: The Contemporary City*. Zone Books.
13 Plantec, P. (2012, January 7). "The Fascinating Story of How Autodesk Came to Be (Part 1)." *Studio Daily*, January 7. Available at: https://www.studiodaily.com/2012/01/the-fascinating-story-of-how-autodesk-came-to-be-part-1/ [Accessed January 21, 2023].
14 Weisberg, D. (2023, March 27). "IBM, Lockheed and Dassault Systèmes." *Shapr3D*, March 27. Available at: https://www.shapr3d.com/history-of-cad/ibm-lockheed-and-dassault-systemes
15 Ibid.
16 Ibid.
17 Eastman, C. (1975). "The Use of Computers Instead of Drawings." *AIA Journal*, 46.
18 Beck Tech. (2021, May 28). "Rebels of Construction—Charles M. Eastman." *Beck Technology*, May 28. Available at: https://www.beck-technology.com/blog/rebels-of-construction-charles-m-eastman [Accessed January 22, 2023].
19 Note, for a full accounting of Chuck Eastman's educational background at Berkeley, with Christopher Alexander and Horst Rittel, where he developed a deep appreciation for human behavior and wicked problems, or, his time at the University of Wisconsin where he began to discuss AI with a group in the psychology program, go to: http://acadia.org/news/CQRYPC [Accessed January 25, 2024].
20 Eastman, C. and Henrion, M. (1977, July 20). *Glide: Proceedings of the 4th Annual Conference on Computer Graphics and Interactive Techniques*. doi:10.1145/563858.563863.
21 Ingram, J. (2020). *Understanding BIM: The Past, Present and Future*. Oxford: Routledge.
22 Ibid.
23 "Vectorworks History: Founding, Timeline, and Milestones" (2020, August 27). *Zippia*. Available at: https://www.zippia.com/vectorworks-careers-1559564/history/ [Accessed January 23, 2023].

24 Jeffrey, C. (2022, November 10). "Silicon Graphics: Gone but not Forgotten." *TechSpot*. Available at: https://www.techspot.com/article/2142-silicon-graphics/ [Accessed January 24, 2023].

25 Kosmos, K. *CADKEY official*. Available at: https://info.kubotekkosmos.com/cadkey-official [Accessed January 24, 2023].

26 *The Software behind Frank Gehry's Geometrically Complex Architecture*. Lian Chikako Chang. https://lianchikako.com/The-Software-Behind-Frank-Gehry-s-Geometrically-Complex-Architecture [Accessed January 24, 2023].

27 Failes, I. (2020, June 3). *A Visual History of 3ds Max*. Befores & Afters. Available at: https://beforesandafters.com/2020/06/04/a-visual-history-of-3ds-max/ [Accessed January 24, 2023].

28 InspirationTuts. (2019, December 27). *3ds Max History*. Available at: https://inspirationtuts.com/3ds-max-history/

29 Note, see ACADIA Conference Proceedings – called a Workshop at that time for more information. Title of the conference: *Architectural Education, Research and Practice in the Next Decade*. Turner, J. A. (ed.) (1986, January 1). *ACADIA Workshop 1986 Proceedings*. Also see eCAADE Conference Proceedings for more information: Title of Conference, *CAAD – Education Research and Practice*. See https://papers.cumincad.org/cgi-bin/works/paper/e59b. CAAD: Education. (1989, January 1). Research and Practice [Conference Proceedings]. See https://papers.cumincad.org/cgi-bin/works/paper/45e6

30 Celani, G. and Veloso, P. (2015). "CAAD Conferences: A Brief History." Conference: *The Next City – New Technologies and the Future of the Built Environment:16th International Conference CAAD Futures 2015* at São Paulo, pp. 47–58.

31 H. Borkin, P. Burgess, K. Cavanaugh, D. Collins, W. Cooper, Chuck Eastman, U. Fleming, J. Garrott, G. Glass, J. Hamer, Yehuda E. Kalay, R. I. MacDonald, J. McIntosh, B. Mitchell, R. Mukerjea, R. Quadrel, G. Stonebreaker, L. Summers, J. Tector, R. Thornton, J. Wade, W. Wake, P. Winsberg, and C. Yessios. See http://acadia.org/

32 IBPSA. (2023, July 28). *Home Page*. International Building Performance Simulation Association. See https://ibpsa.org/

33 Celani, G. and Veloso, P. (2015). "CAAD Conferences: A Brief History" Conference: *The Next City – New Technologies and the Future of the Built Environment:16th International Conference CAAD Futures 2015* at São Paulo, pp. 47–58.

34 See https://manifold.umn.edu/read/chapter-1-lab-space/section/aec5864d-1c9a-4062-bf04-f99125aff29c [Accessed January 25, 2023].

35 Kalay, Y. E., Harfmann, A. C., and Swerdloff, L. M. (1986). "Knowledge-Based Computer-Aided Design: The Computer as Design Partner," in *CAD and Robotics in Architecture and Construction*. New York: Springer US, pp. 41–52. doi:10.1007/978-1-4684-7404-6_3.

36 Kalay, Y. E. and Harfmann, A. C. (1985). "An Integrative Approach to Computer-Aided Design Education in Architecture," February, 1985. [17] p.: [8] p. of ill, CADline. See also, Kalay, Y. E., Harfmann, A. C., and Swerdloff, L. M. (1985). "ALEX: A Knowledge-Based Architectural Design System." *Proceedings of the 5th Annual Conference of the Association for Computer Aided Design in Architecture (ACADIA)*. doi:10.52842/conf.acadia.1985.096.

37 Eastman, C. (1989). "Why Are We Here and Where We are Going: The Evolution of CAD." *Proceedings of the 9th Annual Conference of the Association for Computer Aided Design in Architecture (ACADIA)*. doi:10.52842/conf.acadia.1989.009

38 Bethany. (2017, February 23). "How CAD has Evolved Since 1982." *Scan2CAD*, February 23. Available at: https://www.scan2cad.com/blog/cad/cad-evolved-since-1982/#Setting_the_Stage_for_Large-Scale_Adoption_of_CAD [Accessed January 25, 2023].

39 AA School. See https://www.aaschool.ac.uk/obituaries/paul-stephen-coates-1969-2013 [Accessed January 25, 2024].

40 John Frazer, Biography. Division of Philosophy, Art & Critical Thought. The European Graduate School. See https://egs.edu/biography/john-frazer/
41 Kalay, Y. E. (1987). *Graphic Introduction to Programming*. Hoboken, NJ: Wiley-Interscience.
42 Radford, A. and Gero, J. S. (1988). *Design by Optimization in Architecture, Building, and Construction*. New York: Van Nostrand Reinhold Company.

EPISODE 3

APPROPRIATION (1992–2003)

The trajectory of this episode was inspired by explorations and developments coming from other fields outside of architecture while also recognizing the interconnectedness of a growing digital community. Much of the groundwork for integrating computers into/by architecture was accomplished by a critical leveraging of software and ways of working that were usurped from different fields. Architects found inspiration from already established CAD/CAM processes in the aerospace, automotive, and shipbuilding industries. This appropriation ushered in new forms of experimentation, significantly affecting how architects would design and build. The experimentation was also provoked by 3-dimensional modeling software that was appropriated from other professions and ushered in a new type of formal modeling that brought with it theories on style and topology. The maturing concepts of ubiquitous computing and the Internet of Things (IoT) also provided the long-needed technological spark for the percolating ideas of embedded computation. Ultimately, the appropriation in general, coupled with a critical leveraging of understanding ways of working from different fields, fostered a new wave of architecturally specific software that iteratively redefined architectural processes. Eventually, the profession began to play a role in directing the development of the technology and tools that affected it. It was a time when the profession began to ask what was architectural about computation and not dependent on the inverse, forging its own identity and beginning to break down pre-existing rules and boundaries. The tools would start to foster a recalibration between the artisanal authorship of and the intellectual authorship of Alberti.

DOI: 10.4324/9781032671208-5

Global Organization and Communication

Academia Unites Globally

Almost a decade after the founding of ACADIA in 1981 and the sister organization of eCAADe in 1983, there finally began to be a truly international representation of computation and architecture through several new organizations. ACADIA generally represented North America, while eCAADe generally represented Europe. They held annual geographically anchored conferences to network digital design researchers and professionals. The next wave of academic organizations came about swiftly and fostered a truly global impact, although it should be noted they were still somewhat geographically isolated due to the undeveloped state of the internet at this time.

Sequentially, the first was CAADRIA in 1996 (Association for Computer Aided Architectural Design in Asia),[1] followed immediately by SIGraDi in 1997 (Iberoamerican Society of Digital Graphics),[2] generally representing all of Central and South America. A few years later, ASCAAD (The Arab Society for Computer-Aided Architectural Design) was founded in 2001. These five organizations of ACADIA (North America), eCAADe (Europe), CAADRIA (Asia), SIGraDi (South America), and ASCAAD (Arab World regions of West Asia and North Africa)[3] became the foundational sister organizations, creating an international CAAD network.

The organizations followed a standard template of holding annual conferences that typically integrated workshops, generated peer-reviewed proceedings, and recognized influencers in the field (both people and places) with annual awards. Each organization also had some form of executive committee or board of directors who administrated and steered the organization. The conferences served as a platform for disseminating the unfolding technologies and institutions, which, in turn, were critical in developing digital literacy for future trajectories and workforce training. This template still holds true for the network of sister organizations today as they continue annual conferences and expand digital design literacy.

CAADRIA was the first organization to follow the previously established ACADIA and eCAADe. Co-founded by Thomas Kvan and Tsuyoshi Sasada (namesake of the Sasada Prize), this organization established a much-needed dissemination outlet for Asia. The first conference was held in Hong Kong in 1996 with 32 papers and grew steadily over the years, with around 150 annually[4] in the early 2020s. The conference's founding was a response to what was happening in academia; as the first president stated in a recorded editorial in 1996,

> Computers have established themselves as indispensable tools in the practice of architecture; there are few practices today which do not have access to computers for some aspects of their work … The pervasive

> application of the tools in practice and the ease of access to some form of computing in architectural schools poses a challenge to which architectural education has responded.[5]

Twenty conferences have since been held in Australia, China, Hong Kong, India, Japan, Korea, Malaysia, Singapore, Taiwan, and Thailand.[6] Christiane Herr breaks down the organization's history concerning research funding in Asia, suggesting national governments have historically funded CAADIRA research and thus follow national funding preferences. Regarding the expanding regional participation, she goes on to state, "While the initial CAADRIA conferences featured a significant number of research papers submitted by authors based in Hong Kong, Taiwan, Singapore, and Japan, recent conferences have seen a strong increase of papers submitted by South Korea and especially mainland China-based authors."[7] Regardless, the organization is now responsible for over 2,000 papers, representing a massive contribution to the field as summarized in a comprehensive bibliometric analysis by Bob Martens and Tomo Cerovšek in "The Evolution of CAADRIA Conferences."[8]

Almost in parallel with the development of CAADRIA in Asia was the development of SIGraDI, which has primarily served Latin America and Iberoamerica. It was founded by the pioneer in architectural computing, Arturo Montagu, at the University of Buenos Aires after conversations with colleagues at several universities in Argentina. Arturo was one of the world's leading voices in the region in architectural computing, whose work and teaching influenced generations of professionals and researchers in Latin America and beyond. Through him, many of today's relationships among people in the architectural computing community in this area of the world came to fruition. The first conference was held in Buenos Ares, Argentina, in 1996, and the annual meeting has since moved to various regional countries annually. In 2021, the 25th anniversary of the organization's founding, a massive historical documentary was published as a book recording the collective vitality of the organization.[9] The book provides access to more than 2,800 articles published over the years, as well as mementos, graphic timelines, and photo documentation of the years of conferences.

The last of the sister organizations formed was ASCAAD in 2001 by 17 founding members at Jordan University of Science and Technology. The first conference, however, was not held until 2005 in Dharan, Saudi Arabia.[10] Having started later and covering a smaller geographic region, ASCAAD has always been a smaller organization relative to the other sister organizations. However, the organization has been vital for its regional perspective, and the conferences consistently have moved to various countries throughout the region, including Saudi Arabia, Bahrain, the UAE, Morocco, and Jordan, highlighting the growing concentration of work being done in this part of the world.

Up until 1998, the existing sister organizations produced proceedings from their annual conferences, cataloging and documenting the research in architecture computation. In the case of ACADIA (1981), eCAADe (1983), and CAADFutures (1985), this meant one to two decades of material. Analog dissemination was challenging, expensive, and typically limited. However, toward the end of 1998, CumInCAD (Cumulative Index of publications in Computer-Aided Architectural Design) was founded to serve as an online repository for all the current and future sister organizations. Creating this dedicated digital archive and retrieval system was a significant step toward unifying and advancing CAAD knowledge. CumInCAD was originally designed and released by Bob Martens at TU Wein and Ziga Turk. It was significantly enhanced during the SciX (Open, self-organizing repository for scientific information exchange) project, which took place from 2002 to 2004.[11] As a demonstration of an e-prints archive, SciX was relatively unprecedented; however, with funding from the European Commission, it was a significant demonstration of the feasibility of new alternative models of scientific publishing.

In 2000, a survey by Bo-Christer Björk and Ziga Turk showed that researchers interested in Internet Technologies related to architecture and construction had accessed 50% of the scientific publications they read over the Internet. Additionally, as readers, they strongly preferred freely accessible material to subscription-based material.[12] In 2016, the repository became open-access and was fully relaunched by Tomo Cerovšek. In 2023, CumInCAD now includes bibliographic information of nearly 12,500 records from journals and conferences, including content from the sister organizations.[13] Alexander Koutamanis stated in his very aptly named article "A Biased History of CAAD"[14] that in the process of doing research, patterns emerge from the collected information. These included tendencies, approaches, and principles and ultimately determined the developmental trajectory of an area. His theories were based on a bibliographic study recognizing patterns of work collected on CumInCAD. Looking back at the history of publications in the repository, he found that

> CAAD only established effective mechanisms for the production of publications in the 1990s, a decade generally characterized by an explosive growth in the number of scientific publications. The numbers also reflect the availability of material for CumInCAD, i.e., most digital publications that could be directly included date back to the mid-1990s.[15]

There were only 16 papers from the 1960s in CumInCAD and 185 from the 1970s, which then grew to nearly 1,000 in the 1980s and more than tripled in the 1990s with over 3,000 publications. It is on track to exceed this number in the 2000s.[16]

Only a few years after the founding of CumInCAD, the "Architectural Computing Alliance" was formed as a consortium uniting the five international CAAD organizations of eCAADe, ACADIA, CAADRIA, SIGraDi, and CAADFutures. Out of this alliance, another major dissemination outlet came to fruition in the *International Journal of Architectural Computing* (*IJAC*), which was first released in 2003. *IJAC* was created as a peer-reviewed journal, remaining to this day as a pre-eminent outlet for Architectural Computing. *IJAC* publishes four issues per year. On a rotating basis, one issue each year is successfully supervised by Editorial Board members from one of the four founding sister organizations and supported by the CAADFutures Foundation. This point is non-trivial as the continually rotating guest editorial boards set the topic for the call and source the peer review process. The global distribution of the organizations thus serves to curate a sort of annual barometer of relevance in architectural computing through publication.

By the end of this episode in 2003, architectural academic computation research now has a global if not still geographically isolated, presence. The founding of organizations in Latin America, South America, and the Middle East and the introduction of *IJAC* and CumInCAD complete a networked presence of academic outlets for research that was not previously available. Moving forward, the profession began to play a more active role in directing the development of the technology and tools affecting it.

Dissemination and the Role of the Internet

The limits of dissemination were very much tied to an understanding of the state of the internet at this time. Given the current pervasive nature of the internet in 2024, it is hard to remember the first web page did not exist before 1991. By 1995, 14% of U.S. adults had access to the internet. Most were using slow, dial-up modem connections. To place this in some context, in 1998, when CumInCAD was created, the internet was only a few years old, and Although 41% of U.S. adults went online that year (up from 36% in 1997),[17] the connection speeds were still 56 kbps and downloading a file with images was an isolated and time-consuming endeavor. This primitive state of the internet, coupled with geographically isolated sister organizations, meant development happened in parallel and within relatively non-intentional, geographically isolated silos. The internet did develop at an astounding rate, however, and by 2003, which marks the end of this episode, close to two-thirds of U.S. children and adults were now online and able to access the internet, with even 31% of these users having broadband internet at home with a high-speed DSL, cable wireless, T-1 or fiber optic connection.[18] While growth was rapid in parts of the world, like the U.S., other regions and countries still lagged behind, making internet access uneven. At this time, nearly 1/3 of U.S. citizens accessed the internet, but that number was only 6% globally.[19] A number that has since shot up to 67% almost two decades later in 2023.[20]

Organizations Reaching Beyond Academia

It should be noted that beyond the primarily academic societies discussed, several additional early influential organizations became powerful outlets for dissemination. Autodesk, which released AutoCAD in 1982 and quickly captured a large market share, held its first user conference in 1993. The conference was primarily a networking and disseminating opportunity for professional users. Out of this first conference, Autodesk University (AU) was born and became an annual event that began to invite speakers and become a forum for thought leadership from within the profession[21] (Figure 3.1). Autodesk University has since settled in Las Vegas as an annual event with international reach. AU provides a broad and influential spectrum of coverage of professional topics ranging from architecture and engineering, construction and civil infrastructure, and even professional business models and AI.

A second influential organization called SmartGeometry was also launched near the end of this episode as an interesting partnership between practice, research, and academia. SmartGeometry (SG) was founded by members of the world's leading architectural and engineering practices and

FIGURE 3.1 The Autodesk University annual user conference emerged as a networking and dissemination outlet for professionals.

educational institutions. It began as an informal network of designers interested in computation and architecture led by Lars Hesselgren, J. Parrish, and Hugh Whitehead, who at the time worked together at YRM (now part of RMJM) in the late 1980s. They held a cross-disciplinary series of design workshops, presentations, and discussions focused on redefining how architects could use the new digital tools. The network grew to include collaborators, including computer scientists including software developer Robert Aish, who developed the parametric design extension to Bentley System's MicroStation software that became the early test platform for the workshops and academics, including Robert Woodbury and Axel Kilian. Kilian was involved in the workshops from 2003–2010 and also contributed to other emerging organizations, including the Advances in Architectural Geometry Symposium by Helmut Pottmann and the Design Modelling Symposium by Christoph Gengnagel. The early SG group also integrated experimental practitioners, including Mark Burry and Chris Williams, to assemble the initial conferences and workshops. Early participants, among others, included Francis Aish, Judit Kimpian, Jenny Sabin, Achim Menges, Jeroen Coenders, and many more. The SG group of contributors grew quickly with practitioners and academics joining, such as Shane Burger, and Xavier de Kestellier, who took on organizing later SG editions. It was an interesting and non-conventional setup that differed from the more formally organized academic conference. In the intro to the *Inside SmartGeometry* book that came out in 2013 which documented years of work from the organization, it states, "In workshop groups, designers can work on projects 'off the books,' away from their offices or university settings, creating pure explorations of technique beyond the confines of the design project."[22] They were generally very concerned with the cross-fertilization of ideas in practice and the creation and application of digital tools. So, as the organization began with a lecture and workshop in 2003, it eventually grew to a four-day curated workshop and two-day public conference, attracting more than 300 international participants (Figure 3.2).

And yet, with all the innovation and the amazing seeds of ideas coming out of the workshops, there was a sentiment of frustration that the architecture profession had not really changed. Hesselgren, Parrish, and Whitehead identified the discrepancy, noting that a decade after the first workshop and digital technology introduction, buildings were largely still being designed the same way. In contrast, digital technologies in other fields had already become much more disruptive.[23] Innovation had accelerated outside of architecture with many technologies such as 3D printing, AR, and 3D scanning, which were innovative workshop ideas that then went on to become commercial successes by outside companies.[24]

Last, a third organization, "Design Computing and Cognition" (DCC), was founded in 2004, and focused on generative design in architecture and engineering. DCC focused on Artificial Intelligence, cognitive science,

FIGURE 3.2 The Smart Geometry curated workshops grew to serve both academics and professionals as seen in the 2011 Workshop at the School of Architecture in Copenhagen.

neuroscience, and computational theories in design. The conferences provided a bridge between the two fields of "design computing" and "design cognition." The first conference was held at MIT in 2004 and pioneered by Ulrich Flemming, then at Carnegie Mellon with a personal research focus on generative design in architecture and engineering. John Gero became the chair of the biennial conference series and was previously the Co-Director of the Key Centre of Design Computing and Cognition at the University of Sydney and then a Professor in Computer Science and Architecture at the University of North Carolina at Charlotte. Outside of his work with DCC, John remains one of the most prolific and influential contributors to architectural computation as the author or editor of 54 books and over 850 papers and book chapters in the fields of design science, design computing, Artificial Intelligence, computer-aided design, design cognition, and design neurocognition.[25]

As the area "design cognition" draws on cognitive science, it was one of the earliest forums to recognize the potential impacts of Artificial Intelligence as providing a paradigm within which design research based on computational constructions can be carried out. As Gero and Goel wrote in the preface to the Proceedings of the Third International Conference on Design Computing and Cognition:

> There are now three sources for design research: design computing, design cognition, and human-centered information technology. The foundation for much of design computing remains artificial intelligence with its focus on ways of representation and on processes that support simulation and generation.[26]

Distributed Collaboration

Early Networked Practices

Looking back again at the primitive internet history during the 1990s, there was enormous optimism and speculation on how it could be leveraged to support collaboration across distances. Distributed collaboration during a time when internet access was in its infancy and working online was very challenging due to limited access to even a slow broadband connection. One of the pioneers was that of the office of OCEAN Net,[27] founded by Michael U. Hensel, Ulrich Königs, Tom Verebes, and Bostjan Vuga in 1994 as an experimental practice in architecture, landscape architecture, and urban design. It was a practice-led but research-based design office focused on computational design in architecture. It was founded in London as a collaborative and interdisciplinary endeavor. For context, in 1994, Microsoft released its first web page, and the first World Wide Web conference was held in Geneva, Switzerland. Cell phones had recently come into existence, were very expensive, and had no screens. Still, not long after the original OCEAN team formed, they were joined by other design teams and established in several European cities, including Cologne, Helsinki, London, Ljubljana, and Oslo, pioneering collaborative work at a distance. These teams fused in 1998 to operate as OCEAN North and included Johan Bettum, Kim Baumann Larsen, Markus Holmstén, Bonsak Schildrop, Birger Sevaldson, and Kivi Sotamaa.[28] The network produced a number of iconic works over the years and still exists today with expanded membership and specialized sub-groups working remotely. Another pioneering group was SERVO, established in 1998 as a young design collaborative that embraced new forms of distributed practice enabled by the advent of telecommunications technologies. The group was founded by four Columbia GSAPP graduate students: Chris Perry, Marcelyn Gow, David Erdman, and Ulrika Karlsson. The work spanned design disciplines to incorporate areas of expertise particular to interactive design and digital fabrication. The group created several high-profile projects with international acclaim and still exists today with offices in Los Angeles and Stockholm.

The Virtual Design Studio

Today, most schools of architecture have some form of remote collaboration lab, or dedicated communication room with monitors, sound, and connection speeds, but the change has come about only recently. The struggles with remote collaboration that the pioneering academics navigated are difficult to comprehend. Understanding the challenges associated with these efforts is mainly because this area has come to fruition perhaps more seamlessly than the early pioneers ever imagined. Marshall McLuhan coined the term "The global village"[29] as a civilization where electronic communication media have dramatically reduced the distance and isolation of people from each other, thus virtually restoring the world to the psychological equivalent of one[30] tribe or village, finally began to see the concept begin to come to fruition in the 1990s.

In 1992, using very primitive equipment with even more primitive connection speeds, some former students of William Mitchell from Harvard experimented with using modems to work together on a sketch design. Nancy Cheng aptly describes early promises:

> Using 2400 baud modems to send e-mail messages and transfer CAD files to and from a common server computer which acted as a bulletin board. From this simple start, it was clear that working far away in different time zones could have interesting benefits. Because the information would wait patiently on the server, one could work on the project as suited an idiosyncratic personal schedule. In addition, for the early stages, ambiguity could profitably be used for spawning new re-interpretations.[31]

The Virtual Design Studio (VDS) documented in Jerzy Wojtowicz's 1995 book *Virtual Design Studio*[32] describes the first comprehensive experiment in the collaborative online studio, which took place in 1993 and included 54 students and tutors of architecture located in five separate universities on a joint two-week-long design experiment. The fact that the participants in this studio were in four different time zones, thousands of miles apart, while addressing and resolving the given problem was unprecedented. This studio brought together students and tutors at Barcelona, MIT, Harvard, Cornell, Washington University, St. Louis, the University of British Columbia, and the University of Hong Kong. The book documented the start of a new paradigm for expanding computer tools beyond that which was strictly technical to incorporate social discussions necessary for design negotiation.

Wojtowicz, who documented the original studio, was a student of Bill Mitchell's in the original VDS along with Nancy Cheng and Branko Kolarevic, who both went on to continue developments in the area. Nancy Cheng continued the work into her teaching in Hong Kong with Thomas Kvan and then at the University of Oregon.[33] Due to her interest in fostering community, she began structuring the virtual studios to increase the amount and quality of exchange. From 1993–1996, she coordinated a series of collaborative virtual design studios, each building upon the successes and shortcomings of the previous years. Cheng established some foundational online collaboration strategies related specifically to architectural design through these experimental studios.

Additionally, in 1997, a group of three different schools around the world, roughly eight hours apart, ran the first non-stop 24-hour virtual design studio ("Multiplying Time: 3 × 8 = 24") over the course of one week (Figure 3.3). The studio was led by Gerhard Schmitt, with several other faculty at the ETH working with Kolarevic at the University of Hong Kong and Brian Johnson at the University of Washington. The collaboration was focused on a common design project working from a common database, taking advantage of the staggered time zones.[34] Kolarevic followed up the initiative in 1998 and 1999 with similar experiments working with different partners and agendas.

Tsuyoshi Sasada, one of the founders of CAADRIA and longtime director of the Sasada lab at Osaka University at the same time was developing numerous networked 3D interactive design systems for collaboration, which he also tested out on inter-university virtual design. He is also responsible for pioneering several tools at the time by adding scripts such as the 3D interactive design tool "NODE" to work easily in a collaborative way with WWW and VRML. These early methods allowed for collaborative models, environments, and operations.

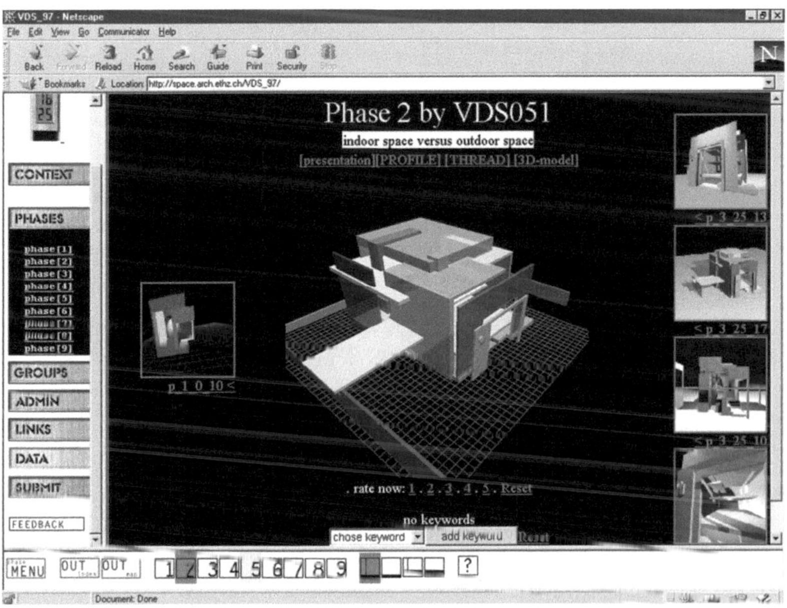

FIGURE 3.3 Virtual Design Studio Webpage showing design entries in the "PhaseX" database that was used for VDS'97 involving students and faculty in Hong Kong (HKU), Seattle (UW), Vancouver (UBC), and Zurich (ETH).

Technology Transfer and Assimilation

Professional Framework

This episode marks a time when the profession begins to forge its own identity, breaking pre-existing rules and boundaries. Much of the groundwork was accomplished by a critical leveraging of software and ways of working that were usurped from other fields. This newfound appropriation fostered experimentation that greatly affected how architects designed and built. Some architects began implementing CAD/CAM processes inspired by the aerospace, automotive, and shipbuilding industries. One of the more famous stories of this appropriation comes from the office of Gehry Partners adopting the software used for aerospace design to build a fish sculpture for the 1992 Barcelona Olympics. This story is even more ironic in that Gehry himself "speaks with a certain degree of pride in his inability to operate a computer," as described by then CTO Dennis Sheldon.[35]

The Boeing 777 was the first commercial aircraft designed entirely by computer from 1992–94.[36] Each design drawing was created on a three-dimensional CAD software system, CATIA, sourced from Dassault Systems and IBM.[37] Serving as a precursor to Michael Grievers launching the idea of Digital Twinning in 2002,[38] and what Dassault would call a "virtual twin,"[39] the process essentially let the engineers assemble a virtual aircraft in simulation to check for interference and verify that the thousands of parts fit correctly. To test the digital plane, Boeing also developed its visualization system called FlyThru, which later became known as IVT Integrated Visualization Tool (IVT) and was used to support large-scale collaborative reviews and production drawings. Boeing was initially sceptical of the approach and constructed a physical mock-up of the nose section based on the CATIA model to verify its results. The mock-up was so successful that additional mock-ups were cancelled. The 777 *"...was completed with such precision that it was the first Boeing jet that didn't need its kinks worked out on an expensive physical mock-up plane."*[40] When Frank Gehry designed the now-famous fish sculpture in Barcelona, the office was faced with the realization of being ill-equipped to design it to the degree that construction was possible. After the contractor failed to translate the vision for the pavilion, Gehry's partner Jim Glymph suggested looking into the French aerospace company, Dassault, to adapt the firm's computer modeling software for building design application called CATIA (Figure 3.4). Dassault Systems first used CATIA as early as 1977 to design the Mirage fighter jet. CATIA was an associative parametric 3D free-form modeler using a point cloud solid modeling engine. Gehry Technologies was the in-house technology company owned by Gehry Partners which grew out of a desire to develop custom computational solutions to deliver the complicated designs of Frank Gehry. Gehry Technologies then developed Digital Project as a bespoke CAD software application based on CATIA V5. The software was important for two reasons. First, it was useful in translating to "buildable" issues, such as rationalizing surfaces into constructable and parametric surface optimization for material and structural assembly. Second, the software served as a true onramp to the use of BIM in creating a single model for construction and demonstrated the capacity for modeling software to do this on increasingly complex building geometries and typologies. The stars seemed to have aligned to a certain extent in that the innovations in this story unfold only through their application and their specific use in a design context. As Glyph points out, "These conditions were the result of a convergence of technical and social practices, which created a site where the function of the digital model could take various forms."[41]

It was important the office develop a methodology of working with computation that did nothing to change the original sketch and physical model-based design process of Frank Gehry. The physical models were scanned and manipulated, and subsequently, new models were made from the computer data after it was optimized and rationalized. Eventually, a final computer model became the database for all dimensions and coordinates. The BIM "master" model became the construction documentation and shop drawing base. The story was made all the more powerful because the BIM model created a balance shift of who controlled the information.

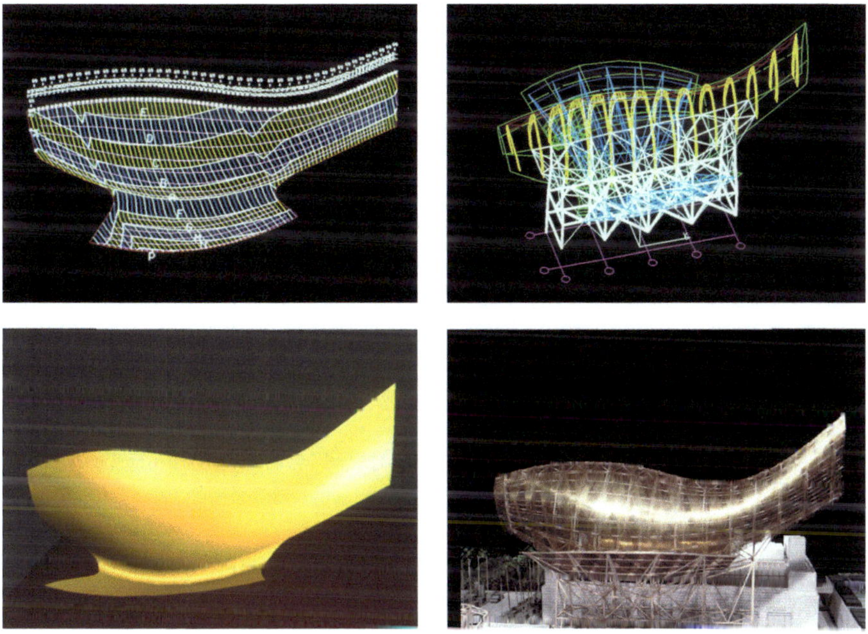

FIGURE 3.4 The Fish Sculpture by the office of Frank Gehry ushered in a new era of software appropriation by developing the bespoke Digital Project based on CATIA V5.

Gehry Technologies eventually became a stand-alone company in 2002, serving as a consultancy service to the AEC industry with a high-profile client list. The company was acquired by Trimble in 2014, which now owns SketchUp software and specializes in on-site location and surveying technologies such as GPS devices, laser rangefinders, and navigation systems. Many will identify the legacy of Frank Gehry's architecture through his nearly six-decade-long career of iconic and daring buildings circling the globe. However, it should also be noted the innovation in software and design technologies, along with fabrication and construction methodologies, have influenced generations of practitioners and educators in the AEC industry.

Software Explosion – Challenging the Stasis

The episode marks the release of a second wave of influential tools, including Rhino, Sketchup, and Revit, which were positioned to compete with the ubiquitous AutoCAD. Forged by an explosion of profession-driven software and a critical leveraging of understanding ways of working from different fields, the appropriation again came to the fore.

The beginning of software appropriation embraced not just modeling but also pure visualization in ways that were not previously possible. Many of these visualization programs were developed for other industries outside of architecture and adopted by the architectural community. LightWave 3D was released in 1994 by NewTek, having evolved from the even earlier rendering and animation software VideoScape 3D (1988) as a visualization tool with stellar rendering capabilities, including radiosity, realistic reflections, caustics, and render nodes. After internal disputes led to the demise of NewTek in 2004, the LightWave 3D team formed a new company called Luxology and released a similar visualization product called Modo. It was quickly adopted as the most used software for movies, video games, and the general CG community as a precise and easy modeler. It was used in many feature films at the time and adopted by a few in the architectural community to exploit the pioneering visualization capabilities. Ironically, Modo was eventually acquired by Foundry, a UK-based company, and quickly lost its user base, while LightWave 3D remains to this day a popular software used in many feature films and animations.

Arguably, however, the most impactful of the appropriated software released at this time were several free-form software programs adopted by the architectural community. Blender was released in 1995, while Maya and Rhino were both formally released in 1998. Architects quickly adopted these new software offerings for their visualization and rendering capabilities, but also for what they offered regarding 3D modeling using NURBS (Non-Uniform Rational Basis Splines). These programs introduced a new way of modeling to the architectural community, and the modeling freedom managed to liberate a massive cohort of designers with the capability to create designs like never before. Maya quickly became a popular tool in architecture for fluid, smooth modeling that was heavily influenced by the forms of Zaha Hadid and her presence at the AA Design Research Lab. It was also adopted for early designs by several high-profile architects, including MAD Architects, Morphosis, Asymptote, UN Studio, Reiser + Umemoto, and Greg Lynn, all of whom fostered its acceptance in the community. The formal inspiration for these new free-form design was fueled by the earlier work of Archigram, Candela, Nervi, Buckminster Fuller's work with geodesic domes, inflatables, among many others. There was a response to the dynamics of natural forms referencing D'Arcy Thompson's *"On Growth and Form"* (1917)[42] and the later natural inspirations made clear by Frei Otto and Bodo Rasch in their book *Finding Form* (1995),[43] among others. The term "blob" was first used by the Czech-British architect Jan Kaplický for the "Blob Office Building" in London in 1986[44] and later popularized by Greg Lynn's writing and work, signaling a new era in thinking about forms and processes that challenged traditional notions of static formal purity.

Blender, a free and open-source software, was developed in 1994 but was not launched until 1995.[45] Like Maya, it also started as an in-house Digital Content Creation (DCC) app for a Dutch 3D animation studio called NeoGeo in the mid-1990s. Like Maya, it was geared toward general animation and VFX artist workflows and was capable of modeling, animation, and video editing.[46] While Blender had a lot of similarities and market overlap with Maya, it did not succeed as a commercial project. Rather than be shut down, it was re-released as open source to make the code base accessible to independent developers to continue its development. As open-source software, it consequently garnered a more fringe but highly passionate user base in the design community because of the open-source aspect.

Maya was a free-form modeling software geared toward animation and special effects that was initially the most widely adopted by the architectural community. Although it never really moved into the mainstream because of the difficulties in producing construction documents, it played a vital role for those interested in non-Euclidian formal experimentation. It was adopted as a very popular design tool, where the early models were then often exported to another software, such as AutoCAD, that was more geared for the professional creation of building documentation for construction. Maya was originally an animation product based on code from *The Advanced Visualizer* by Wavefront Technologies and was developed in close coordination with Disney. The software was primarily suited for movie animation and special effects, where it is still used to this day.[47] Silicon Graphics Inc. acquired Alias and Wavefront Technologies, Inc. in 1995,[48] but because the Wavefront technology was still under development, Silicon Graphics merged it with Maya. Following a series of acquisitions, Maya was bought by Autodesk in 2005.[49]

Rhino was the third of the free-form software released in 1998. It differed slightly from Maya and Blender in being more precise and suited for architecture but, like the others, offered good rendering and visualization capabilities and some animation capabilities. Rhino was developed by Robert McNeel and associates and started as an application to run within AutoCAD using AGLib from Applied Geometry. AutoCAD was, at the time, the most ubiquitous CAD program worldwide. In 1997, the last build of AccuModel for AutoCAD was released, followed by the release of Rhino V1 in October 1998. Michael Gibson, hired at McNeel as an intern, created a mesh modeling software called Sculptura. After several years of development, Sculptura was integrated with NURBS, and its name was changed to Rhinoceros. Rhino quickly became immensely popular as an easy-to-learn free-form surface modeler. It was based on NURBS (Non-Uniform Rational Basis Splines) geometry, which made for mathematically precise (as opposed to the approximations of Bezier curves) models that were easy to interact with in 3D space. The key point of NURBS is that arcs, lines, and free-from curves can all be modeled with NURBS precisely thanks to the weights built into the NURBS concepts, which allows for a uniform representation of all geometry in one curve format rather than the separation into arcs, lines, free form curves, etc.[50] NURBS then can accurately represent both standard geometric objects and free-form geometry like car bodies and human bodies.[51] While Rhino could create accurate 2D representations, it was never fully adopted as a tool directly applicable to the creation of construction documents. Yet even though it was not utilized for CD production, it became the software of choice for explorations with many simultaneously emerging digital fabrication tools such as 3D printing, laser cutting, and CNC routing. Finally, its user base has outlasted many other modeling software primarily because of the plugins that have been released over the years, including Grasshopper (parametric visual scripting), Ladybug (climatic analysis), and VisualARQ (BIM), which will be covered in later episodes.

Another highly impactful modeler, Sketchup by @last Software, was released only two years after the previously mentioned free-form modeling software. The software filled an entirely different niche by allowing users to create 3D schematic models very easily and was targeted specifically for architects and designers. In collaboration with Google, the developers created a plug-in for Google Earth, allowing users to geolocate their models. Google subsequently acquired Sketchup and released it for free to exponentially increase the user base, allowing users to see how their model looked in its surroundings.

Parametric Design Reaches the Masses

Returning to the developments resulting from the SmartGeometry Group, it is important to highlight the contributions made toward parametric modeling and associative geometry into mainstream architecture practice. Additionally, this group contributed knowledge to accelerate the acceptance of early-stage three-dimensional structural analysis and late-stage clash detection, which are standard practices today.[52] Early workshops provided inspiration to many in the professional domain. This was especially true for Robert Aish in his pursuit of creating parametric software as the Director of Research for Bentley Systems. In 2003, he led the development of Generative Components (GC) as the project lead for Bentley Systems, released in 2005. It had the greatest impact on the London architecture community, eventually being developed on top of the popular Microstation software.[53] Aish played a pivotal role as a software designer and developer and has deeply understood design thinking and how architecture was conceptualized and delivered. Aish's influence didn't end with GC, as he would later become Director of Software Development at Autodesk, where he led the development of DesignScript, which in turn went on to become Dynamo.

Eventually, the profession played a role in directing the development of the technology and tools that affected it. It was a time when the profession began forging its own identity, breaking down pre-existing rules and boundaries. Perhaps one of the earliest uses of parametrically driven design, even preceding that of the more radical explorations by Gehry's office, was that of the International Terminal, Waterloo Station in London by Nicholas Grimshaw in 1993 in Microstation, which had the parametrically driven 36 identical but twisted and bowstring arch. By deploying a single parametric model to address each of the unique structural arches, Branko Kolarevic points out,

> a highly complex hierarchy of interdependence could be parametrically modeled, allowing iterative refinement, i.e., the dimensional fine-tuning of the project in all stages of its development, from conceptual design to construction.[54]

Several years later, in 1999, Norman Foster's office employed the clarity of parametric concepts to address the complexity of the roof of the Great Court at the British Museum. The structure was unprecedented for the unique way it enclosed the space with a glass roof made from 3,312 panes of glass, no two of which were the same. Hugh Whitehead, who led the Specialist Modeling Group (SMG) at Foster's office, spearheaded the effort. Interestingly, no parametric modeling software was used, but the roof membrane was scripted with equations by Chris Williams, a consultant for the engineering office of Buro Happold, and Williams then ran a dynamic relaxation script to find the point distribution riding on top of the mathematically defined surface.[55]

Not long after this time, a massive gap was filled in the area of parametric BIM, more specifically geared toward professionals, with the introduction of Revit by Autodesk. Autodesk already had 3D Studio Max as software for exploring geometry and AutoCAD, a complicated 3D modeling software

FIGURE 3.5 The International Terminal, Waterloo Station in London (1993) by Nicholas Grimshaw stands as one of the earliest parametrically driven design projects.

used primarily for building drafting and documentation. With the release of Revit Autodesk, the company would join the BIM market with Nemetschek (makers of ArchiCAD, AllPlan, and Vectorworks) and Gehry Technologies with the CATIA-based Digital Project discussed previously.

Like most software, Revit was initially developed in 1997 by the small company called Charles River Software, led by Leonid Razi and Irwin Jungreis.[56] One of the key differences for Revit software in the marketplace, unlike many other software mentioned thus far, was that the specific application was for architects with a deep understanding of documentation, construction, and engineering. The company was renamed Revit Technology Corporation in 2000 and purchased by Autodesk in 2002. As a BIM software, the goal was to allow architects to create a parametric three-dimensional model that included both the geometry and non-geometric design and construction information. In 1996, the control over parametric components could also be done with ArchiCAD and Vectorworks, as discussed in Episode 2, but the difference was Revit offered a graphical "family editor" to take the place of using a programming language, and the model captured all relationships between components, views, and annotations.[57] Another distinguishing point was how Revit introduced bi-directional associativity. In simplified terms, all updates were automatic between all three main classes of elements, including *Building Components, Views*, and *Annotations*. Regardless of the changes made, the model remained connected, and all documentation was coordinated. Although the dream of BIM would take a long time to come to fruition, the impact on the process whereby 3D modeling and documentation were the same would become massively impactful as the hordes of AutoCAD users begin to migrate over to Revit.

The parametric BIM programs mentioned above, including Vectorworks, ArchiCAD, Revit, Digital Project, and Generative Components, made huge strides in building performance analysis, including computational fluid dynamics concerning coordination of MEP and structural, but there was also a parallel development of tools for environmental analysis. At a time when there was growing global awareness of environmental issues, specifically the architectural impact of carbon emissions. ArcGIS first came out in 1999 by the company ESRI as a command line-based GIS (Geographic Information System) under the name of ARC/INFO which at the time had the highest level of licensing and was therefore the highest functionality. It was later merged into ArcGIS Desktop and eventually ArcGIS Pro as a single integrated package with an intuitive interface. ArcGIS offered the ability to visualize and understand a project within the context of a location. In addition to the wealth of contextual data, there was also a single point of access to environmental analysis, which could be used to understand the environmental impacts of development projects.

EnergyPlus was also released only a couple of years later, in 2001 which grew out of the BLAST and DOE–2 programs. BLAST (Building Loads Analysis and System Thermodynamics) and DOE–2 were both developed and released in the late 1970s and early 1980s as energy and load simulation tools.[58] With integrated weather files, the goal was for a designer (either architect or engineer) to size HVAC equipment appropriately, carry out studies for life cycling cost analyses, and optimize energy performance. As a whole building simulation tool, it allowed for the first time both energy loads and water requirements to be realistically calculated in a scientific and iterative way.

Novel Ways of Designing

It was within the context of exploration, coupled with the new means of dissemination and the explosion of new software tools, that a number of pioneers leveraged to work in fascinating new ways. Perhaps the most widely recognized was that of the Paperless Studio introduced by Bernard Tschumi at the Columbia Graduate School of Architecture Planning and Preservation in 1993. The widely publicized studios became a defining moment for the discipline to experiment with unfamiliar computer hardware and software and reconsider its relationship within the architectural context. It was also an opportunity to theorize the effects of the digital screen on architectural representation.[59] In this context, Tschumi felt it was an

> appropriate time to question how an engagement with digital technology would further expand the field. This interest coalesced with the resurgence of media theory and architecture's relationship to media, theory, and digital technology.[60]

The success and massive impact of the Paperless Studio primarily hinged on the very well-known and capable group of faculty who ran the studios, including Greg Lynn, Scott Marble, Jesse Reiser and Nanako Umemoto, Bill MacDonald, Sulan Kolatan, Hani Rashid and Lise-Anne Couture, Evan Douglas, and Stan Allen.

One of these faculty members at the time, Greg Lynn, who was already mentioned as contributing to "blob" architecture, went on to help define a new, innovative architectural approach. Using topological geometries to mutate entities, he created unprecedented formal departures that went against preconceived ideas of architecture at the time (Figure 3.6). Lynn developed the concept of folding as a fluid logic of connectivity. His interest was in the topology of interconnections and relations. He pushed the ideas further with the seminal book *Architectural Curvilinearity: The Folded, the Pliant and the Supple*,[61] an essay in *Folding in Architecture* (Vol. 63 No. 3/4 1993) which coalesced a series of essays by leading practitioners and academics of the time including, Jeffrey Kipnis, Bahram Shirdel, Frank Gehry and Philip Johnson. The book's impact transcended formal shape-making to usher in a new acceptance of the potential for the use of computation in design, ensnaring everything from design to construction and mass-customization fabrication processes. Lynn's work also stood on its own merits through his experimentation with animation and special effects software to transform spaces and forms.

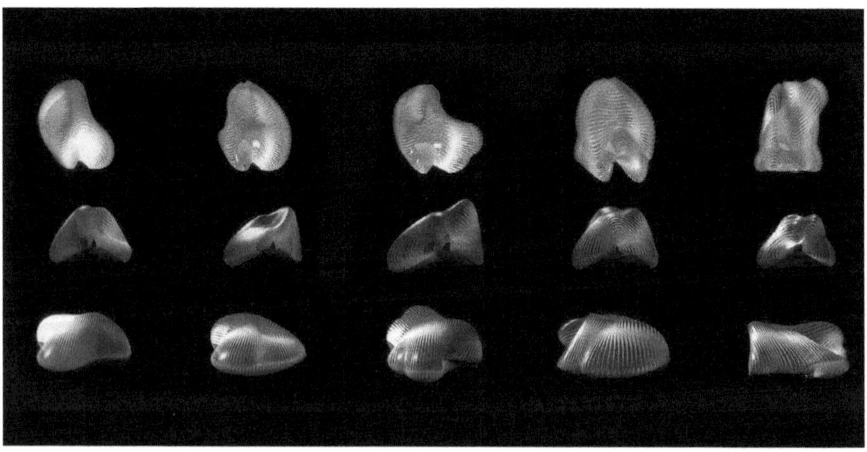

FIGURE 3.6 Greg Lynn created unprecedented formal departures that went against any preconceived ideas of architecture at the time.

By 1999, Lynn released *Animate Form*[62] with an interactive CD of his recent architectural projects. With these projects and accompanying essays, he was able to most clearly summarize his theories on the potential of a dynamic (animated) architectural process – and the potential of this on form and space.[63] The book challenged traditional notions of static formal purity with models of dynamic organization that were responsive to the dynamic and active context in which they are situated. He and several other academics and practitioners began demonstrating a new era of unprecedented design. Credited with coming up with the term "Blob Architecture," the reference had a much more technical origin as Lynn explains,

> When I first used the term it was completely technical. The term Blob modeling was a module in Wavefront software at the time, and it was an acronym for Binary Large Object – spheres that could be collected to form larger composite forms.[64]

This description expanded on his use of the animation software's disposition to model with non euclidian "n" dimensional geometries that meshed together based on proximity. Beyond Kaplický's use of blob mentioned previously, we certainly see the conceptual/ formal explorations of precursors in Fredrich Kiesler's Endless House (1959),[65] the work of Archigram from the 1960s and later, Peter Eisenman, who Lynn worked for.

The first entire blob building, from the standpoint of using computer tools, was the Water Pavilion built in 1993–1997 in the Netherlands by Lars Spuybroek, (NOX), and Kas Oosterhuis (Figure 3.7). The renowned cultural and design theorist Charles Jencks would proclaim the Water Pavilion to be

FIGURE 3.7 The first entire blob building from the standpoint of using computer tools, was the Water Pavilion by Lars Spuybroek and Kas Oosterhuis.

one of the great architectural achievements as the decade was closing.[66] Its shape was fully designed on the computer and directly manufactured with computer-aided tools. Spuybroek would also go on to be attributed with coining the term Non-Standard Architectures as his way of describing the blob geometry. This reached a pinnacle with the show curated by Frédéric Migayrou at the Centre Pompidou entitled "Non-Standard Architectures"[67] in 2003–2004. In addition to some of those already mentioned, the exhibition featured 12 participants and included digital designers and innovators such as Sulan Kolatan and Bill MacDonald of Kol/Mac Studio, François Roche and Stéphanie Lavaux of R&Sie, SERVO, Mark Goulthorpe of deCOI, and Dagmar Richter.[68]

Nearly at the same time, was also the influential work of Ushida Findlay Architects, including the unprecedented Truss Wall House (1993) which was also one of a very early series of experimental homes built to showcase examples of computers and automation. There was also the undulating and reflective Selfridges Building department store facade by Future Systems Office in 2003 (Figure 3.8). Lastly, the famous Kunsthaus Graz (described in the next episode), designed by Colin Fournier and Peter Cook and completed in 2003, also had a major impact on being widely published then.

Similarly, in contrast to the longstanding notion of delineation between interior and exterior relationships, Bernard Cache and others began to formulate new concepts about territorialization and topographic surfaces as a

FIGURE 3.8 The Selfridges building in Birmingham by architect Jan Kaplicky of Future Systems.

means to blur and "fold in" boundaries. Gilles Deleuze provided the context for much of this thought and influence in his 1993 book, *The Fold: Leibniz and the Baroque*,[69] which had a widespread impact on a generation of theorists and digital designers. For Cache, the notion of "fold" was to rethink not only the architectonic relationships but also that between past and present and architecture and the urban context. Lynn's "folding" is one of many terms and concepts, such as affiliation, smooth and striated space, pliancy, and multiplicity, appropriated from Deleuze's Fold.[70] In his 1995 book *Earth Moves: The Furnishing of Territories*,[71] Cache formulated Objectile Theory, which is an open-ended notation allowing for infinite parametric variations. These could be directly fabricated using file-to-factory technologies, thus enabling the serial reproduction of non-identical parts, where ranges of limited variations can be mass-produced at no extra cost.[72] For Cache, the aim was to develop processes involving both hardware and software to this end and pioneered the dream of industrially producing nonstandard objects that could be affordable and accessible.

The CAAD pioneer Paul Coates was also fascinated with forms at the time, using the computer to explore the idea of emergence to generate designs and focus the pedagogical process as a determiner of forms. Pushing some of the earliest notions of agents and Swarm behavior, the longtime programmer argued in the paper *"Agent-Based Modeling"*[73] that a spatial problem must be broken down into low-level machine code. This idea became a search for architectural DNA, a seed to grow from. Implemented through his teaching, he found the most successful experiments revealed that the simpler the seed, coupled with the clearest of generators, the elegant algorithm, the more useful representations of form and space emerged. The premise became his mantra: "Simple rules – Complex outcomes," which he would go on to elaborate on in *Programming in Architecture*[74] in 2010.

Perhaps one of the best examples at the time bridging the theoretical world with built form was the landmark Yokohama Pier Port Terminal in Japan by Foreign Office Architects (FOA) run by Farshid Moussavi and Alejandro Zaera-Polo. The competition was held in 1995, and the project was completed in 2002. The experiment in topology was a hybrid of non-Cartesian infrastructure and versatile social functionality. The office generally employed "technical rigor in their focus on organic growth and the evolution of design 'species' hybridizing uses relating to local and global conditions. Their work addressed a variety of locations and typologies."[75]

Another practitioner and avid theorist of technology and contemporary culture is Neil Denari, who stands as one of the earliest pioneers in integrating computation into his work. The publication *Interrupted Projections* paralleled an exhibition at the TOTO GALLARY- MA in Tokyo in 1996.[76] This began an experimental transition from hyper-detailed machine architecture drawn by hand to the more fluid, post-mechanical paradigm of forms, which he would go on to explore through computation. Denari's linework invoked an instant feeling of fluidity, and their compositions were meticulous.[77]

Following Denari's influence as Director at Sci-Arc (1997–2002), others like Wes Jones, Tom Mayne, and Frank Gehry contributed to pulling the computational design dialogue into the context of Los Angeles and the West Coast of the US. By this time, academics and thought leaders like Greg Lynn, Sylvia Lavin, and Karl Chu (founder of the Institute of Genetic Architecture) were also moving to SCI-Arc and UCLA to explore local influences as they tied back into the broader global discourse. The film and entertainment industry and the network of parallel fields of visualization and animation made for a fertile ground for experimentation. A new generation of leaders would soon follow. In 1999, Heather Roberge and Jason Payne, initially partners at Gnuform and faculty at UCLA, along with Marcelo Spina and Georgina Huljich of P-A-T-T-E-R-N-S and faculty at Sci-ARC and UCLA, respectively, joined a growing number of new voices. These young practices began integrating digital technology with an extensive consideration of form and innovative materials, layering in the distinctive contextual questions of housing, infrastructure, and materiality uniquely positioned within the West Coast context.

This was a time when the World Trade Center buildings fell, and the first war (Iraq) was presented to the public live on television. It was out of this context that the somewhat ominous shared vision of cyberculture emerged, ensnaring the social, cultural, and technological phenomena associated with computation that Christopher Hight explored through a reformulation of architecture's relationship to humanism, modernism and technology in his pioneering book *Architectural Principles in the Age of Cybernetics* (2007).[78] The Hong Kong architect James Law also coined the term "Cybertecture" to symbolize a new kind of design that merges technology and architecture.

Integrating Computation into Everyday Things

In line with the theme of appropriation which defines this episode, we also find that while many were exploring the new forms in architecture, there was a somewhat parallel development by those integrating the broader aspects of computer science and "ubiquitous computing," a term coined in 1988 by Mark Weiser as a post-desktop model of human-computer interaction and discussed in Episode 2. Ubiquitous computing can be defined as computation thoroughly integrated into everyday objects and activities and is often regarded as the intersection of computer science, behavioral sciences, and design. The maturing concepts of ubiquitous computing fostered the development of the Internet of Things (IoT), which refers to the potential for connected devices and their benefits. Embedded computation was consequently born as the architectural application of the concepts, defined as "the convergence of embedded computation and a physical counterpart that satisfies adaptation."[79] The discipline subsequently learned that we could use the tools, but in different ways than they were intended, and that the tools are, in fact, malleable.

Out of the explosion of growth in computer science, fields such as "intelligent environments" (IE) were formed to study spaces with embedded computation and communication technologies, creating spaces that brought digital technology into the physical world. Intelligent environments are defined as spaces in which computation is seamlessly used to enhance ordinary activity. Echoing the earlier adaptive architectural ambitions of Price, Eastman, and Frazer, Michael Mozer, coming out of an entirely different profession, led the almost parallel development of the pioneering Adaptive House in the late 1990s (Figure 3.9). He discussed the "intelligence" of the home as that which arises from the home's ability to predict the behavior and needs of the inhabitants by observing them over time.[80] Instead of being programmed to perform specific actions, the Adaptive House essentially programmed itself by monitoring the environment and sensing actions performed by the inhabitants, observing the occupancy and behavior patterns of the inhabitants, and learning to predict the future states of the house.[81] Another approach was that of MIT's Intelligent Room Project, directed by Michael Coen, which was created to experiment with different forms of natural, multimodal human-computer interaction (HCI) by embedding computational smarts into everything the users encounter. The goal was to allow computers to participate in activities that have never previously involved computation and to enable people to interact with computational systems the way they would with other people.[82] In ubiquitous computing, users engage many computational devices and systems simultaneously while doing ordinary activities and may not even be aware that they are doing so. Weiser described this as "the age of calm technology when technology recedes into the background of our lives."[83] Mahesh Daas pointed out two diametrically opposed perspectives

FIGURE 3.9 The pioneering "Adaptive House" by Michael Mozer and the University of Colorado essentially programmed itself by monitoring the environment and sensing actions performed by the inhabitants.

that prevailed at this time: a life defined by pragmatic convenience and a life controlled by the machine whereby the users become dependent upon their environments.[84]

Embedded Computation in Architecture

Eventually, academia began to assemble comprehensive prototypical projects based on real-world, market-driven developments, although they were often outside architecture and often driven by technical accomplishments. Numerous academic "smart home" and "smart workplace" projects were initiated in the 1990s that relied heavily on technological advancements. Many of the early architects involved in these projects learned by working directly with computer scientists such as Mary Lou Maher, who specifically impacted the study and development of novel interaction and communications technology, particularly with respect to design and creativity. At this time, wireless networks, embedded computation, and sensor effectors became both technologically and economically feasible to implement. This feasibility fueled experimentation with many of the ideas of the early visionary architects and theoreticians outlined above that had been stifled by their day's technological and economic hurdles. John Frazer argued that architecture should be a "living, evolving thing" in his book *An Evolutionary Architecture* (1995).[85] He outlined eight aspects of evolution, all producing change at various scales, and the basis of all such conditions is information. The ideas facilitated a paradigmatic shift from the mechanical to the biological from the standpoint of adaptation. John and Julia Frazer's "Interactivator"[86] project responded physically to visitors and the atmosphere of the environment and stands as the first online virtual interaction with the development of an evolving form in a remote exhibition (Figure 3.10). The system allowed both virtual and actual visitors to make selections or propose (via a bank of switches) genetic information to influence the evolution of the form. Change in the mechanical world was cyclical, but there was no broader development, as the factors were continually repeated with set outcomes. However, the organic paradigm was developmental and reciprocal: It emulated life. Organic theory emerged from nature, an environment that possessed evolutionary patterns producing forms of growth and strategies of behavior, optimizing each pattern to the contextual situation.[87]

There was a growing sentiment that when architecture was built upon a sympathetic understanding of biological systems, it presented a break from how we had constructed our built environment in the past. When architectural space had a true communicative capability, it fostered a heightened sense of attachment. At a time when sensors were beginning to be both technologically and economically feasible, Ted Krueger was questioning how we communicated with our environments, specifically interested in the ability of architecture to extend human perception. He posited that "direct

FIGURE 3.10 Early prototype by John Frazer who argued that architecture should be a "living, evolving thing."

actions in the world are the most robust means of communication, this eliminates the interface as an object or artifact of design and concentrates efforts on crafting the interaction that takes place between autonomous agents."[88] Krueger argued for an intelligent and interactive architecture conceived of as a "metadermis," a socially inhabited body, referencing recent work in the fields of robotics, intelligent structures and skins, and interactive materials.[89] In several pioneering projects, he explored various means of sensory input, considering competing accounts of perception and examining their potential as interface technologies. Usman Haque, with Josephine Pletts and Luca Turin, similarly developed the "Scents of Space" environment, exploring the olfactory sense. Smells can have extremely positive associations, evoking strong emotional reactions as many of our olfactory likes and dislikes are based on emotional associations. Aside from the emotional aspects of personal associations, environments augmented with olfactory enhancement could benefit those suffering from memory loss. Beyond the sensorial innovations, both Haque and Ruari Glynn, who would go on to direct the Interactive Architecture Lab at the Bartlett, advanced the earlier notions of Pask's "conversation theory" now through actual project implementation. As Usman Haque puts it, such systems must define interaction as circular or merely "reacting" and not "interacting." A truly interactive system is a multiple-loop system in which one enters a conversation: A continual and constructive information exchange.[90] Glynn and Haque emerged from the interactive architecture workshop established by Stephen Gage at the Bartlett School of Architecture as a pioneering forum for architectural pursuits in the field. Two major research strands developed out of this group, including 1) *Responsive Behavior, Interactivity, and Performance*: Research predicated on the notion of architecture as time-based, changing its form and behavior rather than static and fixed and 2) *Innovative Design Practice*: Understanding differences between simulated and actual behavior is especially relevant in design, where the observer's engagement is haptic, and the virtual observer's descriptions are inevitably partial and incomplete. At about the same time, Michael Fox also formed the Kinetic Design Group (KDG) at MIT in 1998, focusing on computationally driven, flexible, and responsively adaptable spaces and objects utilizing kinetics.

While the foundational work in academia was playing out, there were those in the professional world who were pushing the boundaries through actual implementation. The previously mentioned Lars Spuybroek (NOX) came to be known for his free-form architecture, a merger between the building, the body, the environment, and technology. His architecture and theories also derived the dynamic forces used to model a building from the occupant's mobility. The Water Pavilion (with Kas Oosterhuis), mentioned earlier for its pioneering accomplishments, also stands as one of the earliest examples of embedded computation in architecture, having an electronic interactive interior where sound and light were transformed by the visitor. Kas Oosterhuis became a seminal figure in the area, publishing several books on digital architecture, including *Programmable Architecture* (2002),[91] *Architecture Goes Wild* (2001),[92] and *Hyperbodies, Towards an Emotive Architecture* (2003).[93] He founded the Hyperbody research group at TU Delft in 2000, specializing in Nonstandard Architecture and Interactive Architecture. Mark Goulthorpe, mentioned as a part of the Non-Standard Architectures Exhibition at the Pompidou, founded the office dECOi atelier in 1991 and has written extensively on the impacts of digital technologies in architecture. Goulthorpe's work was widely known for his collaboration with Mark Burry on the seminal "Hyposurface" project in 2003.[94] This project was an ensemble of thousands of faceted metallic surfaces that could deform physically as a real-time response to electronic stimuli from the environment, including movement by people, light, and sound. Mark Burry himself was also responsible for establishing the Spatial Information Architecture Laboratory (SIAL) at RMIT in Australia in 2001, focused on acoustic design, sound performance, and soundscape research that was accessible not only to architects but also to a wide range of designers.

Early Stages of Digital Making

In parallel to the work in modeling and interactive environments, architects joined the latest tendencies to investigate digital fabrication and developed novel techniques to create buildings. Digital fabrication was born as a design and manufacturing workflow where digital data directly drives manufacturing equipment to form various part geometries. Digital Fabrication was essentially the ability to transfer from CAD (computer-aided design) to CAM (computer-aided manufacturing).

Academic Initiatives

A few academic initiatives had an early focus on digital fabrication. One of the most influential of the time was through the Center for Bits and Atoms (CBA) at the MIT Media Lab, founded by Neil Gershenfeld (2001). The Fab Lab was an early project from the CBA and served as a model lab that could be set up quickly and inexpensively to provide basic fabrication capability for rapid prototyping of almost anything. The idea was these labs would become easy enough to create and set up almost anywhere in the world. The labs would be self-sufficient and useful to the local community to support whatever engineering or fabrication projects they could imagine. The meme of Fab Lab grew out of this driver, which has become a commonplace term today and tied closely to the DIY movement. Vigyan Ashram, a learning center connected to the Indian Institute of Education (IIE) in the small town of Pabal, was the first lab outside of MIT in 2002 to teach various tools and machines focused on locally sourced technological fabrication. In 2001, the pioneering IAAC (Institute for Advanced Architecture of Catalonia) was established as an experienced-based center where one learns by doing through a unique and unconventional approach to current construction models combining technology innovation and architectural design (Figure 3.11). Neil Gershenfield's CBA model was employed as a template to help shape the bold vision to create a new educational pedagogy for the IAAC.[95] The center focused on exploring real solutions in architecture to confront the growing challenges humanity faces, particularly concerning the environment. A recent online 20th-anniversary gathered many educators and practitioners who went through the IAAC program and identified one of the most pioneering aspects of the program. They collectively spoke about the collection and availability of large-scale equipment in a space with students and educators from around the world where they could collaborate and experiment together.[96] Also around the same time, but directly supporting architectural pursuits, was the Fabrication Lab at the Taubman School of Architecture. The FABLab was founded to support research and teaching activities in digital fabrication. The idea was that everyone could bring in their agendas, and they would be supported through a culture of manufacturing and fabrication. These labs would become more commonplace over the next decade as familiarity and active learning became more central to architectural education.

At the time, there were also various targeted conferences specifically geared toward digital fabrication, which served to coalesce the emerging experimentation in the area. Martin Bechthold, who would go on to establish

FIGURE 3.11 The IAAC (Institute for Advanced Architecture of Catalonia) was established as a pioneering experienced-based center where one learns by doing combining technology innovation and architectural design.

the Design Robotics Group at Harvard's GSD along with Kimo Griggs and Marco Steingerg, and coordinated a seminal international symposium in 2000 at the school to both investigate the "current state of technology and to explore potential future developments and their implications on architecture and design practice."[97] This symposium led to the publication of *New Technologies in Architecture II & III: Digital Design and Manufacturing Technique*[98] in 2003 with Daniel Schodek and others as the first real guide to computer-aided design and manufacturing specifically focused on architecture.

Posited to foster an abandonment of the discourse on style, discussed earlier in this episode, almost as abruptly as it began, Branko Kolarevic changed the subject in his edited volume, *Architecture in the Digital Age: Design and Manufacturing,*[99] which came out in 2003 and grew out of a conference held at the University of Pennsylvania in 2002. What united digital architects, he stated, was the "use of digital technology as an enabling apparatus that directly integrates conception and production in ways that are unprecedented since the medieval times."[100] He argued that the complexity of non-Euclidean and topological architecture "is actually drawing architects out of necessity back into being more involved with the making of buildings and more in control of the building process."[101] This book, as much as any, combined a group of contributing authors, such as Bill Mitchell, Hugh

Whitehead, Mark Burry, Jim Glymph, and Bernard Cache, along with Kolarevic, to provide a seminal text to guide the subsequent discourse that would follow over the next decade.

Impacts Beyond Architecture

While many diligently pursued various trajectories mentioned thus far in this episode, a few looked down from far above and documented it well along the way. During the short span of this episode, architect and urban visionary Bill Mitchell published an informal trilogy examining the ramifications of information technology in everyday life. His earlier book, *The Logic of Architecture*,[102] published in 1990, served as a foundation much of the work to transpire over the following decades. It was a guide to the modern framework of design thinking and would document the basis of what would come to be known as computational shape grammars. States Mitchell, "A design problem exists when you can say what you want in the critical language but cannot immediately see how to produce a state in the design world that depicts what you want."[103] In the book, he developed an argument for establishing a grammatical and syntactical language of architectural form. The book was credited by *The New York Times* as having "profoundly changed the way architects approached building design."[104] In 1995, he published the seminal *City of Bits*,[105] which imagined architecture and urbanism and the people who inhabit it in an emerging digital era. Mitchell outlines four contemporary developments necessary for a reconceptualization of architecture and urban space: The digital telecommunications revolution, nanotechnology, or the miniaturization of electronics, the commodification of digital information, and the recent domination of software over materialized forms.[106]

Most importantly, he examined the social and cultural implications of online phenomena and their potential effects on our architectural and urban paradigms of physical space. He argues that in the same way that railroads and later automobiles influenced settlement patterns and economics, computer networks will similarly influence how we live, work, and move.[107]

In *e topia*[108] published in 2000, he picked up where City of Bits left off, arguing that the digital world is a whole new infrastructure that necessitates extending our previous physical definitions of cities and urban design. The last of these books, *M++*,[109] came out in 2004, where he examined the implications of linkages, interconnections, miniaturization, and portability at the individual level. The more separate spatial consequences of cyberspace are now turned toward the flexible and flowing world of interconnected human relationships. Perhaps the most important point here is that he published all of these at a critical time when the appropriation was rampant, when liberating software was exploding, and when the internet was an immense unknown frontier.

Notes

1 CAADRIA – The Association for Computer-Aided Architectural Design Research in Asia. See https://caadria.org/ [Accessed August 5, 2023].
2 "About SIGraDi." See https://sigradi.org/en/about-sigradi/ [Accessed August 5, 2023].
3 Arab Society for Computation in Architecture, Art, and Design. See https://ascaad.org/ [Accessed August 5, 2023].
4 Herr, C.M. (2020). "CAADRIA at Age 25: Mapping our Past, Present, and Future," in D. Holzer, W. Nakapan, A. Globa, and I. Koh (eds.), *RE: Anthropocene, Design in the Age of Humans – Proceedings of the 25th CAADRIA Conference – Volume 2*, Chulalongkorn University, Bangkok, Thailand, 5–6 August 2020, pp. 567–576. doi:10.52842/conf.caadria.2020.2.567.
5 Kvan, T. (1996). "Editorial: The Introduction of Technology," *Proceedings of The First Conference on Computer Aided Architectural Design Research in Asia*, 25–27 April 1996, Hong Kong, p. 1.
6 CAADRIA – The Association for Computer-Aided Architectural Design Research in Asia. See https://caadria.org/ [Accessed August 5, 2023].
7 Herr, C.M. (2020). "CAADRIA at Age 25: Mapping our Past, Present, and Future," in D. Holzer, W. Nakapan, A. Globa, and I. Koh (eds.), *RE: Anthropocene, Design in the Age of Humans – Proceedings of the 25th CAADRIA Conference – Volume 2*, Chulalongkorn University, Bangkok, Thailand, 5–6 August 2020, pp. 567–576. doi:10.52842/conf.caadria.2020.2.567.
8 Cerovšek, T. and Martens, B. (2020). "The Evolution of CAADRIA Conferences – A Bibliometric Approach Source," in D. Holzer, W. Nakapan, A. Globa, and I. Koh (eds.), *RE: Anthropocene, Design in the Age of Humans – Proceedings of the 25th CAADRIA Conference – Volume 1*, Chulalongkorn University, Bangkok, Thailand, 5–6 August 2020, pp. 325–334.
9 "SIGraDi#25." See https://www.sigradi.org/en/news/sigradi25-en/ [Accessed August 7, 2023].
10 "ASCAAD History." See https://ascaad.org/history/ [Accessed August 7, 2023].
11 Martens, B., Björk, B.-C., and Turk, Z. (2002). "The SciX Project: Re-Engineering from Paper-Based to Free Electronic Publishing." *ACADIA Proceedings*. doi:10.52842/conf.acadia.2002.179.
12 Björk, B.-C. and Turk, Z. (2000). "How Scientists Retrieve Publications: An Empirical Study of How the Internet Is Overtaking Paper Media," *Journal of Electronic Publishing*, 6(2), 9.
13 "What is CumInCAD?" See https://papers.cumincad.org/helpdesk/knowledgebase.php?article=1 [Accessed August 9, 2023].
14 Koutamanis, A. (2005). "A Biased History of CAAD, Digital Design: The Quest for New Paradigms." *23rd eCAADe Conference Proceedings*, Lisbon, September 21–24, 2005, p. 631.
15 Ibid.
16 Ibid.
17 "America's Online Pursuits" (2003, December 22). Pew Research Center: Internet, Science & Tech. See https://www.pewresearch.org/internet/2003/12/22/americas-online-pursuits/
18 Ibid.
19 "World Internet Users Statistics and 2023 World Population Stats." See https://www.internetworldstats.com/stats.htm [Accessed August 7, 2023].
20 Ibid.

21 "A Brief History of AU." Autodesk University. See https://www.autodesk.com/autodesk-university/blog/brief-history-AU-2015 [Accessed August 9, 2023].
22 Peters, B. and Peters, T. (2013). *Inside SmartGeometry*. Hokoken, NJ: John Wiley & Sons ltd. See https://onlinelibrary.wiley.com/doi/book/10.1002/9781118653074 [Accessed August 9, 2023].
23 Jordana, S. (2013, July 5). "Practice 2.0: 10 Years of Smart Geometry." *ArchDaily*, July 5. Available at: https://www.archdaily.com/398406/practice-2-0-10-years-of-smart-geometry
24 Ibid.
25 John Gero. See https://sites.google.com/view/johngero/ [Accessed August 10, 2023].
26 Goel, A. K. and Do, E. Y.-L. (2010). "Design Computing and Cognition: An Introduction." *Artificial Intelligence for Engineering Design, Analysis and Manufacturing, 24*(1), 1–2. doi:10.1017/s0890060409990205.
27 "About OCEAN.net." See https://www.ocean-net.org/about-ocean-net/ [Accessed August 10, 2023].
28 Ibid.
29 McLuhan, M. (1962). *The Gutenberg Galaxy: The Making of Typographic Man*. London: Routledge, p. 31.
30 Ibid.
31 Wojtowicz, J. (1995). *Virtual Design Studio*. Hong Kong: Hong Kong University Press.
32 Ibid.
33 Bradford, J. W., Cheng, N., and Kvan, T. (1994). *Virtual Design Studios*. eCAADe Proceedings. doi:10.52842/conf.ecaade.1994.163.
34 Kolarevic, B., Schmitt, G., Hirschberg, U., Kurmann, D., and Johnson, B. (2000). "An Experiment in Design Collaboration." *Automation in Construction, 9*(1), 73–81.
35 Sheldon, D. (2002). *Digital Surface Representation and the Constructability of Gehry's Architecture*. Doctoral Thesis, MIT, pp. 1–340. Available at: https://dspace.mit.edu/handle/1721.1/16899
36 Eden, P. (ed.) (2008). *Civil Aircraft Today: The World's Most Successful Commercial Aircraft*. London: Amber Books Ltd., p. 106.
37 Norris, G. and Wagner, M., (1999). *Modern Boeing Jetliners*. Minneapolis, MN: Zenith Imprint, p. 133.
38 "Digital Twin: Bringing MEP Models to Life." *Autodesk University*. Available at: https://www.autodesk.com/autodesk-university/article/Digital-Twin-Bringing-MEP-Models-Life-2021 [Accessed January 27, 2024].
39 Dassault Systèmes (2020, February 6). "Dassault Systèmes Opens Up New Horizons: 3DEXPERIENCE from things to life." *Dassault Systèmes*. Available at: https://www.3ds.com/newsroom/press-releases/february-6-2020-dassault-systemes-opens-new-horizons-3dexperience-things-life
40 Norris, G. and Wagner, M. (1989). *Modern Boeing Jetliners*. Minneapolis, MN: Zenith Imprint, p. 21. See also, https://web.archive.org/web/20190919185120/https://newrepublic.com/article/154944/boeing-737-max-investigation-indonesia-lion-air-ethiopian-airlines-managerial-revolution [Accessed August 15, 2023].
41 Glymph, J. (2005). "Evolution of the Digital Design Process," in Branko Kolarevic (ed.), *Architecture in the Digital Age: Design and Manufacturing*. New York: Taylor & Francis, pp. 101–120.
42 Thompson, D. W. (1992). *On Growth and Form: The Complete Revised Edition*. Garden City, NY: Dover Publications.
43 Frei O. and Rasch, B. (1995). *Finding Form*. Stuttgart: Edition Axel Menges.
44 Margolius, I. and Kaplicky, J. (2022). *For the Future and for Beauty*. Prague: Edition Axel Menges GmbH.

45 "History – Blender.org." See https://www.blender.org/about/history/ [Accessed August 13, 2023].
46 Pouchnikov, D. (2023, March 9). "Blender vs Maya for Architectural Design – UH Studio." *UH Studio.* See https://uhstudio.com/posts/blender-vs-maya-architecture-design
47 "Best Books About 3d Maya." See https://web.archive.org/web/20101125035450/http://www.mayabooks.org/ [Accessed August 15, 2023].
48 Carlson, W. E. (2017, June 20). *Computer Graphics and Computer Animation: A Retrospective Overview.* Columbus, OH: The Ohio State University Press, p. 244.
49 Ibid., p. 261.
50 Farin, G., Hoschek, J., and Kim, M.-S. (2002). *Handbook of Computer Aided Geometric Design*. Amsterdam: Elsevier.
51 "What Does NURBS Mean and Why Should I Care?" McNeel Wiki. See https://wiki.mcneel.com/rhino/nurbs [Accessed August 17, 2023].
52 Peters, T and Peters, B. (2013). *Inside SmartGeometry: Expanding the Architectural Possibilities of Computational Design*. Germany: Wiley, p. 13.
53 Day, M. (2005, January 19). "Generative Components." *AEC Magazine*, January 19. See https://aecmag.com/news/generative-components/ [Accessed January 12, 2024].
54 Kolarevic, B. (2004). "Chapter 2: Digital Morphogenesis," in *Architecture in the Digital Age: Design and Manufacturing.* London: Taylor & Francis, p. 18.
55 Williams, C. J. K. (2001). "The Analytic and Numerical Definition of the Geometry of the British Museum Great Court Roof." *Mathematics & Design, 200,* 434–440.
56 Peicho, R., (2020). *BIM for Architectural Design Research and Representation*. Master's thesis. Available at: https://repozitorij.uni-lj.si/IzpisGradiva.php?lang=slv&id=121118 [Accessed March 3, 2024].
57 Ingram, J. (2020). *Understanding BIM: The Past, Present and Future.* Oxford: CRC Press, p. 29.
58 Big Ladder Software. *Introduction: EnergyPlus Essentials — Energyplus 9.6.* Available at: https://bigladdersoftware.com/epx/docs/9-6/essentials/essentials.html [Accessed September 23, 2023].
59 Audisho, E. (2020). "Liveness, Mediation and the Simulated: Effects of the Digital Screen on Architectural Representation Post–1990." *Interstices: Journal of Architecture and Related Arts, 20*(20), 75–92. Available at: https://interstices.ac.nz/index.php/Interstices/article/view/648
60 Ibid.
61 Lynn, G. (1993). "Introduction." *Folding in Architecture*, 63(3/4), 8–15. Berlin: Academy Editions.
62 Lynn, G. (1999). *Animate Form.* London: Princeton Architectural Press.
63 Ibid.
64 Rappolt, M. (2007, March 21). "Greg Lynn." *ICON Magazine*, March 21. Available at: https://www.iconeye.com/back-issues/greg-lynn-icon-005-september-2003 [Accessed January 17, 2024].
65 Kiesler, F. "Model for the Endless House." *Whitney Museum of American Art.* Available at: https://whitney.org/collection/works/7371 [Accessed January 18, 2024].
66 Jencks, C. (2022). *The New Paradigm in Architecture*. New Haven, CT: Yale University Press, p. 223.
67 "Non-standard Architectures." *Centre Pompidou.* See https://www.centrepompidou.fr/en/program/calendar/event/cpBeKA [Accessed January 18, 2024].
68 Ibid.
69 Deleuze, G. (1993). *The Fold: Leibniz and the Baroque.* London: Burns & Oates.

70 See Kolarevic, B. (2004). *Architecture in the Digital Age: Design and Manufacturing*. London: Taylor & Francis, p. 3; and Deleuze, G. (2006). *The Fold*. London: Bloomsbury Academic, p. 10.
71 Cache, B. (1995). *Earth Moves: The Furnishing of Territories*. Cambridge, MA: MIT Press. p. 88.
72 Carpo, M. (2013). *The Digital Turn in Architecture 1992–2012*. Chichester: John Wiley & Sons, p. 146.
73 Coates, P. and Schmid, C. (1999). "Agent-Based Modeling," in A. Brown, M. Knight and P. Berridge (eds.), *Architectural Computing: From Turing to 2000* [eCAADe Conference Proceedings] CAADRU, University of Liverpool, UK.
74 Coates, P. (2010). *Programming Architecture*. London: Taylor & Francis.
75 "Foreign Office Architects." *Icon Magazine* Online, 007, November 2003. Iconeye.com. Retrieved July 17, 2023.
76 Denari, N. "Interrupted Projections." *Canadian Centre for Architecture*. See https://cca-bookstore.com/products/denari-interupted-projections-denari-interupted-projections [Accessed October 5, 2023].
77 Neil D. @ work. *Archinect*. See https://archinect.com/features/article/64628/neil-denari-work [Accessed October 5, 2023].
78 Hight, C. (2007). *Architectural Principles in the Age of Cybernetics*. London: Taylor & Francis.
79 Fox, M. and Kemp, M. (2009). *Interactive Architecture*. Princeton, NJ: Princeton Architectural Press, p. 12.
80 Mozer, M. C. (2005). "Lessons from an Adaptive House," in *Smart Environments: Technologies, Protocols, and Applications*, edited by D. Cook and R. Das. Hoboken, NJ: J. Wiley & Sons, pp. 273–294.
81 Mozer, M. C. (1999). "An Intelligent Environment Must be Adaptive." *IEEE Intelligent Systems and their Applications, 14*(2), 11–13.
82 Coen, M. (1998). "Design Principles for Intelligent Environments." *Proceedings of the Fifteenth National Conference on Artificial Intelligence*, Madison, WI, p. 1.
83 Weiser, M. and Brown, J. S. (1995, December 21). "Designing Calm Technology Xerox PARC." *PowerGrid Journal*, v 1.01, July 1996. See http://powergrid.electriciti.com. Also appeared as Chapter 6, "The Coming Age of Calm Technogy" in the book *Beyond Calculation – The Next Fifty Years of Computing*, by P. J. Denning and R.M. Metcalfe. Berlin: Copernicus/An Imprint of Springer-Verlag.
84 Senagala, M. and Nakamura, C. (2006). "Going Past the Golem: The Emergence of Smart Architecture." Published in *Proceedings of the ACADIA International Conference*, Louisville, KY, p. 375.
85 Frazer, J. (1995). *An Evolutionary Architecture*. London: Architectural Association.
86 Frazer, J. H., Rastogi, M., and Graham, P. (1995). "The Interactivator." *Architectural Design, Architects in Cyberspace*, pp. 80–81.
87 Kronenburg, R. (2002). "Introduction," in *Transportable Environments 2*, edited by R. Kronenburg, J. Lim, and W.Y. Chiu. London: Spon Press, p. 4.
88 Krueger, T. (2006). "Eliminate the Interface." *Journal of Architectural Education, 56*, 4.
89 Krueger, T. (1998). "Autonomous Architecture." *Digital Creativity, 9*, 43–47.
90 Haque, U. (2006, August). "Architecture, Interactions, Systems." *AU: Arquitetura & Urbanismo, 149*, p. 2.
91 Oosterhuis, K., Bouman, O., Lénárd, I., and Oosterhuis, K. (2002). *Programmable Architecture*. Milan: L'Arca edizioni.
92 Oosterhuis, K. (2001). *Architecture Goes Wild*. Rotterdam. 010 Publishers.
93 Oosterhuis, K. (2003). *Hyperbodies: Towards an E-motive Architecture*. Berlin: Princeton Architectural Press.
94 Burry, M. (1999). "Paramorph," in S. Perrella (ed.), *AD Profile 139: Hypersurface Architecture II*. London: Academy Editions, pp. 78–83.

95 IAAC. (2021). IAAC 20th Anniversary Celebration – “20 years, 20 speakers” [Video]. Available at: https://iaac.net/20th-anniversary-event/?fbclid=IwZXh0bgNhZW0CMTAAAR07rI40VusDz-x2lUJ3KrCBIBOmIZm6K81RD38riV9WXaHHdaedQD7jEqU_aem_3k3QCc2GURlBpccAv1hdPQ

96 Ibid.

97 *New Technologies in Architecture II & III: Digital Design and Manufacturing Technique* (2003, September 6). Harvard Graduate School of Design. See https://www.gsd.harvard.edu/publication/new-technologies-in-architecture-ii-iii-digital-design/

98 Bechthold, M. (2003). *New Technologies in Architecture: Digital Design and Manufacturing Techniques, II & III*; Second International Conference Harvard University Graduate School of Design, November 2001; Third International Conference Rakennusteolliusuus RT Ry Helsinki, June 2002, Proceedings. United States: Harvard University, Graduate School of Design.

99 Kolarevic, B. (2004). *Architecture in the Digital Age: Design and Manufacturing*. London: Taylor & Francis.

100 Ibid., pp. 3–15.

101 Ibid., p. 3.

102 Mitchell, W. J. (1990). *The Logic of Architecture: Design, Computation, and Cognition*. Cambridge, MA: MIT Press.

103 Ibid., p. 64.

104 Grimes, W. (2010, June 16). “William J. Mitchell, Architect and Urban Visionary, Dies at 65.” *The New York Times*, June 16. Available at: https://www.nytimes.com/2010/06/16/us/16mitchell.html

105 Mitchell, W. J. (1996). *City of Bits: Space, Place, and the Infobahn*. Cambridge, MA: MIT Press.

106 Silver, D. (2001). “Review of *City of Bits: Space, Place, and the Infobahn*.” CAA Reviews, February 13, 2001. See http://caareviews.org/reviews/397 [Accessed October 12, 2023].

107 Mitchell, W. J. (1996). *City of Bits: Space, Place, and the Infobahn*. Cambridge, MA: MIT Press. p. 110.

108 Mitchell, W. J. (2000). *E-topia: Urban Life, Jim–But Not as We Know It*. Cambridge, MA: MIT Press.

109 Mitchell, W. J. (2004). *Me++: The Cyborgs Self and the Networked City*. Cambridge, MA: MIT Press.

EPISODE 4

EXPERIMENTATION (2004–2012)

By the time 2004 arrived, the architectural world was well acquainted with the implementation of digital toolsets in the design process. The previously nascent and distributed corners and outposts of digital design had now mobilized into a global network. Academic and professional leaders were actively engaged in not just leading their more enigmatic interests, but now there was also a collective realization the way they researched, taught, practiced, and transformed the built environment was fundamentally changing. No singular trajectory could now define this timeframe. What characterized this moment, more than almost anything, was the dynamic energy spent on exploring and embracing experimentation. The early part of this episode reflects an attitude of openness built on the trajectories of investigation and optimism. However, the global banking crises and economic downturn further revealed how interconnected production and opportunity were within the built environment. These crises manifested architectural theories that percolated over the previous 15 years and tethered the period of experimentation to the next stage of more focused inquiry by the mid-2010s.

By 2004, an academic and professional diaspora had begun. Young researchers and practitioners were eager to set up new places to try their hand where the digital toolset would serve as a catalyst for what they were doing. The emergence of experimental offices, not tied to long histories of research or practice, led to a proliferation of widespread innovation and opportunity. Fundamental to this experimentation was still a vital awareness that preceding accomplishments were critical to building the foundation upon which much work of the time was taking place. The ability to bring design work to realization during this time often relied upon finding new forms of collaboration. Additional aspects like hardware/software evolution, the global network via conferences and publications, and the academic and

DOI: 10.4324/9781032671208-6

professional pioneers collectively paved the way for this next generation of digital designers to now come in and take a vital role in the architecture design community. During this time, researchers also concentrated on development in which procedural and methodological applications started to enhance existing fields (urbanism, sustainability, and gaming) and reconfigure other areas (manufacturing, scripting, and visualization). One of this episode's most compelling and distinguishing marks was the growing intelligence around existing and new digital fabrication tools. Hanratty's CNC invention from five decades earlier started to cross over into architecture more directly and link to parametric design, and robotic fabrication emerged as a completely new opportunity offering a wide range of possibilities.

Exploring Modalities in Digital Procedures and Communication

The Role of Publications

As 2004 arrived, several books and publications on digital design methodology highlighted a growing awareness of the importance of new software and hardware in the design process. A growing curiosity about the new digital toolset and affiliated design procedures drove the rapid expansion of involvement for many different voices. Indeed, academic publications continued to provide the foundation of theoretical and projective implications on the design process. However, by the end of this episode, documented exploration and experimentation were a shared domain by the professional and academic design communities, with each making valuable contributions.

It is challenging or even counterproductive to suggest that only a handful of books summarized this highly active time of publication; however, several books served as guideposts for what would frame future steps forward. *Digital Tectonics* (2004), edited by Neil Leach, David Turnbull, and Chris Williams, was an early attempt to gather voices synergistically through projects and writing from that period that articulated the new role of craft, making, and digital design in the built environment. Respected academics and practitioners who could speculate on the arrival of digitally fabricated architecture provided a starting point for discourse. Specifically, these contributors focused on how digital technologies brought form, space, and structural behavior into greater focus. A long list of books emerged over the following eight years, capturing overlapping parts of the developing narrative of the changes in academia and practice. Books like Neil Gershenfeld's *FAB: The Coming Revolution on Your Desktop—From Personal Computers to Personal Fabrication*[1] (2005) helped to broaden the audience and enlarge the tent for those interested in personal computing and digital fabrication. At the same time both books came out, Malcolm McCullough offered an important reminder in his book *Digital Ground: Architecture, Pervasive Computing, and Environmental Knowing*[2] (2005) about the role and theories of place in a world that was now squarely at the intersection of ubiquitous computing and digital design.

Other books during this time focused on new methodologies, cataloging approaches, language, and projects that became tantamount to guidebooks for those attempting to familiarize themselves with some of the new digital procedures. Lisa Iwamoto's *Digital Fabrications: Architectural and Material Techniques*[3] (2009) became one of this genre's more widely recognized books, providing a clear taxonomy of work produced by a group of practitioners and academics. There were other authors who similarly cataloged projects and methods to Iwamoto's book, such as *From Control to Design: Parametric Architecture* (2008), edited by Albert Ferré and Tomoko Sakamoto, and *Contemporary Digital Architecture Design & Techniques* (2010), edited by Jacobo Krauel.

Some books looked forward while others cataloged new methodologies, and then there were also those that tied new digital theory to a broader digital lineage. In the case of *Computational Design Thinking*[4] (2011), Achim Menges and Sean Ahlquist provided a curated edition of seminal texts by a broad range of authors, "from which a conceptual model for critical computation in design thinking in architecture may originate."[5] Many of these texts and authors had served, or would continue to serve, as thought leaders for the future generation of computational design leaders. By 2012, Mario Carpo gathered some of the most important theoretical texts on digital design theory published by Architectural Design (*AD*) over the past 20 years into an edited collection to provide a much-needed curated path titled *The Digital Turn in Architecture*.[6] Like Michael Hays's[7] or Kate Nesbit's[8] important anthologies of architectural theory, Carpo's *Digital Turn* identified the rapidly changing directions posited by various academics and practitioners within the computational design field and signaled a shift in the theoretical landscape.

International conferences were not a new modality in the academic context or even the digital design field. However, a global network of academic organizations by the first decade of the 21st century brought forward a new awareness of activity that had not previously existed. The autocatalytic effect, discussed in Episode 0, was amplified further as the conferences, proceedings, and digital modes of communication began to reach a more diverse and broader audience. These conferences became not just platforms for sharing new findings but essential feedback loops for work and research for those hailing from a context where no such opportunities existed.

A survey of conference themes from 2004–2012 suggests an array of far-reaching topics that pivoted from the previous fifteen years to new areas such as digital fabrication methodology[9], information systems, communication technologies,[10] geospatial reconfiguration,[11] as well as cultural and urban ecology.[12] With the global network in place and the vehicles for dissemination and communication development like IJAC and CumInCad, conferences for more specialized areas of research and work launched during this time.

Frei Otto, the German architect and structural engineer, brought a greater awareness of the potential of natural systems inspiring efficient and structurally sound architectural surfaces in their publication *Finding Form* in the late 1960s.[13] However, it was the geometer Helmut Pottmann, along with fellow authors Andreas Asperl, Michael Hofer, and Axel Kilian, who published the book *Architectural Geometry*[14] in 2007 and provided a more precise and comprehensive examination of the increasingly complex geometries being introduced in architecture design. Pottman's work, in particular, brought about a more acute understanding of the inherent shortcomings of the modeling limitations for complex geometries by the software modeling programs used in architectural applications.[15] The following year, in 2008, the first Advances in Architectural Geometry (AAG) conference was held in Vienna and chaired by most of the same authors of the book. This bi-annual conference highlighted the role of "modern geometric computing provides a variety of tools for the efficient design, analysis, and manufacturing of complex shapes."[16] The conference added an important voice to the exploration of technical and theoretical complex geometry and computation's evolving role at the time. It also provided a platform to invite the contributions of computer graphics researchers, architects, and engineers to submit research work and create a cross-disciplinary platform for the emerging field of architectural geometry in digital design.

Pavilions and Competitions

Similar to international conferences, competitions were not a new modality for engagement. Yet, several garnered specific attention for how they would exemplify the opportunity to test the "digital tectonics" proffered by Leach, Turnbull, and Williams in 2004. For most of this period, pavilions and temporary installations garnered significant attention. Pavilions offered a unique opportunity to experiment with form, material, and assembly while minimizing requirements for other aspects of a more permanent structure. The PS1 Young Architects Program Museum of Modern Art and the Serpentine Pavilion in London were two of the more widely known examples during this time.

The PS1 started in 1998 and had several critical works done in the early 2000s,[17] setting the tone for the next decade and a half. Young practices were afforded to work through ideas of digitally mediated positions on a larger stage with well-supported budgets. Concepts like emergent behavior and prescriptive mapping, as in the case of Hernan Diaz Alonso's "SUR" 2005 installation.[18] Or there was MOS's "Afterparty" in 2009 using "complex structural arch systems defining hyperbolic surfaces – juxtaposed with a rough thatched roof"[19] creating a type of performative cooling stations. By 2010, SO-IL dematerialized the space with "Pole Dance," providing a "participatory environment that reframes the conceptual relation between humankind and structure."[20] Equally important were the finalists in these and other years who provided insight across relevant issues of fabrication methods, interactive architecture, and design methodology for various topics. Additional noteworthy contributions came in the years after this episode and served as a barometer for how the focus on form and fabrication shifted to social and environmental issues.[21]

At the same time as the early PS1 Competitions took place, the Serpentine Pavilion Exhibition in London also provided an opportunity for experimentation with more established practices. While not all installations were investigations into the use of new digital toolsets, many provided forays into this arena by professional offices.[22] Similar to the PSI Competition, additional offerings in subsequent years shift from techniques and methodology toward broader questions about social and cultural issues.[23]

Other competitions captured the fascination of the digital design community, creating a buzz for the formal, structural, and methodological assembly techniques illustrated through the temporary pavilion's typology. Coming out of the AADRL10 Pavilion competition, the [C]Space DRL 10 Pavilion by Alan Dempsey and Alvin Huang (2008) illustrated just such an example (Figure 4.1). The pavilion was located at Bedford Square in London and merged unique flat

FIGURE 4.1 The [C]Space Pavilion by Alan Dempsey and Alvin Huang was constructed in 2008 as part of the tenth-anniversary celebration of the AA's Design Research Laboratory. The pavilion, located in Bedford Square in London, was the winning entry of the global competition.

fiber-reinforced concrete elements into a single continuous curved form. The [C]Space Pavilion exemplified similar installations at this time by using discrete parts that were meticulously produced, choreographed, and assembled by a large team of volunteers.[24] These hands-on assemblies often extended the classroom into a form of *digital barn raising*, bringing students and professionals into contact for a collaborative learning experience and an essential component of the active learning process for many students and faculty during this time.

Emerging Websites and Social Media

Dissemination also began to find a new home via the maturing medium of the internet. As a vehicle for communicating image-laden information related to complex modeling and methodological research, websites' burgeoning social media platforms were in the very early stages. A Pew Research study showed that during the decade following 2005, there was a nearly 10× factor increase in adult social media usage – from 7% to 65%.[25] The drastic increase in use meant platforms like email and early website adopters became more strategically important for work, research, and branding. By the start of 2010, some design firms started to recognize the value of communication, marketing, and even commerce related to website presence. It would take the confluence of global practice/interest combined with a technological platform to communicate to an audience that allowed for a rise in awareness of what was taking place. The building blocks had taken shape for the past fifteen years with the precipitous stacking of internet and social media technology. Search engines like Netscape, Yahoo, Mozilla, and Google were all in play. Sharing platforms such as Flickr (2004), YouTube (2005), Twitter (2006), and Reddit (2006) were being launched. In 2007, Apple also released the first iPhone, starting the portable computing revolution advocated by Mark Weiser in Episode 2.

The degree of introduction of digital tools into design education and the architecture profession was uneven and a topic for debate through the early 2000s.[26] Still, as students left academic institutions and firms, a diaspora of digital designers spread, broadening experimentation, and taking new design practices and educational institutions into many new directions. The following years would provide various forays into wide-ranging hypotheses about new possibilities.

Parametric Design

As outlined in Episode 0, Luigi Moretti defined parametric architecture in 1971 as an architecture governed by mathematical logic underpinned by computer techniques and analytical decision making.[27] However, parametric design as a more precisely defined instance of computational design would take another 20 years to find additional specificity. Yehuda Kalay, in *Modeling Objects and Environments (Principles of Computer-Aided Design)* (1989),[28] would extend this definition to parametric modeling, where "computational representation of geometric relationships that are 'automatically updated and visualized on the screen' upon parameter change." By the early 2000s, the term parametric architecture and parametric design were gaining widespread use in the computational design community.[29] An analysis of keyword terminology usage in the central architecture publication repositories from 1978–2018 reveals the term "parametric design" was used at almost a 2:1 ratio to other terms like "generative design" or "performance-based design" and a 10:1 ratio to terms such as "algorithmic design" and "evolutionary design."[30] Facilitating this was a consensus around the definition of parametric design. By 2003, Branko Kolarevic had extended Kalay's definition to provide instantiation of design solutions, given that parameters applied to relationships and not geometry.[31] Shortly after that, others like Mark Burry,[32] Robert Aish and Robert Woodbury,[33] Daniel Schodek,[34] Rivka Oxman,[35] Michael Meredith, and Mutsuro Sasaki[36] would all publish similar definitions.

For those examining the structural implications of parametric design, optimization was a factor that became integral to the definition and working methodology.[37] Mark Burry and his colleagues Dominik Holzer and Richard Hough advanced this idea in their journal article 2007, *Parametric Design and Structural Optimisation for Early Design Exploration*,[38] on combined architectural geometry with structural systems. For several preceding decades, Burry had developed his research framework through ongoing work on Antonio Gaudi's vision for the Sagrada Familia (Figure 4.2). His familiarity and investment with the project, dating back to 1979 when he was still completing his degree at Cambridge, allowed him to introduce CAD to various analog procedures a decade later and rapidly accelerate the construction process.[39]

He went on to quickly accelerate an entire repertoire of digital hardware and software tools over the next two decades, which would lead to

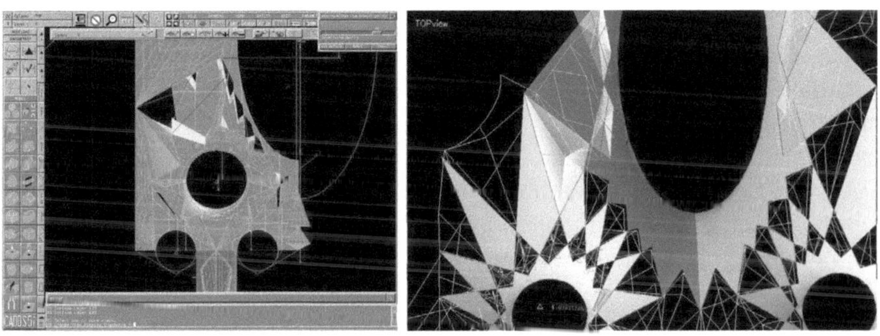

FIGURE 4.2 Mark Burry's early work in 1991 on a parametric model using CADDS5 for the Rose Window. The Sagrada Familia served as a pivotal opportunity to demonstrate emerging parametric design methods on a constructed project requiring complex geometric translation.

facilitating his position as a leading voice on parametric design and application in construction.

There were those who contributed to the discourse from more broadly positioned definitions. For his part, Patrik Schumacher declared parametric design "a new hegemonic paradigm for architecture."[40] He presented Parametricism as a *"research programme based upon the parametric paradigma"*[41] delivered through five primary points. Beyond operations and processes, Schumacher posited a worldview of architecture as an autopoiesis, a system of society that co-evolves with other important autopoietic subsystems like art, science, politics, and even the economy in the book *The Autopoiesis of Architecture, Volume I: A New Framework for Architecture* (2011).[42] While this first book laid the foundations for an autopoietic system, a second book was released a year later: *The Autopoiesis of Architecture, Volume II: A New Agenda for Architecture* (2012),[43] which addressed the "specific, contemporary challenges and tasks that architecture faces." Schumacher would go on to elaborate on his position with the edited publication *Parametracism 2.0* in 2016,[44] where he gathered a large number of practices using digital design methodologies to contribute to the discussion.

Throughout this timeframe, many continued their work from an earlier decade, able to now integrate more advanced digital modeling programs with earlier theories and ultimately provide foundational texts for future generations of practitioners. As mentioned in Episode 3, Paul Coates would build off his work with John Frazer and their work at the University of East London.[45] In 2010, he published *Programming Architecture*,[46] which provided a clear introduction to algorithmic design and the use of computer technology through an introduction to coding for design applications. As a more specific working methodology of parametric design, algorithmic design found a more pronounced correlation between parts and the traceable algorithms used to control the geometry output. Another example would be Mark and Jane Burry's work on the Passion Façade of the Sagrada Familia.[47] Also, in 2010, Robert Woodbury published *Elements of Parametric Design*.[48] This text built off the past two decades of work on parametric design and directly tied into work done earlier in the decade.[49] Specifically, Woodbury's 2010 publication presented design methodology derived from calculations and systematic operation. Woodbury's text presented geometric strategies built upon a mathematical foundation essential to deploying parametric geometry into the design process. Woodbury began his introduction with the premise that parametric modeling represents change, owed in no small part to Ivan Sutherland, who first presented this in his 1963 thesis when he included parametric change in his Sketchpad system. Woodbury's text fused architecture and computer science through a prescriptive understanding of geometry and algorithms. Others like Wasim Jabi and Kostas Terzidis would expand on parametric design from the generative design position.[50] Generative design was perhaps the most open-ended definition and aligned for some, like Mitchell[51] and Frazer,[52] with the earlier works of cybernetics. Primarily, those working in this space generally utilized evolutionary processes, cellular automata, self-organization, swarm methodology, and shape grammars.[53]

During this episode, there was an emerging consensus around what defined specific ways of working, but this was far from universally agreed upon. Some dove deep into the technical aspects of controlling the software and subsequent outcomes, and others leveraged the opportunity to disrupt and engage broader tendencies of the computational field. This would be further explored in subsequent years, but it was becoming clear the impact of computation on the design process was maturing rapidly.

Many firms and designers contributed to the growing body of built work defining parametric design. The case can easily be made that the remainder of those discussed throughout this episode were, in some capacity, working parametrically. Firms like Zaha Hadid Architects, with their projects like the MAXXI (2010) and the Eli and Edythe Broad Museum (2012) or Coop Himmelb(l)au's BMW Welt (2007) and the Dalian International Conference Center (2012) illustrated formal and material complexity. Other projects, like Herzog & de Meuron with AI Weiwei's Bird's Nest, became symbolic for the wide exposure it would receive at the center of events like the 2008 Beijing Olympics.

To focus in more closely, Office dA was a compelling test case for how an early firm implemented parametric design strategies at various scales into actual built works. Mónica Ponce de Leon and Nadar Tehrani formed Office dA in 1991, shortly after graduating from the Harvard School of Design. The timeframe of their operation and shared mutual interests allowed them to bridge the "pre-digitized" and the "overtly digitized" contexts of boutique offices of the 1990s through the early 2010s. They most often foregrounded the material and fabrication parameters to drive the design process compared to many, at that time, who wrestled with translating the digital model to realization. The interior work of the Ventulett installation (2006), Rhode Island School of Design Library (2006), and the BanQ Restaurant (2008) displayed a striking material playfulness. The free-standing work of projects like Tongxian Gatehouse (2003) (Figure 4.3) and The Macallen Building (2008) revealed a calibrated architecture still committed to craft and innovation through digital processes. What would perhaps be equal, if not more profound, would be de Leon's and Tehrani's separate and second act as academic deans at various institutions for the following decades, covered in the next episode.

Digital Fabrication

While parametric design framed a broad methodological foundation upon which many would build a position for architectural experimentation,

FIGURE 4.3 Built in 2003, the Tongxian Gatehouse is located 30 miles outside of Beijing in a community of over 200 artists. It serves as the first phase of a larger development, using local materials and labor to fit into the context.

translating the digital to the physical would represent one of the most seismic shifts within the computational toolset development and application of this moment. Digital fabrication applied to architectural design had ties back to the mid-1990s, and Patrick J. Hanratty's introduction of CAD/CAM in the late 1950s was a critical moment of origin. However, by the mid-2000s, momentum gathered, aligning with a larger level of proficiency, access, theoretical underpinning, and experimentation. As publications during this timeframe underscore, there was a deep interest in the work and methodology for translating digital work into physical work. Perhaps most importantly, this was a global phenomenon that was happening rapidly. Branko Kolarevic reinforced this point in his chapter on Digital Production in his 2003 book *Architecture in the Digital Age*.[54] In the text he pointed out how the deep connection between

> Euclidean geometry in the building brought about drafting instruments, such as the straightedge and the compass, needed to draw straight lines and circles on paper, and the corresponding extrusion

> and rolling machinery to produce straight lines and circles in the material.[55]

He goes on to suggest

> This reciprocity between the means of representation and production has not disappeared entirely in the digital age. Knowing the production capabilities and availability of particular digitally-driven fabrication equipment enables architects to design specifically for the capabilities of those machines.[56]

As mentioned earlier in the episode, conferences often provided a backdrop for a concentrated exploration of ideas. The Fabricate ACADIA+AIA conference held at the University of Waterloo and the University of Toronto in 2004 was a clear investment into the research and work done by academics and practitioners together utilizing digital fabrication technology. This conference brought together an influential group that would go on to shape this discourse for the next fifteen years. A departure from the previous decade of global conferences focusing primarily on various forms of collaboration and visualization, Fabricate paved the way for a shift in the discourse toward the physical manifestation of current research.

There were several early pioneers garnering attention in the field for work they were completing in an array of different platforms and locations. Andrew Kudless, starting in 2004, quickly gained international recognition for several projects, including Manifold Screen (2004), P_Wall (2006), and C_Wall (2006) (Figures 4.4 and 4.5), followed by several temporary pavilions were influential for their innovation and craft, but also the inclusion of readily accessible materials, illustrated steps for fabrication, and working through these projects with students. The latter became a template for many who would bring this working methodology into an educational context for research and teaching.

Achim Menges provided another early voice focusing attention on the specific field of digital fabrication as the founding director of the Institute for Computational Design and Construction (ICD) at the University of Stuttgart. Joining Jan Kippers, who was already directing the Institute of Building Structures and Structural Design (ITKE), the two crafted one of the most highly innovative collaborative research and fabrication programs, interweaving digital fabrication and structural and material experimentation. Much of Menges's early published work was in partnership with Kippers, Michael Hensel, and students in the ICD/ITKE programs. The volume of publications combined with the start of the annual ICD/ITKE Research Pavilions in 2010 created a global network of influence in the developing field. The Pavilions provided some of the most daring experiments in material

FIGURE 4.4 Completed in 2004, Manifold Screen presented novel material and performance outcomes, using a honeycomb structure following a biomimetic design strategy to meet diverse performance requirements.

FIGURE 4.5 The P-Wall Project, commissioned by the SFMOMA in 2009, is an exploration into material performance and self-organizing systems. The 150 plaster cast tiles create a formally expressive wall as part of the SFMOMA's permanent collection.

and methodological output at that time and over the next decade (Figure 4.6).

By 2011, the maturing of various types of work and resulting material outcomes was globally evident. Bob Sheil and Ruairi Glynn from the Bartlett School of Architecture and Mari Skavara from Codica Ltd. founded the FABRICATE[57] organization to bring together those interested in the growing sophistication of digitally fabricated design work. FABRICATE, however, also aimed for a broad audience, bringing "together pioneers in design and making within architecture, construction, engineering, manufacturing, materials technology, and computation."[58] Like many organizations, this was done through conferences, publications, and websites, with the first conference taking place in London in 2011. FABRICATE helped to refine the technical methodology and expertise related to digital fabrication through a more rigorous focus on research methodology and establishing high standards of production output.

FIGURE 4.6 ICD/ITKE Pavilion was constructed in 2012 through robotic fabrication using carbon and glass fiber composites.

Several publications would reinforce the trajectory during the eight years of this episode, focusing on implementing digital fabrication. These publications, similar to those mentioned earlier focusing on parametric design, served as a guide for a broader audience eager to understand and apply specific methodologies or acquire greater expertise for research, teaching, or practical application. One of the early contributions was *Digital Design and Manufacturing*[59] (2004) by Daniel Schodek, Martin Bechthold, James Kimo Griggs, Kenneth Kao, and Marco Steinberg, providing an early cataloging and detailed history and manufacturing perspective of the digital fabrication toolset. As mentioned previously, Lisa Iwamoto's *Digital Fabrications*[60] book was, by contrast, a primer speculating on the more experimental application possibilities in the US and Europe. Nick Dunn's *Digital Fabrication in Architecture* (2012)[61] and Chris Beorkrem's *Material Strategies in Digital Fabrication* (2012) both continued cataloging geometric modeling and fabrication methodologies to provide a collection similar to Iwamoto's book, with the distinction that these books also provided a range of built work by larger firms, case studies, and step-by-step guides on implementing fabrication techniques.

Robotic Fabrication

Digital fabrication would occupy much of the spotlight and energy within the discourse of parametric design from 2004–2012. The same was true that robotic fabrication would garner considerable attention as a subset of digital fabrication during this period as many started to explore the growing possibilities. By the mid to late 2000s, there was a deep fascination with the flexibility and range afforded by the robotic arm as the digital fabrication tool of choice. While a familiar tool in the automotive and other manufacturing industries, there was a growing sense that the robotic arm could unlock a range of previously unavailable opportunities related to the dream of mass customization if harnessed and linked with the newfound parametric design software capabilities.

In the early 2000s, Fabio Gramazio and Matthias Kohler formed their experimental practice to concentrate on installation and building opportunities. By 2005, they took over the research chair positions at the ETH in Zürich with the intent of being

> the world's first robotic laboratory to explore the intersections between architecture and robotics … creating a new research field merging interests in computational design, material innovation, and automated fabrication.[62]

By foregrounding robotic fabrication as the research and production tool of choice, they ushered in a striking body of work for its range of work and outcomes (Figures 4.7 and 4.8), While later work from the Gramazio and

Kohler Research Group continues to be discussed in the next episode, their early commitment to robotic fabrication long stood as a cornerstone to advancing the development of this particular fabrication capability within the design field.

Gramazio and Kohler were not alone in the 2000s, as many others created pioneering work, especially within the academic context. The variability and flexibility of the arm amplified interest in a range of research directions. From pipe bending to wire-cutting and drilling to cutting, the robotic arm was highly customizable for various production output needs. Sigrid Brell-Cokcan and Johannes Braumann were early advocates for the broader adaptation of robotic fabrication. One of their most significant contributions was the formation of the *Association of Robots in Architecture* (RobARCH)[63] in 2010 to cultivate interdisciplinary users from the creative design fields. They quickly realized that adapting the technology would spread into many areas tangential to the creative fields, thus pushing the reach into a transdisciplinary sphere of discourse and impact. Brell-Cokcan and Braumann would go on to publish several significant papers on the further advancement in the programming of robotic arms for the purposes of deeper user interface and customized mass production, solidifying their position as leading voices in the field.[64]

FIGURE 4.7 Robotic fabrication process for the "Stacked Pavilion" in Wettswil am Albis, Switzerland, by Gramazio and Kohler in 2009. The wooden structure consists of 16 contorted elements made from 372 slats.

FIGURE 4.8 The temporary "Stacked Pavilion" completed in 2009. The elements were constructed by a digitally controlled robot that cut and precisely placed the slats according to an algorithmic pattern.

Other critical academic contributions also emerged by the end of the 2000s. The University of Michigan's Taubman's College of Architecture and Urban Planning started advancing the collective discourse on robotic fabrication by the early 2010s. Led by the arrival of Monica Ponce de Leon as Dean of the College and Wes McGee as Director of the Fabrication Lab and active research collaborator with many faculty, the school quickly developed a wide range of work exploring different methodologies and materials. There were also important developments at locations such as the GSD, where Martin Bechthold's Design Robotics Group (shortly after becoming the Material Processes and Systems Group) initiated work on robotics and ceramic fabrication in 2010. On the West Coast, one of the shifts in focus around implementing robotic fabrication was Sci-Arc's introduction of the "Robot House" in 2011 by Peter Testa and Devyn Weiser. With support from Dean Eric Own Moss, Testa and Weiser conceived the Robot House as a lab for evaluating architectural instrumentation and representation instead of exclusively concentrating on fabrication and material-driven research. Early on, the output from the Robot House was diverse and driven by a heterogeneous pedagogical framework.

What became increasingly important about Sci-Arc and other academic institutions on the West Coast was an entirely different set of production and material opportunities for implementing digital technology at this time. Some of this was the byproduct of access to a different manufacturing and fabrication network, tied more directly to the film industry, and some resulted from Silicon Valley's persistence to be at the forefront of technological innovation. Practitioners like Greg Lynn (FORM), Heather Roberge and Jason Payne (Gnuform), Roland Snooks and Robert Stuart-Smith (Kokkugia), and David Erdman (SERVO) would take full advantage of the rich fabrication culture deeply rooted in the synthetic.

Collaborating and Engagement

As mentioned in Episodes 2 and 3, the formation of research centers and labs to focus on using an expanded computational toolset extended back for several decades. By the mid-2000s, the network of expertise and research interests established an equally diversified level of organizations and research entities committed to disseminating computational design and fabrication information.

In 2005, Mette Ramsgard Thomsen formed The Centre for Information Technology and Architecture (CITA) at the Royal Danish Academy of Fine Arts, Schools of Architecture, Design and Conservation. With Ramsgard Tomsen's research focus on architecture and computer science, the Centre was founded on three primary research concentrations: 1) Digital Formations, investigating complex modeling and Building Information Modelling as a new design tool for architecture and digital fabrication; 2) Behaving Architectures, investigating new programmable materials and smart textiles; 3) Interface Ecologies investigating real-time modeling, interface design, and intelligent programming.[65] Martin Tamke joined the team a year later in 2006, brought design-based research, and expanded CITA's material /fabrication interests further.

TEX-FAB was also formed in 2008 to bridge academic institutions across Texas while drawing from the resources of some of the largest cities in the US. The organization's focus identified the growing dialogue between academia, professional designers, and manufacturers on issues related to digital design and fabrication. To explore this relationship, TEX-FAB, created by Andrew Vrana, Kevin Patrick McClellan, Brad Bell and joined by Kory Bieg in 2010, hosted annual conferences that drew regional and leading international voices to conduct workshops and serve as speakers. Workshops drew participation from throughout the southwest and were led by industry leaders like Chris Lasch, Raja Isaa, Ronnie Parsons, and Gil Akos of Mode Collective, Marc Fornes, Sean Ahlquist, Jason Kelly Johnson, Nate Miller, and David Fano, among others. The organization was unique for offering a two phase competition that drew global entries where phase one finalists displayed full-scale proto-typing of their proposal at the annual ACADIA conference, and a winner was selected. For phase two of the competition, the winner typically had six months to work with a national manufacturer and digital fabricator like the A. Zahner Co. and Kreysler and Associates to realize the full-scale installation (Figures 4.9 and 4.10). The outcome of the collaboration became the central piece, anchoring the larger exhibition for the annual TEX-FAB conference and workshops held annually at a School of Architecture in Texas. With participants in all the phases of the organizational modalities coming from across the AECO industry and from parallel design fields, TEX-FAB created a model that strategically worked in a regional capacity but with a broader audience and network.

Digital Futures[66] represents yet another formation of collaboration, research, and network reach formed in 2011 by Neil Leach and Philip Yuan. Initiated as a collaborative venture bringing together students from the University of Southern California (USC) and Tongji University, the format Leach and Yaun saw as a festival of activity primarily consisted of workshops, lectures, and conferences. Multiplying in popularity, attendance, and scope, the reach of the conferences had global participation from the foremost thought leaders in digital design and fabrication. As Digital Futures grew over the next decade, it added conference papers, book publications, an international Ph.D. program, and eventually, a peer-reviewed journal.[67] Unlike the organizations in Episodes 2 and 3 (i.e.,

FIGURE 4.9 The winning entry by Justin Diles for the 2015 TEX-FAB Competition. FRP components are under construction on the fabrication floor of Kreysler and Associates.

FIGURE 4.10 "Plastic Stereotomy" fully assembled for TEX-FAB 5: Plasticity, located in the University of Houston Gerald D. Hines School of Architecture atrium.

ACADIA, eCAADe, SIGraDi) defined by large regions or countries, Digital Futures sought to be untethered to location, country, city, or even an academic institution. The open platform and content accessibility were important for the continued rapid dissemination of information and the growth of awareness and knowledge developing in the field.

One of the more unique partnerships also formed in this time period was the Center for Architecture Science and Ecology (CASE), launched in 2008 and led by Anna Dyson. CASE was an academic and professional partnership between Rensselaer Polytechnic Institute (RPI) and Skidmore, Owings & Merrill (SOM). RPI and SOM created CASE to develop innovative solutions to global environmental challenges. One of the most notable aspects of the research was how the center leveraged computational toolset for ecologically sustainable design solutions used in architectural applications. Building Performance was becoming more central to implementing the digital toolset, and the academic/professional partnership of RPI/SOM exemplified the shifting business model of building solutions with a more concentrated focus on ecological issues. While sustainability was not a novel concept, implementing computation to work toward optimized solutions was emerging as a field with immense potential by the end of the 2000s and early 2010s.

Beyond the new partnerships and collaborations emerging at this time, many conferences and symposia were influential in spreading knowledge about using computational tools and the design application process. Often, these events would provide dedicated multi-day software workshops for users ranging from beginner to advanced. Conferences associated with the Facade Tectonics Institute (2007) or Facades+ (2012) concentrated on the building envelope and a growing interest in computation applied to building performance. Industry experts were able to provide up-to-date information, demonstrations, and case studies on a range of affiliated issues. Simulation for Architecture and Urban Design (SimAUD),[68] which started in 2009, was important because it brought together researchers in the emerging visualization fields related to architecture and urban design. The latest software was making this a rapidly growing area of interest, and the methodology for working in this space was opening up entirely new inquiries. SimAUD brought together industry leaders and academics from several fields, such as computer science, urban design, architecture, sustainability, and VR.

Toward the end of these eight years, Scott Marble authored and edited *Digital Workflows in Architecture* (2012).[69] Like others mentioned during this period, this book identified a deepening trajectory of capacity and interest within the AECO industry's network. Organized into three sections: *Designing Design, Designing Assembly*, and *Designing Industry*, the book provided a platform to include conceptual, procedural, and operational underpinnings of some of the most technical and advanced buildings leveraging digital toolset at that time. Scott Marble outlines the book's thesis in the introduction:

> The assimilation and synthesis of digital communications among architects, engineers, fabricators, and builders is dramatically altering how we work and our relationship to the tools we use. New digital capacities are restructuring the organization and hierarchy of design from autonomous processes to collective workflows.[70]

The Digital Workflows publication foreshadowed a deepening concentration of intelligence in developing and applying digital toolsets to projects from professional offices.

Modeling, Analysis, and Communication

While a large amount of energy and focus went to digital fabrication during this time, significant work was still done in other areas, such as modeling, analysis, and communication, that continued the trajectories of existing research. Largely falling under the umbrella of modeling and communication, some topics brought in much broader levels of pre-existing research, such as information visualization, sustainability, and urban infrastructure, while gaming and advances in BIM would see new stages of development and UI resulting from technological advancement.

By the mid to late 2000s, implementing a more robust digital toolset to visualize information and the design process was gaining traction. Out of

Edward Tufte's shadow of the earlier part of the 1990s and 2000s, people like Manuel Lima and David McCandless in their book *Visual Complexities* (2011)[71] started to shape a focus on how to use large and often voluminous information down to salient points. The increasing focus on the abundance of information produced, consumed, and interconnected certainly impacted architecture as the role of the diagram took on a more important function, interpreting design intent for anything from historical context and design process to financial impact and post-occupancy data points. These graphic manipulations created a scenario where navigating degrees of increased complexity was desirable and, at times, an aesthetic manifestation. Coming at this from the other side was to operate not from source content but from the potential of the toolset itself. As Casey Reas and Ben Fry suggested, when introducing Processing in 2001, they linked graphic design with computer science.[72] By "sketching" via the programming code needed to produce the visual output in the software, there was a fundamental shift to tie into different systems of operation – primarily via a computer science lexicon (Figure 4.11). Reas and Fry created Processing from the lineage of the MIT Media Lab and the Visual Language Workshop. Specifically, Processing emerged from the Design By Numbers System created from John Maeda's Aesthetics and Computation Group (ACG), which started in 1996. The Design By

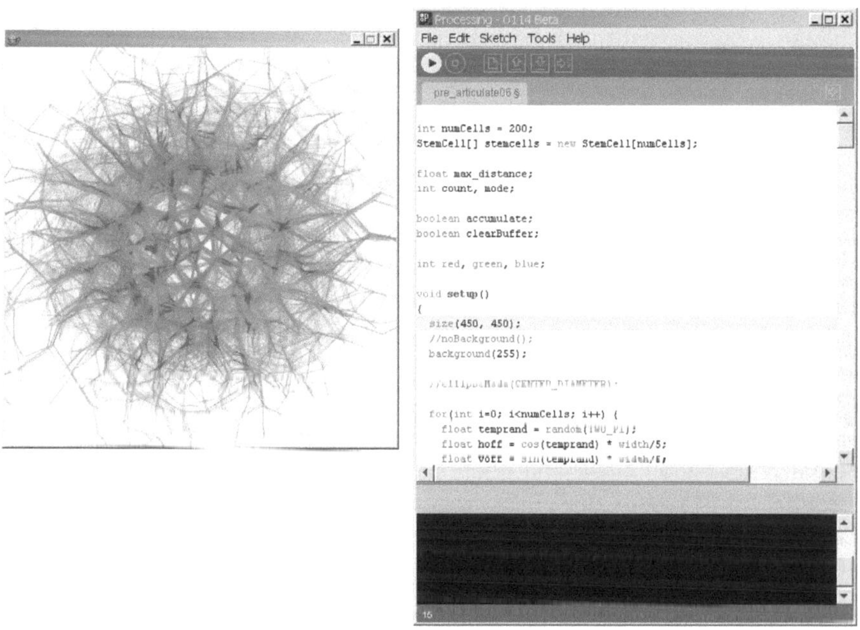

FIGURE 4.11 Early Processing image and code taken from Processing 1.0 IDE running on Windows.

Numbers System brought computation into a visual reality through graphics and programming language.[73]

Growth and implementation were rapid across many disciplines, but within architecture, the resonance existed in the manifestation of programmable authorship, where agency and output had long been a theoretical discourse but had struggled to find technical implementation.

What Reas and Fry would provide in Processing and Reas would go on to articulate in the 2010 book *Form+Code in Design, Art, and Architecture*[74] is the translation of the computer as a tool, which now became a medium, by directly interfacing with the coding.

While some modeling and visualization software were new to the industry at this time, others were continuing to build upon the successes of the past several decades. Building Information Modeling (BIM), as discussed in Episodes 2 and 3, had a well-established history by the early 2000s. However, it was clear that by the mid-2000s, BIM was finding rapid market integration in the AECO industry. From 2007 to 2009, the adoption of use went from 28% to 48%, representing a 75% increase for the AECO industry in those two years alone.[75] While BIM was not new as a digital tool, one feature that led to broader acceptance and use was the ability to share and work from the same model. Starting in 2004 with Revit 6, Autodesk provided capabilities for creating a central file, allowing firms or subcontractors access to only the layers or elements of the model they needed to modify. Cloud computing and later discussion of interoperability and AI extension of modeling capabilities would extend well beyond this initial step; the opportunity to find collaborative space that worked in parallel with the growing nature of the professional framework became an important development at this time.

While Autodesk's Revit was a prominent player within the field of BIM during this time, there were undoubtedly many other software applications that extended the discussion of Chuck Estman's dream of "Building Description System." Graphisoft's ArchiCAD and Nemtschek's Allplan pioneered with the Apple OS, while others like Bentley MicroStation (AECOsim Building Designer) and Dassault Systèmes CATIA worked with academic and industry partners. All these companies helped push toward consistency and adoption of BIM during this time. The Industry Foundation Classes (IFC) was formed in the mid-1990s by several AECO companies to standardize computer-aided design data exchange for the AECO industry. The platform was a neutral, non-hierarchical, and freely available platform. Steps like this were essential to standardizing BIM, regardless of software choice or when moving from one trade to another, and began to find more significant levels of integration. BIM tools also enhanced their capabilities to incorporate sustainability and energy analysis outcomes, responding to an emerging global environmental awareness. This ability to assess environmental impact was an important development at this moment and time.

Sustainability and building performance were not new topics of research or application. However, these topics continued to gain focus through the end of the 2000s and the early 2010s, echoed by software applications that were more customizable software and allowed further upstream decision making. The interdisciplinary integration and choreography of expertise were essential to the advancement of various sectors of the AECO industry. Sustainability linked to building performance and optimization metrics developed a much more rigorous quantification-based assessment to understand building assembly. A report in 2005 came out comparing the top 20 Building Energy Performance Simulation Programs.[76] The market did not lack data points for gathering information on energy performance on many different levels. One program that stood out due to being authored by *architects* for *architects* was Ecotect. Created by Square One Research and Dr. Andrew Marsh in the mid-1990s, they were able to slowly build a following for the iterative-based software that focused on lighting and room acoustics. Autodesk acquired Ecotect in 2009, and like many of these early energy performance programs, Autodesk absorbed Ecotect into different programs or core functionality of Revit. Vasari was another architecture-friendly software used in building analysis/performance development. The software featured geometric and parametric capabilities developed by Autodesk in November of 2010[77] for early schematic decision making. Vasari focused on wind, climate, day, and electric lighting analysis, whole building energy analysis, solar analysis, and solar studies. Like Ecotect, Vasari was discontinued and absorbed into most of the core functionality of Revit in 2015. In the early stages, the overlay of analysis related to building performance at an early stage of the schematic design phase was an important step in expanding the digital toolset to arrive at more optimized design outcomes. Optimization in this regard was calibrated to various criteria, and certainly, sustainability issues determined many of these outcomes. Life-cycle cost, programmatic distribution, geometric refinement, and material implementation were all a part of this newfound spectrum of issues feeding the building performance feedback loop with the new digital toolset.

In 2003, Bentley Systems introduced the program Generative Components (GC). As a BIM parametric solid modeling software, GC was unique at that time for providing 3D associative modeling capabilities.[78] The software was commercially released in 2007 after a multi-year test run with the SmartGeometry group largely facilitated through Robert Aish, who played a central role in SmartGeometry and Bentley Systems as their Director of Research.[79] GC spread in popularity and market infiltration over the next decade. While, ultimately, not achieving the same level of widespread usage of Grasshopper for Rhino or Dynamo for Revit, GC retained a loyal user base and remained one of the workshops offered by SmartGeometry.

Like many other software, Geographic Information Systems (GIS) made significant advancements during this time. The ArcGIS platform dominated the market with its 9.0 release in 2004. 3D GIS was popularized in 2005 by the broad-based introduction of Google Earth, which had been created four years earlier by Keyhole Inc. Combined with Google Maps, which also launched in 2005, these two programs gave users access to global spatial data in an entirely new way affording urban planners and architects ease of access to information that had not previously been available. GIS became a tool for understanding environmental and spatial impact, especially concerning urban growth and infrastructural development. More sophisticated Environmental Impact Assessments (EIA) became more common during this period, significantly impacting the mapping of the hydrological layers, terrain formations, and wildlife habitats to understand the broad-based environmental impact the best.

New Heuristics, New Outcomes

In the face of new opportunities, directions, and working methodologies, many new pedagogies and stylistic positioning emerged during this period. While Cecil Balmond would suggest in his 2002 book *Informal*[80] that at the end of Postmodernism, there was no longer a need for new manifestos to be authored or styles created,[81] there were still those individuals or groups who pushed for a more distinct stylistic positioning. Several new heuristics were presented in rapid succession by digital designers who combined the unique blend of historical and theoretical context with methodological and procedural output. Many of these voices leveraged publication and academic platforms to communicate to a broad and receptive audience what constituted the basis of their work.[82] This symbiosis was compelling in this period if for no other reason than it promulgated a sense of certainty with regard to the new digital methodologies, even if, at times, it was difficult to distinguish what differentiated the work itself. Of course, Parametricism was the most recognizable of these proposed paradigms, and Patrik Schumacher was unabashedly arguing for a stylistic reformulation of what constituted avant-garde architecture at this moment. As written about earlier, Schumacher would draw immense attention to how parametric design as a methodology would be more synthetically distributed across a theoretical framework and applied to design. However, this was not the only new trajectory gathering momentum during this period. There were groups starting to concentrate on ideas and applications that gave a sense of momentum to a wide array of new directions.

Digital Morphogenesis and Emergence

In Branko Kolarevic's 2000 journal article "Digital Morphogenesis and Computational Architecture,"[83] he identifies several early building blocks and contributors that set the stage for what became Digital Morphogenesis and Emergence in the mid-2000s. Identifying themes such as Topological,

Isomorphic, Metamorphic, Parametric, and Evolutionary Architectures, Kolarevic credits people like Greg Lynn, Bernard Cache, John Frazer, William Mitchell, and Marcos Novak (who coined the term "transarchitecture"), among others, who laid the groundwork for the operational implementation of these architectural procedures. The line drawn to Emergent Architecture and linked to morphological and biomimetic systems is picked up several years later by a trio of academics who intertwine some of these principles and players with a more concentrated focus on the use of computational tools and procedural outcomes toward negotiating complex systems of input to produce biomimetic architectural forms. Michael Hensel, Achim Menges, and Michael Weinstock led the most succinct call for architecture, each bringing overlapping and synergistic perspectives to this area of exploration. Working out of the Architectural Association in London to deliver a new master's degree entitled "Emergent Technologies in Design," along with Chris Wise, director of Civil Engineering at the Imperial College in London, they would launch a new framework for implementing design computation, materials, and organizational systems. By the late 2000s, Hensel, Menges, and Weinstock had moved digital morphogenesis and emergence into a part of the global discourse through their publications, academic leadership positions, and research (Figure 4.12). Specifically, from 2004–2010, they edited five editions of

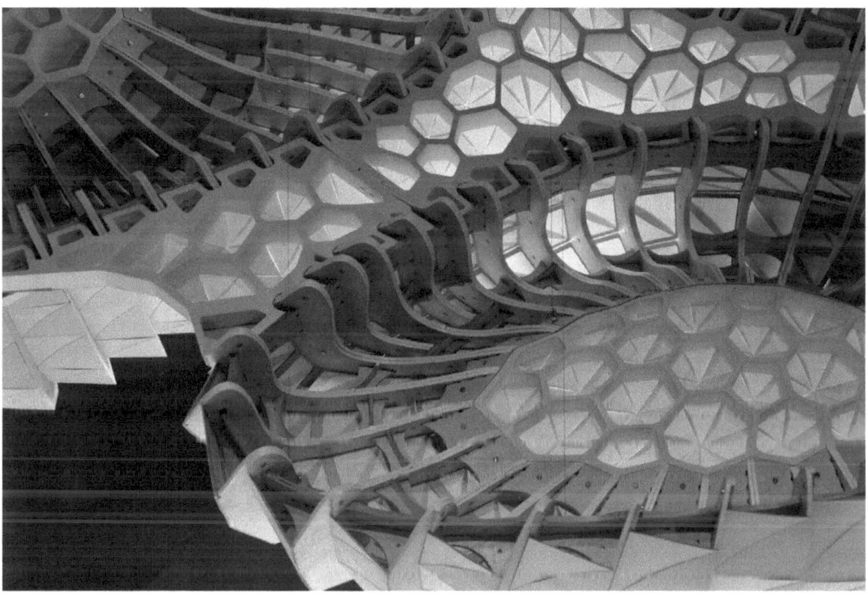

FIGURE 4.12 "HygroScopec: Meteorosensitive Morphology," created by Achim Menges in collaboration with Steffen Reichert in 2012. The design team relied on wood for its anisotropy and hygroscopicity capabilities to achieve the desired material performance.

Wiley's *Architecture Design Journal* outlining the principles associated with morphogenetic design.[84] As well, the Sabin+Jones LabStudio at the University of Pennsylvania launched in 2005 and was one of the earliest collaborations between an architecture and biology department, running experimental research and design studios from 2005–2011 by Jenny Sabin and Peter Jones. This work was later documented in the 2017 book *LabStudio: Design Research Between Architecture and Biology*[85] and was a leading contributor to the growing consensus that biomimetic research was maturing.

Additionally, there were newly established offices that were geographically untethered, where the work and the principals reflected a freedom to engage across methodologies and collaborations. KOKKUGIA (Roland Snooks + Robert Stuart-Smith) and Supermanoeuvre (Dave Pigram + Ian Maxwell) made important contributions to the discourse of morphogenic design (i.e., digital automata, biological systems, generative design, self-organizing behavior) through a number of their projects. These offices were instrumental in both their work and their contribution as educators who worked across several different institutions at this time. Tom Wiscombe, founder of EMERGENT, would indirectly join this broader cohort after leaving Coop Himmelb(l)au's office. His work, similar to KOKKUGIA and Supermanoeuvre, employed digital tools to explore natural, biological, and adaptive systems. Wiscombe's work in particular, pushed a synthetic quality that many were exploring between the refinement in visualization, fabrication, and interactive technologies.

Exuberance and Elegance

Running in parallel to the morphogenetic and emergent design theories, another group articulated a new aesthetic as the anchor point for their theory of Elegance. This theory was built on refusing any type of linguistic mandate in architecture taken from post-modernism or critical modernism.[86] Led by Ali Rahim, Hina Jamelle, and Mark Foster Gage, others joined this effort, such as Hernan Diaz, Marjan Colletti, and Preston Scott Cohen (Figure 4.13). As Gage identified in his 2007 essay on Elegance, *Deus Ex Machina: From Semiology to the Elegance of Aesthetics. Architecture Design*: "the ability to cultivate differentiation and even curate mutation within the sameness of design outcomes is essential to expressing *Elegance*."[87]

For his part, Marjan Colletti would contribute to this discussion through his work, teaching, and his edited collection of essays for AD entitled *Exuberance: New Virtuosity in Contemporary Architecture,* where he would introduce a "new baroque" to combat the turmoil of the global political, economic, and ecological landscape of the post-2008 global banking breakdown, abandoning irrational extravagance, and instead embracing a more pervasive optimism in the discourse and potential of design itself to be performative and therefore active in discourse.[88] Exuberance and Elegance, like Schumacher's use of Parametricism, continued the exploration of new

FIGURE 4.13 Contemporary Architecture Practice (C.A.P.) – Ali Rahim and Hina Jamelle's 2004 proposal for the 10,000-square-foot, 3-story Flagship Store for Reebok in Shanghai, China.

digital theory, aesthetics, style, and even vocabulary to appropriate new territories in the digital design landscape.

The Birth of Graphic Scripting

Scripting[89] and Visual Basic Programming Language[90] were not new in computer science by the 2000s. However, these building blocks provided valuable new steps for software development, graphic user interface, and agency for the design process in architecture. As academic and professional communities began to understand the potential of leveraging deeper computational power, "scripting" became a multivalent term with varying capacities depending on the application and the user. At the most basic level, graphic scripting utilized the customization capacity embedded in most graphic and modeling software available at that time.[91] At the other end of the spectrum was the capacity to build high-level authorship upon the platform afforded by the software, in some instances resulting in coding. In this instance, designers were using a range of scripting languages such as Maya MEL, Rhino VB, C#, Python, and Processing.[92]

As mentioned in support of Ben Fry and Casey Reas's development of Processing, we must identify John Maeda as an important pioneer for what he started in the broadest sense with the Aesthetics and Computation Group (ACG)[93] in 1996. The ACG research initiative laid the groundwork for the research that became highly influential in helping to bring graphic scripting into the design process.[94] The link to physical output from the graphic scripting process was a decisive shift in the conversation from the preceding decade and, indeed, a shift from focusing on software output taking place up until that point.

In 2005, the young duo of Ben Aranda and Chris Lasch put out *Pamphlet Architecture 27: Tooling*.[95] This recipe for "rules that exist pre-material,"[96] supported by their work, provided an onramp to those attempting to implement this approach into their design process. With an obvious set of operational categories, such as spiraling, packing, weaving, blending, cracking, flocking, and tiling, the book leveraged algorithmic procedures to produce parametrically controlled results. The growing community of those interested in scripting embraced the opportunity to experiment and exchange ideas with others who were also finding useful "recipes" for geometric operations.

Many, like Aranda and Lasch, explored various methods, scales, and materials that helped deepen the burgeoning discourse. One of the clearest examples was the 2008 curated exhibition and website by Marc Fornes and Skyler Tibbets entitled "Scripted by Purpose." The exhibition at the FUEL Gallery in Philadelphia and the parallel website hosted a selection of 20 young offices, research groups, and individuals. Each contributed work that utilized different computational programming languages compiled toward their interests and was diversly represented in digital art, design tools, form-finding, optimization, problem-solving, and digital fabrication.[97]

Marc Fornes and THEVERYMANY would emerge as one of the strongest advocates for parametric design and the visual scripting process. Fornes described his approach to scripting and fabrication as built on encoded protocols and defined through computational syntax using Python programming language. The programming language relies on external libraries of Rhinocommon, and sequencing takes place through the Rhino3D software environment[98] (Figure 4.14).

By 2011, Mark Burry authored *Scripting Cultures: Architectural Design and Programming*,[99] providing a clear summary of the work done by the community of scripting designers at that time. While the work included was a helpful reference that indexed current work, perhaps more important was how Burry used a large cross-section of academic and professional colleagues to curate a conversation about scripting across the historical, contemporary, and future trajectory. Neil Leach, John Frazier, Achim Menges, and Brady Peters all forecast the deeper integration of the visual and graphic aspects of a multi-environment interface, suggesting that scripting, if successful, would move to the background of the digital design process both as a function of assimilation into the larger culture and as a function of the software/hardware capabilities.[100]

Emerging Structural and Material Systems Awareness

As software provided greater geometric modeling capabilities, architects realized there was a need to better understand the geometry, structural forces, and materials involved in these outcomes. Again, following Balmond's earlier publication, *Informal* in 2002,[101] where he synthesizes his

FIGURE 4.14 "nonLin/Lin" was fabricated in 2011 for the FRAC Centre by Marc Fornes and THEVERYMANY. The project represents an early prototypical work in mesh segmentation and structural stripes. Each module is made from 6,367 non-linear, 1mm thick aluminum stripes.

architectural engineering and design work, Jessie Reiser and Nanako Umemoto published *Atlas of Novel Tectonics*[102] in 2007. Reiser and Umemoto proposed "asserting the primacy of material and formal specificity over myth and interpretation"[103] and focused on short lessons on the role of matter, force, and material science in architecture. The book included what would be, up to that point, mostly a series of their high-profile digital projects but foreshadowed structural and material operational strategies that would inform discourse for the upcoming decade. Martin Bechthold's *Innovative Surface Structures: Technology and Applications* (2008)[104] came from a different but equally influential perspective. Here, he offered an in-depth look at the new capabilities of utilizing computational tools combined with digital fabrication techniques to produce surfaces. The book specifically examined the innovative use of cementitious, composites, glass, and other smart materials in computationally derived shell and tensile structures.

Participatory Environments | Participatory Toolmaking

While many explored the directions afforded by the new digital tools during this period, a subset of designers actively engaged with extending the responsiveness of the architecture itself and the environment it created. In the example of the designer/code/robotic arm/agile environments/user, the tool or toolset took on a different and more integrated relationship as a constellation of constituent parts. Bob Sheil identified this more broadly as an effort to reconfigure the entire design process in his introduction to *Protoarchitectures* (2008).[105] As a clear trajectory developed from the parametric capabilities, the digital theories extended into more dynamic and animated environments, resulting in spaces that invited or required user participation. For the designers working in this area, including digital tools and space in the design process didn't present an antithetical proposition but was actually synergistic. As computational design evolved, these architects and designers understood the importance of agency in decision making and toolmaking. Ultimately, this meant the design process constantly evolved during this time and fostered the development of new toolsets associated with their pursuit of new forms of participation.

Software and Hardware Applications

As mentioned earlier in this section, Ben Fry and Casey Reas released Processing in 2001. While the software would take time to penetrate academic and professional offices,[106] the early adopters would find the coding interface and the resulting graphic outcomes to be primary reasons to adopt this software for parametric design applications. Building or constructing code/design outcomes manipulated by data points or user input was a new approach. Processing was one of the earliest examples geared toward this user interface and graphic production outcome.

Set against the backdrop of the corporate juggernaut of Autodesk was the small but growing software company of Robert McNeel and Associates, which was responsible for Rhino. While McNeel had supported Rhino Software for some time, the mid-2000s transformed the CAD software industry for what would take place with parametric customization within the software. Starting in 2007 and 2008, Rhino provided a level of interaction that was not previously possible. In 2007, David Rutten released the first version of Grasshopper[107] inside *Explicit History*. It took another seven years for this to come out as a separate plug-in, and this gets discussed further in the next episode. Still, the roots of Grasshopper are defined midway through this decade, and early adopters begin to realize the potential of how the future of the software would operate. Simultaneously, in 2008, for the release of Rhino 4.0, Raja Issa developed Paneling Tools.[108] Paneling Tools provided 2D and 3D customizable geometric interfaces with surfaces in a "define and apply" process. Working from RhinoScript,[109] the integrated functionality initiated a more comprehensive range of explorations into surface articulation and variable surface geometry. The software grew in customizable "leaps-and-bounds" starting in 2010 because it built on the early plug-in capabilities and prioritized user development and functionality. Food4Rhino.

com[110] launched in 2009 and had just over 10k downloads by 2012. That number would reach 10 million by 2023.[111] By early 2012, developers had built plug-ins ranging from geometric operations to Kuka|prc,[112] providing robot language code directly from Grasshopper and a live physics engine called Kangaroo Physics.[113] There were also specialized functionality plug-ins like "Shortest Walk Gh"[114] and "WeaverBird,"[115] which performed a range of topological mesh operations.

Beyond Rhino, several other developments in the software and hardware space aligned with the spirit of customizable tools and distilled interfaces. Arduino initially started as a project called "Wiring" by Hernando Barragán[116] in 2003 under the supervision of Massimo Banzi and Casey Reas while at the Interaction Design Institute Ivrea (IDII) in Italy. In 2005, Massimo Banzi, David Cuartielles, Tom Igoe, Gianluca Martino, and David Mellis initiated the Arduino Project, working from several sources, including Barragán's, to provide an open-source platform for novice users interested in electronic projects connected to the digital environment. The Arduino,[117] continues to be a commonly used hardware device due to its small size, cost, and flexible application possibilities, especially in the DIY community.[118]

Interactive Environments

In 2009, *Interactive Architectures*[119] by Michael Fox and Miles Kemp was published, providing a clear arc from the kinetic and cybernetics of the 1960s to the newfound investment of the 2000s now made possible by emergent technologies and embedded computation. The driving force behind the renewed interest in interactive environments was the technologically influenced and changing patterns of human interaction with the built environment. This was the beginning of an intensification of social and urban change, coupled with the responsibility of issues of sustainability, amplifying the demand for adaptive architectural solutions. In the context of architectural needs, the ability to adapt to changing needs is paramount in contemporary society. These issues continued to emerge as a driving force behind developing trajectories in the next episode. At the time, however, the interactive capacity, combined with the dynamic functionality of the architecture itself, provided a territory to explore and examine further that had been mapped out by earlier pioneers. The caveat was the computational investment in the process, and at times, the resulting environment would extend the outcomes into new dimensions entirely.

Categorization into a particular methodological approach was counterproductive for many practitioners during this period. Many were agnostic in their process to the toolset and moved across various platforms, material explorations, and techniques to produce a diversified body of work. Technology transfer from similarly integrated interactive developments in other fields began to continue to predicate, impact, and evolve with interactive architecture. Such transfer was apparent concerning innovations in aerospace design, automotive design, interface design, and digital media. Interestingly, developmental forecasting could be retrospectively viewed in industries other than architecture, which were precursors to architectural applications. At the time, "Nearly 80 percent of all innovations within automobiles are derivatives of electronic systems."[120] Until recently, nearly all innovations were related to manufacturing and fabrication.[121] The "drive-by-wire" technologies in the automotive industry replaced traditional mechanical and hydraulic control systems with electronic control systems using electromechanical actuators and human-machine interfaces. This technology, of course, was predicated on fly-by-wire technology in the aircraft industry. Both were derivatives of the application of embedded computation, which was now quickly taking center stage with respect to the built architectural environment. A boom in sensor innovation and manufacturing signaled the availability of previously unimaginable means for gathering data and information.[122]

It was a time when many courses were taught through hands-on prototyping to explore ideas within an architectural framework. The circuit board (microcontroller) and the software (a variant of C++) combined to be deployed by artists, hobbyists, and designers for various applications. As application sophistication increased, users started to deploy the Arduino toward issues related to IoT applications, wearables, 3D printing, and embedded environments. In 2010, Jason Kelly Johnson and Andy Payne released the Firefly Primer for Rhino,[123] ushering in a wave of experiments that directly brought the parametric software's functionality into the physical space. It was eventually a comprehensive set of tools to integrate microcontrollers and other input/output devices. Firefly was particularly important in academia working in interactive design, bridging the gap for those working with Arduino and enabling data flows between the physical and digital worlds. Later, in 2012, the Raspberry Pi Model B was released after three years of development to wide acceptance and fanfare. Developed by Eben Upton, Rob Mullins, Jack Lang, and Alan Mycroft at the University of Cambridge's Computer Laboratory, the Raspberry Pi was created as a very low-cost computer to retail for approximately $35. Conceived as a single-board computer for educational applications, its cost and adaptability quickly facilitated its adoption into a much larger context of uses ranging from weather monitoring to robotics.

Still, there started to be a pivot point in responsive and dynamic systems projects that impacted the social discourse and thinking. In 2012, Alisa Andrasek (biothing) and Jose Sanchez created an emergent "urban toy" for the general public to engage called BLOOM (Figure 4.15). A series of brightly colored pink recyclable PET plastic, the project allowed the user to interlock the pieces in a wide range of variable configurations – all staged to create indeterminacy and contingency.[124] The genesis for the design was the city of London's celebration of the 2012 Olympic and Paralympic Games.

FIGURE 4.15 The BLOOM Games, deployed in Greenwich, next to *Cutty Sark*, and reconfigured by the public. Design and production by Alisa Andrasek and Jose Sanchez. Commissioned by the Greater London Authority as part of the Wonder Series to celebrate the 2012 Olympics and Paralympics.

The design would also go on to be deployed in additional European and United States sites in subsequent years and later served as a tangential research parallel for Sanchez's online and VR games that built off of urban and culture/community engagement.[125]

The early cybernetic theories of Cedric Price's work, taken up by Peter Cook and Archigram from the 1960s to the 1970s, would come to some minor level of expression in Cooks Graz Kunsthaus (2003) done with Colin Fournier. Identified by its vibrant blue glass, bulbous shape, and the BIX media facade, done by the Edler brothers out of Berlin,[126] engaged with the public as a giant multimedia device. However, work done at a more intimate scale seemed to draw the most attention during this period. In the UK, Ruairi Glynn, Director of the Interactive Architecture Lab at the Bartlett School of Architecture at University College London and FABRICATE founder, provided an important voice to the growing field of computationally interactive art and architecture. His highly interdisciplinary work cut across areas such as psychophysics, cybernetics, cognitive psychology, robotics, puppetry, animation, interaction design, and performance and provided a platform to work with some of the leading cultural institutions and commercial clients worldwide. SERVO, mentioned in Episode 3, continued to contribute recognized work in the field, such as their Lattice Archipelogics in collaboration with Smart Studio (2002) and the Dark Places Santa Monica Museum of Art (2008) (Figure 4.16).

Philip Beesley, an architect, artist, and educator, is perhaps one of the best-known voices emerging from this time. Beesley was recognized for his installations that meticulously integrated sensors, actuators, and controllers to create fully immersive and responsive environments. His work in the early 2000s was the start of a wide range of collaborative and speculative installations based on the principles of responsive architecture. Beesley has written and spoken extensively on his interest in architecture becoming a living and natural system. He even ties directly into Price's Fun Palace and the theories of Responsive Architecture in *Situated Technologies Pamphlets 4: Responsive Architecture/Performing Instruments.*[127] In this publication, Philip Beesley and Omar Khan discuss the general principles and precedents for defining a responsive architecture. His *Hyozolic* series (2007–2012) creates a "metabolic architecture," and *Meniscus* (2008) and *Sargasso* (2011) are pivotal for the integration of biomimetic effects and scientifically integrated principles into architecturally derived design processes. Beesley has also found highly successful collaboration and cross-pollination with other disciplines, most notably in the fashion industry with Iris Van Herpen, where

FIGURE 4.16 The Dark Places Exhibition, in 2006, curated by servo and located in the Santa Monica Museum, California. The installation served as a display for the video art exhibition allowing viewers to interact with the videos at a control panel and view them at the end of the armature.

they collaborated on innovative couture since 2012 on finely detailed, hand-crafted, three-dimensional fabric, directly integrating digital fabrication and computational design. These few examples laid the groundwork for others who would come along during after period to build on the foundation to create advancements based on a refinement of the computational tools in both the dynamic parts, interface, and effects created.

Building Automation (BA), or what would become the Smart Building Movement, was well underway at this time. Large advancements from the early 1980s took place, assisted by integration related to the interconnection between computational technologies and building systems. Moving well beyond lighting and HVAC, BA gained momentum due to wireless technologies and the integration of Internet of Things (IoT) devices coming to market. Data collection and remote monitoring allowed enhanced decision making both upstream and post-occupancy. By the end of 2012, a re-focusing on human-centric design parameters was coming online to be more personalized and customizable to the user. These were a direct result of the software and the computational capacity now available to be integrated into the physical properties of the built structures.

The Next Steps in Digitizing the Profession

By the time the late 2000s arrived, big and small firms were assimilating technology into their modalities of practice. In many instances, this assimilation was at the highest level, such that leadership on these topics came from the industry and the profession. Optimism and a desire for partnership replaced the previous divide between academia and the profession. Specialized groups within firms were strategically focused and important for advancing the conversation heading into the decade's second half.

Continued Professional Advancement

Many offices led the way in advancing software, and the implementation into the ways built work was coming out of pioneering practices became more sophisticated throughout this period. Offices like Frank Gehry, Zaha Hadid Architects, and Morphosis employed computational tools from the earliest moments in the design conception process all the way through to on-site construction.

Buildings like the Eight Spruce Street Skyscraper, New York City (2011) by Frank Gehry Architects, the Perot Museum, Dallas, TX (2012) by Morphosis, and the Heyder Aliyev Centre, Azerbaijan (2012) by Zaha Hadid Architects all represented a broader portfolio of work from architects that spent this period exemplifying the potential of computational design using post rationalization strategies[128] and also working with engineering, construction and manufacturing partners who were equally equipped for the task. The buildings from this period demonstrated significant sophistication in implementing non-standard geometries into standardized construction and manufacturing processes. Maybe no other firm exploited this aspect more than SHoP Architects. While SHoP's Dunescape, mentioned earlier in the episode, was pioneering for early forays into the fabrication process, perhaps the choreography of software, hardware, and AECO relationships led to the innovation in some of their earliest commissions. The work of the Porter House (2003), 290 Mulberry (2009/2013), and the Barclay Center (2012) (Figure 4.17) all leveraged aspects of the software to fabrication in a way that brought novel solutions to the industry. By reworking the processes within the AECO industry, SHoP was able to arrive at architectural solutions and find innovation both in the design and the construction outcomes.

While Gehry, Hadid, Morphosis, and, to some extent, SHoP identified how these tools assisted in bringing complex geometries into reality, other offices used the same toolset to manifest a different approach and outcome. Foster and Partners, Grimshaw, and even Barkow Leibinger provided an alternate take on implementing the computational technology available at that time. In the case of Foster and Grimshaw, the pre-existing and long track records of completed projects provided a framework for adapting to how the tools and architectural design process would adapt accordingly. Foster and Partners utilized projects like The Swiss RE Headquarters UK (2004), The Glasshouse, Gateshead, UK (2004), and the Kogod Courtyard, Center for American

FIGURE 4.17 Barclays Center was designed by SHoP Architects in 2012 in Brooklyn, New York. The facade is fabricated from 12,000 uniquely shaped panels in weathered steel that reference the color and scale of adjacent brownstone blocks.

Art and Portraiture at the National Portrait Gallery, Washington, DC (2007) to pioneer processes developed by the in-house Specialist Modeling Group (SMG) led by Hugh Whitehead.[129] Whitehead's leadership was paramount to using parametric modeling to guide the introduction of pre-rationalized geometry to some of the most successful projects during this period.[130]

For Grimshaw, projects like the Southern Cross Railway Station, Melbourne, Australia (2006) or the Paul O Gorman Building at University College, London, UK (2007) provide additional examples of building form or performance integration as driving parameters in the design outcome. In the case of Barkow Leibinger, a firm that was less defined by a particular stylistic or formal outcome, was able to leverage an experimental making approach with a wide range of materials and manufacturing techniques like laser cut steel structural cantilever canopy in the Gate House, Ditzingen (2007), or the glass curtain wall system of the TRUTEC Building in Seoul, Korea (2008) or the precast concrete facade of the Tour Total Building in Berlin (2012) (Figure 4.18).

FIGURE 4.18 The Kogod Courtyard at the Smithsonian Institution Courtyard in Washington, DC, completed in 2007 by Foster and Partners. Structurally, the roof is composed of three interconnected and undulating vaults, creating a rigid shell supported by only eight columns.

Upstream Manufacturing and Consultancy

As outlined earlier, introducing OpenBIM concepts made interoperability and collaboration more seamless during this time. It also meant that consultants were no longer brought in downstream but could be integrated into the design process and work more strategically due to the growing digital modeling and UI capabilities shared across the industry. Entrepreneurial-minded practitioners and forward-thinking manufacturers helped reconfigure the thinking so that consultants were a part of the design process from the beginning to assist with a more seamless outcome. The consultants' value was heightened when digital fluency allowed for a more integrated exchange from the very beginning. In many instances, software and hardware fluency, beyond AutoCAD, expanded in many directions for the AECO industry.

Front Inc. was founded in 2002 by Michael Na Min Ra, Marc Simmons, Bruce Nichol, and Martin Riese. Coming out of the curtain wall consultancy paradigm, Front immediately broadened its capabilities and area of operation. Working to bridge from design to construction and pushing out from New York to China and throughout Southeast Asia, Front broadened its footprint and worked with some of the most progressive offices and the enclosing facade systems for projects of this period. Some of those included Seattle Central Library, Seattle, OMA (2005); CCTV Headquarters, Hong Kong, SOMA (2008); Yas Island Marina, Abu Dhabi, Asymptote, (2009); Eli and Edythe Broad Museum, East Lansing, Zaha Hadid Architects (2012); Barclays Center, Brooklyn, SHoP Architects (2012).

Another example of strategic building information consultancy during this time was CASE Inc. CASE Inc. was founded in 2008 by David Fano, Federico Negro, and Steve Sanderson. All three founders came out of the SHoP Architecture office, constituting an important component of their digital leadership at the time of their departure. CASE Inc. was able to differentiate itself from others in this space based on previous experience with implementing innovative software and building solutions at moments having the greatest impact on design, fabrication, cost, and client interaction outcomes. Before being bought by WeWork in 2015, CASE Inc. was a multi-faceted consultancy operation working with owners and operators of all aspects of the AECO industry. From technical software work to softer skillset support like educational training, CASE Inc. operated in many directions simultaneously. This space was not homogenous or limited to just a few participating groups like Front and CASE. In some ways, the smaller, more agile companies have continued to morph as the digital environment has changed. SITU was started in 2005 by Basar Girit, Aleksey Lukyanov-Cherny, Wes Rozen, and Bradley Samuels in Brooklyn, New York. This office worked simultaneously on their work and the consultancy and direct fabrication for other offices. Situ has carved a unique position as designers and architects, not strictly consultants, by staying agile in their own business approach while maintaining a deep knowledge of digital fabrication expertise specializing in the latest technologies.

In the early 2000s, more traditional manufacturers and specialists working in the construction industry also began to adapt their practices to using computational tools for both software and hardware. Like the architecture and engineering firms of this period, some had a longstanding pre-existing model of innovative work, and the implementation of the digital toolset made for a logical extension of pre-existing working methodologies. For some, this control over the toolset ensnared their continued involvement, if not control over the building process. For others, this moment afforded new opportunities to explore additional business sectors. It was a time that fostered, sometimes out of pioneering necessity, a new era of digitally fluent architectural fabricators.

For the A. Zahner Company, founded in 1897 by Andrew Zahner, over a century of innovation in the architectural metalwork industry led great grandson L. William (Bill) Zahner to understand the unique moment the digital frontier offered relative to architectural metalworks, particularly facade systems. As a result of this foundation, Zahner initiated work with noted architects such as Frank Gehry in the late 1990s on the MoPoP and the Stata building at MIT. By the early 2000s, the A. Zahner Co. was one of the most advanced metalworks companies working globally to synthesize computational design software with advanced metallurgy for firms such as Herzog & de Meuron on the de Young Museum (2005), REX/OMA the Wyly Theater (2009), Cooper Union Foundation Building, Morphosis (2011), and Zaha Hadid on the Broad Museum (2012) (Figure 4.19).

Boston Valley Terracotta, a company started in 1981, was not working with multiple generations of leadership at the helm but was working to preserve a quickly disappearing craft of terracotta facade system previously relegated to only restoration of buildings built over the past century. While the restoration of the earlier architecture work continues to this day, the ability to pivot and build off the pre-existing knowledge to use advanced fabrication tools made them an interesting case study. They initiated a progressive strategy of implementing parametric modeling and robotic moldmaking to help generate new opportunities for architects regarding innovative terracotta cladding systems. Located just south of Buffalo in Orchard Park, New York, the company directly worked with the University of Buffalo and the School of Architecture to leverage some of the early educational and onboarding needs as a baseline. The new methods were not just effective in helping to work on contemporary architecture design, but they were also equally used in the work geared toward the restoration of historic facades and the construction of high-performance buildings.[131]

Compared to Zahner and Boston Valley, Gate Precast worked with Morphosis at the Perot Museum of Nature and Science (2012) in Dallas, TX,

FIGURE 4.19 The Eli and Edyth Broad Art Museum, located on the campus of Michigan State University in East Lansing, Michigan. It was completed in 2012 by Zaha Hadid Architects, with A Zahner Co. serving as the facade sub-contractor.

providing a different perspective of how manufacturing was changing rapidly during this time. The plant in Hillsboro, TX, provided architectural precast for projects in that region and directly worked with Morphosis's team early in the design process to identify ways to integrate the precast process to meet the design parameters, variability vs standardization metrics, and cost control. As Thom Mayne would describe it, the "embedded" relationship with Gate created a paradigm shift for future working partnerships with manufacturers and contractors.[132] This project would lead to opportunities to take Gate's architectural precast sector and begin to stretch it into more complex outcomes, such as the Solomon Victory Theater in the WWII Museum, New Orleans (2009) by Voorsanger Mathes The Frost Museum of Science, Miami (2013) by Grimshaw, or the Glassell School of Art, Houston, (2018) by Steven Holl.

Conclusion

What characterized this episode, more than almost anything, was the dynamic energy spent on exploring and embracing experimentation with an attitude of openness and optimism, building out new trajectories of investigation. The research concentrated on development in which procedural and methodological applications started to enhance existing fields like urbanism, sustainability, and gaming. New innovations also started to reconfigure other areas like manufacturing, scripting, parametric design, and visualization. Academic publications provided the foundation of theoretical and projective implications impacting the design process. One of this episode's most compelling and distinguishing marks was the growing intelligence around digital fabrication tools. There was a spreading interest in the increasingly accessible translation of digital to physical space. The maturation of the internet served as a vehicle for communicating image-laden information and new forms of collaboration, and a growing curiosity about new digital toolsets and affiliated design procedures drove the rapid expansion of involvement for many. Ultimately, by the end of this episode, the exploration and experimentation were a shared domain by the professional and academic design communities.

Notes

1 Gershenfeld, N. (2005). *FAB: The Coming Revolution on Your Desktop—From Personal Computers to Personal Fabrication*. New York: Basic Books.
2 McCullough, M. (2005). *Digital Ground: Architecture, Pervasive Computing, and Environmental Knowing*. Cambridge, MA: MIT Press.
3 Iwamoto, L. (2013). *Digital Fabrications: Architectural and Material Techniques*. Princeton, NJ: Princeton Architectural Press.
4 Menges, A. and Ahlquist, S. (2011). "Computational Design Thinking," in *Computation Design Thinking*. Hoboken, NJ: John Wiley & Sons.
5 Ibid., p. 9.
6 Carpo, M. (ed.) (2013). *The Digital Turn in Architecture 1992–2012*. Weinheim: Wiley.
7 Hays, K.M. (1998). *Architecture Theory Since 1968*. London: MIT Press.
8 Nesbitt, K. (1996). *Theorizing a New Agenda for Architecture: An Anthology of Architectural Theory 1965–1995*. Princeton, NJ: Princeton Architectural Press.
9 Beesley, P., Cheng, N.Y.-W., and Williamson, R.S. (eds.) (2004). "Fabrication: Examining the Digital Practice of Architecture," *Proceedings of the 23rd Annual Conference of the Association for Computer Aided Design in Architecture* and the *2004 Conference of the AIA Technology in Architectural Practice Knowledge Community*, Cambridge (Ontario), November 8–14, 2004.
10 Bourdakis, V. and Charitos, D. (eds.) (2006). "Communicating Space(s)," *24th eCAADe Conference Proceedings*, Volos (Greece), September 6–9, 2006, p. 914. doi:10.52842/conf.ecaade.2006.
11 See Dave, B., Li, A., Gu, N., and Park, H. (2010). "New Frontiers," *Proceedings of the 15th International Conference on Computer-Aided Architectural Design Research in Asia CAADRIA 2010*; and Schmitt, G., Hovestadt, L., Van Gool, L., Bosché, F., Burkhard, R., Colemann, S., Halatsch, J., Hansmeyer, M., Konsorski-Lang, S., Kunze, A., and Sehmi-Luck, M. (eds.) (2010). "Future Cities," *28th eCAADe Conference Proceedings*, ETH Zurich (Switzerland), September 15–18, 2010, p. 904. doi:10.52842/conf.ecaade.2010.
12 Johnson, J. Cabrina, M. and Steinfeld, K. (eds.) (2012). "ACADIA 12: Synthetic Digital Ecologies, ACADIA 12: Synthetic Digital Ecologies," *Proceedings of the 32nd Annual Conference of the Association for Computer Aided Design in Architecture (ACADIA)*, San Francisco, October 18–21, 2012, p. 588. doi:10.52842/

conf.acadia.2012; Chiarella, M. and Tosello, M.E. (eds.) (2011). "Sigradi 2011: Augmented Culture," *Proceedings of the 15th Iberoamerican Congress of Digital Graphics*, Argentina, Santa Fe, November 16–18, 2011, p. 579. See https://papers.cumincad.org/cgi-bin/works/Show?sigradi2011_000; and Bennadji, A., Sidawi, B. F., and Reffat, R.M. (eds.) (2010). "CAAD – Cities – Sustainability," *5th International Conference Proceedings of the Arab Society for Computer Aided Architectural Design (ASCAAD 2010)*, Fez (Morocco), October 19–21, 2010, p. 361. See https://papers.cumincad.org/cgi-bin/works/Show?ascaad2010_000

13 Trostel, R., and Schleyer, F. K. (1967). *Tensile Structures: Design, Structure, and Calculation of Buildings of Cables, Nets, and Membranes*. Otto, F. Pneumatic structures. Trostel, R. Calculation of membranes. Otto, F. Tension anchoring in the foundations. Cambridge, MA: MIT Press.

14 Pottmann, H., Asperl, A., Hofer, M., and Killian, A. (2007). *Architectural Geometry*. Bentley Institute Press.

15 Killian, A. (2024, February 29). Email, personal communication.

16 Killian, A., Hofer, M., and Pottmann, H. (2008). *Advances in Architectural Geometry, 1*(1).

17 SHoP Architects Dunescape by SHoP Architects (2000) and Playa Urbana / Urban Beach by William E. Massie (2002) serve as important projects because of the material and methodological contributions they made to the dialogue of digital fabrication in the early 2000s.

18 "SUR at MoMA PS1." *Architect Magazine*, February 7, 2014. See https://www.architectmagazine.com/project-gallery/sur-at-moma-ps1-3671 [accessed November 8, 2023].

19 "MoMA PS1 Afterparty." *MOS*. See https://www.mos.nyc/project/moma-ps1-afterparty [accessed November 8, 2023].

20 "Pole Dance." *SO – IL*. See http://so-il.org/projects/pole-dance [accessed November 8, 2023].

21 David Benjamin/The Living (2014), Andrés Jaque/Office for Political Innovation (2015), and Jenny Sabin (2017) all contributed important work through winning entries for the PS1 Competition and show the evolving focus on how digital fabrication becomes directed by different questions in the years after 2012.

22 Toyo Ito (2002), Álvaro Siza and Eduardo Souto de Moura (2005), Olafur Eliasson and Snøhetta's Kjetil Thorson (2007) are notable examples of temporary pavilions utilizing digital fabrication technology.

23 Sou Fujimoto (2013) and Bjarke Ingles (2016) provide examples of the later work directed toward larger issues beyond just material and fabrication methods.

24 Dempsey, A. and Obuchi, Y. (2010). *Nine Problems in the Form of a Pavilion*. London: Architectural Association, pp. 34 and 92.

25 See https://www.pewresearch.org/internet/2015/10/08/social-networking-usage-2005-2015/#fn-14740-1

26 For a review of digital tools and media used in architectural education and practice during the early 2000s see: Breen, J. (2004). "Changing Roles for (Multi)Media Tools in Design – Assessing Developments and Applications of (Multi)Media Techniques in Design Education, Practice and Research." *Proceedings of the 22nd International Conference on Education and Research in Computer Aided Architectural Design in Europe (eCAADe)*. doi:10.52842/conf.ecaade.2004.530; Henri, H. A. (2003). "New Design Methods for Computer Aided Architectural Design Methodology Teaching." *International Journal of Architectural Computing, 1*(1), 72–91. doi:10.1260/147807703322467441; Fatah gen. Schieck, A. (2008). "Exploring Architectural Education in the Digital Age." *Proceedings of the 26th International Conference on Education and Research in Computer Aided Architectural Design in Europe (eCAADe)*. doi:10.52842/conf.ecaade.2008.861

27 Moretti, L. (1971). "Ricerca Matematica in Architettura e Urbanistica." *Moebius, 4*(1), 20–53.
28 Kalay, Y. E. (1989). *Modeling Objects and Environments*. Chichester: Wiley.
29 Caetano, I., Santos, L., and Leitão, A. (2020). "Computational Design in Architecture: Defining Parametric, Generative, and Algorithmic Design." *Frontiers of Architectural Research, 9*(2), 287–300. doi:10.1016/j.foar.2019.12.008
30 Ibid.
31 Kolarevic, B. (ed.) (2003). *Architecture in the Digital Age: Design and Manufacturing*. London: Spon Press.
32 Burry, M. (2003). "Between Intuition and Process: Parametric Design and Rapid Prototyping," in B. Kolarevic (ed.). *Architecture in the Digital Age: Design and Manufacturing*. New York: Taylor & Francis, pp. 149–162.
33 Aish, R. and Woodbury, R. (2005). "Multi-level Interaction in Parametric Design," in *Smart Graphics*. Heidelberg: Springer, pp. 151–162. doi:10.1007/11536482_13
34 Schodek, D., Bechthold, M., Griggs, J. K., Kao, K., and Steinberg, M. (2005). *Digital Design and Manufacturing: CAD/CAM Applications in Architecture and Design*. Hoboken, NJ: John Wiley & Sons, Inc.
35 Oxman, R. (2006). "Theory and Design in the First Digital Age." *Design Studies, 27*(3), 229–265. doi:10.1016/j.destud.2005.11.002
36 Meredith, M. (2008). "Never Enough (Transform, Repeat Ad Nausea)," in T. Sakamoto and A. Ferré (eds.), *From Control to Design: Parametric/Algorithmic Architecture*. New York: Actar, pp. 6–9. Also see Sasaki, M. (2008). "Matsuro Sasaki," in T. Sakamoto and A. Ferré (eds), *From Control to Design: Parametric/Algorithmic Architecture*. New York: Actar, pp. 72–115.
37 Eggert, R. J. (2005). *Engineering Design*. London: Pearson/Prentice Hall.
38 Holzer, D., Hough, R., and Burry, M. (2007). "Parametric Design and Structural Optimisation for Early Design Exploration." *International Journal of Architectural Computing, 5*(4), 625–643. doi:10.1260/147807707783600780
39 See https://egs.edu/biography/mark-burry [accessed November 3, 2023].
40 Schumacher, P. (2009). "Parametricism: A New Global Style for Architecture and Urban Design." *Architectural Design, 79*(4), 14–23. doi:10.1002/ad.912
41 See https://www.patrikschumacher.com/Texts/Parametricism [accessed November 3, 2023].
42 Schumacher, P. (2011). *The Autopoiesis of Architecture, Volume I: A New Framework for Architecture*. Berlin: Wiley.
43 Schumacher, P. (2012). *The Autopoiesis of Architecture, Volume II: A New Agenda for Architecture*. Berlin: Wiley.
44 Schumacher, P. (2016). *Parametricism 2.0: Rethinking Architecture's Agenda for the 21st Century*. Berlin: Wiley.
45 Coates, P., Healy, N., Lamb, C., and Voon, W. (1996). "The Use of Cellular Automata to Explore Bottom-Up Architectonic Rules." *Eurographics UK, Chapter 14th Annual Conference*, March 26–28, 1996, London, Eurographics Association, UK; Coates, P., Broughton, T., and Jackson, H. (1999). *Exploring Three-Dimensional Design Worlds Using Lindenmayer Systems and Genetic Programming Evolutionary Design by Computers*. San Mateo, CA: Morgan Kaufmann, pp. 323–341.
46 Coates, P. (2010). *Programming Architecture*. Oxford: Routledge.
47 Burry, J. R. and Burry, M. C. (2006). "Gaudí and CAD." *Journal of Information Technology in Construction (ITcon), 11*(32), 437–446.
48 Woodbury, R. F. (2010). *Elements of Parametric Design*. Oxford: Routledge
49 Aish, R. and Woodbury, R. (2005). "Multi-level Interaction in Parametric Design," in: Butz, A., Fisher, B., Krüger, A., and Olivier, P. (eds.). *Smart Graphics. SG 2005. Lecture Notes in Computer Science, vol 3638*. Heidelberg: Springer. doi:10.1007/11536482_13; Woodbury, R., Aish, R., and Kilian, A.

(2007). "Some Patterns for Parametric Modeling," in *27th Annual Conference of the Association for Computer Aided Design in Architecture*. Halifax, Dalhousie University, pp. 222–229.
50 Jabi, Wassim. (2013). *Parametric Design for Architecture*. London: Laurence King Publishing; Terzidis, K. (2003). *Expressive Form: A Conceptual Approach to Computational Design*. Oxford: Taylor & Francis.
51 Mitchell, W. J. (1975). "The Theoretical Foundation of Computer-Aided Architectural Design." *Environment and Planning B: Planning and Design, 2*(2), 127–150.
52 Frazer, J., Frazer, J., Liu, X., Tang, M., and Janssen, P. (2002). "Generative and Evolutionary Techniques for Building Envelope Design," in *Generative Art 2002, 5th International Conference GA2002*. Generative Design Lab, pp. 3.1–3.3.
53 Caetano, I., Santos, L., and Leitão, A. (2020). "Computational Design in Architecture: Defining Parametric, Generative, and Algorithmic Design." *Frontiers of Architectural Research, 9*(2), 287–300. https://doi.org/10.1016/j.foar.2019.12.008
54 Kolarevic, B. and Malkawi, A. (2005). *Performative Architecture: Beyond Instrumentality*. Oxford: Routledge.
55 Ibid., p. 52.
56 Ibid.
57 See http://www.fabricate.org/
58 See http://www.fabricate.org/home-7-2-2-2/ [accessed October 25, 2023].
59 Schodek, Daniel L. (2005). *Digital Design and Manufacturing: CAD/CAM Applications in Architecture and Design*. Chichester: Wiley.
60 Iwamoto, L. (2013). *Digital Fabrications: Architectural and Material Techniques*. Princeton, NJ: Princeton Architectural Press.
61 Dunn, Nick (2012). *Digital Fabrication in Architecture*. United Kingdom: Laurence King Publishing.
62 See https://vimeo.com/149328392 [accessed October 26, 2023].
63 See https://robotsinarchitecture.org/
64 See Brell-Cokcan, S. and Braumann, J. (2010). "A New Parametric Design Tool for Robot Milling, ACADIA 10: LIFE in:formation, On Responsive Information and Variations in Architecture." *Proceedings of the 30th Annual Conference of the Association for Computer Aided Design in Architecture (ACADIA)*, New York, October 21–24, 2010, pp. 357–363. doi:10.52842/conf.acadia.2010.357; Braumann, J. and Brell-Cokcan, S. (2011). "Parametric Robot Control: Integrated CAD/CAM for Architectural Design, ACADIA 11: Integration through Computation." *Proceedings of the 31st Annual Conference of the Association for Computer Aided Design in Architecture (ACADIA)*, Banff (Alberta), October, 13–16, 2011, pp. 242–251. doi:10.52842/conf.acadia.2011.242; and Braumann, J. and Brell-Cokcan, S. (2012). "Digital and Physical Tools for Industrial Robots in Architecture: Robotic Interaction and Interfaces." *International Journal of Architectural Computing, 10*(4), 541–554.
65 See https://innochain.net/cita/ [accessed October 30, 2023].
66 See https://digitalfutures.international/
67 See https://digitalfutures.international/history/ [accessed October 30, 2023].
68 See https://www.simaud.org/
69 Marble, S. (ed.). (2012). *Digital Workflows in Architecture: Design–Assembly–Industry*. Berlin: De Gruyter.
70 Ibid., pp. 7–8.
71 Lima, M. (2011). *Visual Complexity: Mapping Patterns of Information*. Princeton, NJ: Princeton Architecture Press.
72 See https://medium.com/processing-foundation/a-modern-prometheus-59aed94abe85 [accessed November 9, 2023].
73 "Design By Numbers." See https://dbn.media.mit.edu/whatisdbn.html [accessed November 1, 2023].

74 Reas, C., McWilliams, C., and LUST. (2010). *Form+Code in Design, Art, and Architecture*. New York, NY: Princeton Architectural Press.
75 *2009 McGraw-Hill Construction, Smart Market Report*. (2009). McGraw-Hill Construction, 2 Penn Plaza New York, NY 10121.
76 *Contrasting The Capabilities of Building Energy Performance Simulations Programs – A Joint Report* (2005). D. Crawley (U S Department of Energy) Washington, DC, USA; J. Hand (Energy Systems Research Unit) University of Strathclyde Glasgow, Scotland, UK; M. Kummert (University of Wisconsin-Madison Solar Energy Laboratory) Madison, Wisconsin, USA; B. Griffith (National Renewable Energy Laboratory) Golden, Colorado, USA; V1.0 July, 2005.
77 See https://www.caddmicrosystems.com/blog/project-vasari-graduates-from-autodesk-labs/
78 Aish, R. and Woodbury, R. (2005). "Multi-level Interaction in Parametric Design," in *Smart Graphics*. Heidelberg: Springer, pp. 151–162. doi:10.1007/11536482_13/.
79 Aish, R. (2005). *Introduction to Generative Components: A Parametric and Associative Design System for Architecture, Building Engineering and Digital Fabrication*. Bentley White Paper, 1–15.
80 Balmond, C., Smith, J., and Brensing, C. (2002). *Informal*. London: Prestel, p. 15.
81 Ibid.
82 Architecture Design (AD) was the most notable of these publications, providing a platform for some of the most important debates on digital design issues. Mario Carpo's Digital Turn 1992–2012, (Carpo Mario. 2013. *The Digital Turn in Architecture 1992–2012*. Chichester: Wiley) is the most succinct listing the new heuristics referenced in this section.
83 Kolarevic, B. (2000). "Digital Morphogenesis and Computational Architectures." *SIGraDi'2000 - Construindo (n)o Espacio Digital (Constructing the Digital Space)*, 98–103. https://papers.cumincad.org/.
84 See Hensel, M., Menges, A., and Weinstock, M. (2004). *Emergence: Morphogenetic Design Strategies*. Oxford: Routledge. Hensel, M., Menges, A. and Weinstock, M. (2006). *Techniques and Technologies in Morphogenetic Design*. Oxford: Routledge; Hensel, M. and Menges, A. (2008). *Versatility and Vicissitude*. Oxford: Routledge; Hensel, M., Menges, A., and Weinstock, M. (2010). *Emergent Technologies and Design: Towards a Biological Paradigm for Architecture*. Oxford: Routledge; and Menges, A. (2012). *Material Computation: Higher Integration in Morphogenetic Design*. Chichester: John Wiley & Sons.
85 Sabin, J. E. and Jones, P. L. (eds.) (2017). *LabStudio: Design Research Between Architecture and Biology*. Oxford: Routledge.
86 Foster Gage, M. (2007). "Deus Ex Machina: From Semiology to the Elegance of Aesthetics." *Architecture Design, 77*, 82.
87 Ibid., pp. 82–85.
88 Colletti, M. (ed.) (2010). *Exuberance: New Virtuosity in Contemporary Architecture*. Manila: Wiley.
89 Introduction to Scripting Languages. www.jbiet.edu.in [accessed November 3, 2023].
90 Vick, P. (2004). *The Visual Basic.net Programming Language*. Cocos (Keeling) Islands: Addison-Wesley.
91 Burry, M. (2013). *Scripting Cultures Architectural Design and Programming*. Hoboken, NJ: Wiley, pp. 36–37.
92 For a full list of scripting languages, see Ibid., pp. 36–37.
93 Aesthetics + Computation Group: MIT Media Laboratory. See https://acg.media.mit.edu/ [accessed November 3, 2023].
94 Schiffman, J. and Jared M. (2001, January 1). *Aesthetics of Computation: Unveiling the Visual Machine*. Thesis, Massachusetts Institute of Technology. See https://dspace.mit.edu/handle/1721.1/31103

95 Aranda, B. and Lasch, C. (2006). *Tooling*. Princeton, NJ: Princeton Architectural Press.
96 Ibid., p. 8.
97 See http://www.scriptedbypurpose.net/ [accessed November 13, 2023].
98 See https://theverymany.com/art-of-the-prototypical [accessed November 13, 2023].
99 Burry, M. (2013). *Scripting Cultures Architectural Design and Programming*. Hoboken, NJ: Wiley.
100 Ibid., pp. 64–65.
101 Balmond, C., Smith, J., and Brensing, C. (2002). *Informal*. London: Prestel Pub.
102 Reiser, J. and Umemoto, N. (2006). *Atlas of Novel Tectonics*. Princeton, NJ: Princeton Architectural Press.
103 Ibid., p. 23.
104 Bechthold, M. (2008). *Innovative Surface Structures: Technology and Applications*. London: Routledge.
105 Sheil, R. (ed.) (2008). *Protoarchitecture: Analogue and Digital Hybrids*. Hoboken, NJ: John Wiley & Sons, p. 7.
106 See https://medium.com/processing-foundation/a-modern-prometheus-59aed94abe85 [accessed November 14, 2023].
107 "Algorithmic Modeling for Rhino." *Grasshopper*. See https://www.grasshopper3d.com/ [accessed November 11, 2023].
108 "Paneling Tools for Rhinoceros 5". See https://wiki.mcneel.com/_media/labs/panelingtools.pdf [accessed November 11, 2023].
109 R. M. Associates (n.d.). "RhinoScript Guides." Rhino3d. See https://developer.rhino3d.com/guides/rhinoscript/ [accessed November 11, 2023].
110 See https://www.food4rhino.com/en/stats?lang=en#downloads [accessed November 15, 2023].
111 Ibid.
112 *KUK*. (2011, October 21). Food4Rhino. https://www.food4rhino.com/en/app/kukaprc-parametric-robot-control-grasshopper
113 *Kangaroo Physics*. (2010, December 29). Food4Rhino. https://www.food4rhino.com/en/app/kangaroo-physics
114 *Shortest Walk gh*. (2010, December 23). Food4Rhino. https://www.food4rhino.com/en/app/shortest-walk-gh
115 "Weaverbird – Topological Mesh Editor." *Grasshopper*. See https://www.grasshopper3d.com/group/weaverbird [accessed November 15, 2023].
116 *Home*. (2016, January 1). https://arduinohistory.github.io/
117 "Home." *Arduino*. See https://www.arduino.cc/ [accessed November 4, 2023].
118 *Is Arduino Suitable for Industry?* (2022, October 19). Boot & Work Corp. S.L. See https://www.industrialshields.com/blog/arduino-industrial-1/is-arduino-suitable-for-industry-475
119 Fox, M. and Kemp, M. (2009). *Interactive Architecture*. Princeton, NJ: Princeton Architectural Press.
120 Leen, G. and Heffernen, D. (2001). "Vehicles without Wires." *Computing and Control, 12*(5), 205–221.
121 Senagala, M. (2005). "Kinetic and Responsive: A Complex-adaptive Approach to Smart Architecture." Paper presented at the SIGRADI International Conference, Lima, Peru.
122 Fox, M. and Kemp, M. (2009). *Interactive Architecture*. Princeton, NJ: Princeton Architectural Press.
123 See http://www.grasshopper3d.com/profile/firefly
124 Andrasek, A. (2015) "Indeterminacy & Contingency: The Seroussi Pavilion and Bloom by Alisa Andrasek." *Architural Design, 85*, 106–111.
125 Fairs, M. (2016). "Video games will become 'new tools' to solve architecture's global challenges." *Dezeen*, March 7, 2016. Available at: https://www.dezeen.

com/2016/03/07/jose-sanchez-block-hood-video-game-tools-solve-global-challe nges-architecture/ [accessed November 15, 2023].

126 "Realities:United." See https://realities-united.com/realitiesinfos/ [accessed November 16, 2023].

127 Beesley, P. and Kahn, O. (2018, March 23). *Responsive Architecture/Performing Instruments – The Architectural League of New York*. New York: The Architectural League of New York.

128 Dritsas, S. (2012). "Rationalisation of Complex Building Envelopes." *Proceedings of the 17th Conference on Computer Aided Architectural Design Research in Asia (CAADRIA)*. doi:10.52842/conf.caadria.2012.007

129 Peters, B. and De Kestelier, X. (2006). *The Work of Foster and Partners Specialist Modelling Group*. St Albans: Tarquin Publications. See also Aish, R. (2005). *Introduction to Generative Components: A Parametric and Associative Design System for Architecture, Building Engineering and Digital Fabrication*. Bentley White Paper, 1–15.

130 Menges, A. (2006). "Instrumental Geometry." *Architectural Design, 76*(2), 42–53. doi:10.1002/ad.239

131 See https://bostonvalley.com/about-2/ [accessed November 22, 2023].

132 See https://gateprecast.com/case-study/perot-museum-of-nature-and-science/ [accessed November 22, 2023].

EPISODE 5

LEGITIMACY (2013–2018)

The previous episode, covering almost a decade of development was a time of unprecedented exploration and experimentation serving to dissipate the strength of any prevailing paradigm. As the numerous trajectories gained definition, it became increasingly difficult to understand any coherence within the still rapidly evolving technological context that ensnared everything from social and cultural issues to politics and the state of the planet. The last episode also generated numerous books that curated countless taxonomies of everything from parametric design to digital fabrication, robotic fabrication, interactive architecture, and materiality in an endless jostle for credibility. Now, however the taxonomies and explorations narrowed, and it was in part looking back on the context of explorations and in part looking at the contemporary world that a few provided a new overall contextual curation. This episode captures an interesting time after the waters of exploration and experimentation had calmed to a certain extent. It was a time when fewer trajectories prevailed, and research had to demonstrate a degree of legitimacy to survive.

Perspectives

Building on Digital Foundations

The first much-needed curation came from Mario Carpo, who followed up the seminal *Digital Turn in Architecture*[1] (2013) with the *Second Digital Turn*[2] (2017) as part of the "Writing Architecture Series" edited by Cynthia Davidson. The first book focused on how adopting the early modeling tools enabled a style of the first digital age. In the *Second Digital Turn*, Carpo argues that architects are coming to terms with the tools they have

DOI: 10.4324/9781032671208-7

appropriated and that they are no longer tools for making but tools for thinking.[3] The book came out at nearly the same time that OpenAI was founded in 2015, far before even the first Large Language Model (LLM) was published in the form of ChatGPT or any real reckoning of the influence of data. From within this context, Carpo forecasts new modes of thinking based on information retrieval and simulation with unprecedented access to massive amounts of data.

The Stack: On Software and Sovereignty[4] by Ben Bratton was also published almost simultaneously in 2016 and took on an inclusive theory of the technological world, which included architecture and urban planning. In the book, he outlines six layers or "stacks" (earth, cloud, city, address, interface, and user), which are understood independently but also as part of a larger evolving and coherent model of planetary computation. Similar to Kevin Kelly's inclusivity of the *Technium* discussed in Episode 0, Bratton covers both hard and soft systems that are enmeshed, not just computationally but physically as well.[5] Phil Bernstein in *Architecture | Design | Data* (2018)[6] and Dennis Sheldon's in *The Disruptors* volume of *AD* (2020)[7] would both make the point that there was a growing professional world grappling with diverse challenges and opportunities. The new technologies captured in Bernstein's *Data* and Bratton's *Stacks* profoundly changed the building industry. This change impacted fundamental business models, workflows, roles, and responsibilities.[8] To impact the potential role of computation during this time, architects and the profession were forced to examine broader issues such as agency (control), methodology (processes), and value (utility).[9]

Also published at the same time in 2016 was a critical anthology edited by Rivka and Robert Oxman: *Theories of the Digital in Architecture*,[10] which essentially collected articles and original texts from notable individuals working in many of the prevailing taxonomies of the time. The edited volume interlaces ten areas of influence within a historical perspective to provide an overall meta-theory to serve as a foundation for new ways of design thinking.[11] As much as any publication at this time, the Oxman's thematic trajectories catalogued the diversity within the field of design computation into the following sections: *Form, Performance/Generation, Parametrics, Morphogenesis, Tectonics, Materialization, Material Fabrication, Responsive/Dynamic/Adaptive*, as bundled within sections on Theory and Epistemology.[12] The last notable publication identified here is *Paradigms in Computing: Making, Machines, and Models for Design Agency in Architecture*[13] (2015) by David Gerber and Mariana Ibanez. The book similarly collects explorations into paradigms tied together by using the "digital" as a genotype of agency. While not inclusive or historically grounded, the collection provides a valuable glimpse into the range of trajectories and contexts at the time.

Deepening Research Trajectories

While the previous episode was noted for the numerous books that served for documenting new trajectories through collections of explorations, now, the work of this episode shows a more direct lineage and research framework building off the previous foundations of experimentation covered in Episode 4. It was a time when these trajectories coalesced and strengthened. The biological/ecological research usurped work in morphogenesis and responsive/interactive/dynamic systems. It signaled the beginning of a shift from the mechanical to the biological in terms of adaptation in architecture.[14] The work in materiality remained somewhat autonomous but became increasingly ensnared in the worlds of biological and fabrication research. The appropriation of intelligent and smart materials were generalized terms for materials with one or more alterable properties. Coming out of the previous decade's research and publications on exploratory material research,[15] there was an increased connection between the material and applied sciences. The work expanded into a range of areas via the deepening research regarding building technology, building performance, and, in some instances, still tied to biological systems. As a foreshadowing of this synthesis, Mori pointed out:

> We can theoretically produce materials to meet specific performative criteria; this transformation often takes place at the molecular level, where materiality is rendered invisible.[16]

The frontiers of fabrication also increasingly embraced biological and even sustainable agendas through the evolving works of several key individuals like Jenny Sabin, Dana Cupkova, Achim Menges, and Philippe Block, who, by this point, had over a decade of consistent research. Last, the vision of everything parametrically variable and mutually adaptive begins to transcend pragmatic processes and serves as an umbrella for other "isms" that are both formal and performance-driven. During this short but important time, this episode introduces critical synergistic forces into computational design. Within both the research and practice fields, activity builds upon preceding work and finds ways to combine innovation in more rigorous research and impacts in the built environment. As the foregrounding of parallel fields in the hard and social sciences emerges, architectural computation is informed of emerging directions that will take hold over the next decade.

Steps Toward Deeping Research

CumInCAD 2.0

The trajectories of development in architectural computation have always been incremental. In this episode, the narrowing of topics followed a preceding moment characterized by broader exploration and experimentation. These previous years were fueled by the catalytic effect of conferences being accessible online, instantly published pavilions, competitions, and buildings, and social media as a critical component to dissemination and awareness. A subtle but important shift began to take place from tectonics of techniques and methodology toward broader questions about social and cultural issues.[17]

In contrast to the instant and often image-based dissemination of the Internet and social media was the revamp of the indexing and dissemination of all the sister organizations of architectural computing through CumInCAD, which was initially launched by Bob Martens and Ziga Turk in 1998. As mentioned in Episode 2, CumInCAD was significantly enhanced during the SciX (Open, self-organizing repository for scientific information exchange) project, which took place from 2002 to 2004.[18] However, it was in 2016 that the repository entered a new phase and truly started to have a global impact. Tomo Cerovsek's work to deploy CumInCAD 2.0 as a fully Open-Access and cloud-based bibliographic repository of CAAD research was monumental.[19] It included over 12,300 records, most with fully searchable abstracts and texts (Figure 5.1). Publishing a peer-reviewed paper at one of the conferences automatically filters it into the repository. As Cerovsek and Martins identified in their *eCAADe* journal article on these efforts, they set out to "build a 'collective memory' of scientific publications from conference proceedings of CAAD associations; and to make this memory unconditionally accessible to the scientific community as a web-based bibliographic repository of works."[20] The repository instantly became a barometer of relevant trajectories and a way

FIGURE 5.1 CumInCAD 2.0 was launched as a fully Open-Access and cloud-based bibliographic repository of CAAD research.

of measuring global research contributions. Combined with *IJAC* (*The International Journal of Architectural Computing*),[21] the global network of research awareness and interaction was now securely in place.

Diversification in Research Platforms

Architecture Design (*AD*) has almost a 100-year publication history tracking, contributing, and even helping to direct the critical architecture and design discourse. Starting in the late 1990s with the John Wiley and Sons acquisition, the publication began to more clearly involve a wide range of current and projective issues related to digital technology, as well as social, cultural, and environmental themes. For much of this time, Helen Castle served as editor, while Neil Spiller has more recently assumed that role. From Mario Carpo's Digital Turn to the more recent hypothesis about post-human architecture for future space exploration, *AD* has served as a valuable barometer of the transformation of design computation over the 30+ years from the 1990s through the 2020s, more than most publications.

Although not explicitly focused on computation, another important journal, *TAD* (*The Journal of Technology Architecture and Design*), was launched in the US in 2016 through the Association of Collegiate Schools of Architecture (ACSA). In its conception, *TAD* was a focused platform for peer-reviewed research in architectural technology, which consistently included computational architecture.[22] Architecture is an academic discipline and has always been separated from the profession of architecture, which means professional and trade publications have typically been driven by images and narrative as opposed to academic journals that focus on research and analysis.[23] However, because many funding institutions do not recognize architecture as a specific field, research is often rationalized within the scope of other related disciplines. *TAD* has navigated and supported the cross-disciplinary nature of this current research status by including one-third of its authors from disciplines outside of architecture.[24]

Spurred on by the highly publicized work of the ICD/ITKE programs led by Achim Menges, Jan Kippers, Michael Hensel, the NCCR, the BRG led by Phillip Blocke, as well as the Gramazio and Kohler Research Group at the ETH, many students at the time initiated Ph.D. and doctoral studies specifically in architecture and computation. Some programs, such as MIT, had offered a Ph.D. in Design in Computation since the early 2000s. The program at MIT was started by Bill Mitchell. Takehiko Nagakura, Larry Sass, George Stiny, and Terry Knight also joined as faculty with their own foundational work in specific areas of focus. Other programs like the Ph.D. in Architecture and Digital Theory at the Bartlett (UCL) provided a different pathway. Directed by Frédéric Migayrou and Mario Carpo, the program explores research in a range of computational theoretical and methodological tracts. By the mid-2010s, it was becoming more commonplace to have options for pursuing an advanced degree with a specific focus on computation, expanding legitimate research in the field. Perhaps most importantly, the trajectories congealed through the wealth of explorations in other fields outside of architecture, which fostered the architectural acquisition (as opposed to the appropriation) of developments in robotics, ecologies, and biomimetics, among other things, fostering a necessity of interdisciplinary collaboration.

Interdisciplinary programs became one of the ways that research gained greater traction during the mid-2010s, especially as the decade progressed and advances in computer science accelerated. The ATLAS Institute at the University of Colorado launched to slow beginnings in the late 1990s, nearly 20 years later, it would become a model for innovative educational programming, bringing in faculty and industry mentors from across the state. Of particular note are the leadership roles that design computational researchers Mark D. Gross and Ellen Yi-Luen Do played in the institute's diversification. Gross was appointed Director in 2014, with research contributing to the areas of modular robotics, sketch tool applications, and human/computer interaction. Ellen Yi-Luen Do joined ATLAS in 2017 with expertise in connected ubiquitous computing and a long track record of publications in wearable technology, digital sketching technologies, and haptic digital technologies.[25]

Next Generation Computational Design

Biological/Ecological Paradigms

A number of significant books were released in this short period within a context of increased environmental and ecological awareness and an understanding of the problems forecast by many as a "call to action" regarding both the planet and associated social and cultural issues.[26] These books responded to a need to investigate the role design would play in addressing some of these growing issues. However, it is important to situate these publications and the broadening discourse in what could be a natural application from Ahlquist and Menges's *Computational Design Thinking*[27] (2011) mentioned in Episode 4. Ahlquist and Menges framed systems thinking in design as a means by which architecture is no longer understood as a series of "isolated static entities" and would also leverage computation to help navigate *"inter-relational, complex behavior-based systems."*[28] In that vein, Gareth Doherty and Mostafavi Mohsen, dean at Harvard's Graduate School of Design, re-released their popular book *Ecological Urbanism*[29] in 2016. This was the book's second release (originally in 2010) but now included many built case studies and notable people endorsing the cause. The book took a global approach and integrates the importance of recognizing the many complex contributing forces and political, economic, and technological hurdles to make the case that design is the key factor capable of reconciling urbanism with the environment.

Another book with almost the same name came out in 2014, making the case for the same level of global, social, and ethical stewardship. In *Ecological Urbanism: The Nature of the City*,[30] Susannah Hagan argues that "urbanism needs to become environmentally literate, and environmental design needs to become culturally literate."[31] The prevailing theory at this time was that ecological urbanism was fluid and global. Again, in 2014, *Projective Ecologies*[32] by Chris Reed and Nina-Marie Lister further supported this premise. In this book, the contributors bring up many of the same issues of urbanism, culture, societies, and design in general within the context of ecological and systems thinking. The book takes a broad perspective of ecologies with a bent toward landscapes and with an understanding there is no linearity to such systems, but rather, they are sprawling and without direction or narration. The idea they put forth is that such ecosystems depend upon change and adaptation and we, as designers, need to understand them and how to work within such contexts.

Diving even deeper into the ecologies of landscapes with a cybernetic bent was *Responsive Landscapes: Strategies for Responsive Technologies in Landscape Architecture*,[33] which came out in 2016 by Bradley Cantrell and Justine Holzman. It was an interesting take on rationalizing interactive architecture within the context of ecological landscapes. The argument was made with a wealth of built project case studies, which demonstrate that when our landscapes are cybernetically hybridized with technologies, they can better respond and adapt to the more dynamic and temporal qualities of the time. The reconciliation of responsive technologies and landscape architectural theory relies on sensing, processing, and feedback within the larger context of "distanced authorship."[34]

The ecological trajectory grew in scope, usurping work of other previously standalone areas of inquiry, including biological and morphogenesis research, and most of that in the responsive/interactive and dynamic field. Shifting from landscape to larger scales, additional books came out at the time focusing on a broader ecology and global urbanism but focused specifically on how things interact with the environment around them. One of the most influential was *Adaptive Ecologies: Correlated Systems of Living* (2013)[35] by Theodore Spyropoulos, the longtime director of the Design Research Laboratory (AADRL) at the Architectural Association in London (Figure 5.2). The book included essays from several recurring individuals, including Mark Burry, John Frazer, and Patrik Schumacher, among others, and examined a collection of organizational systems as an evolving ecology. The model of architecture and urbanism they speculate in the book is one of governance through emerging collective interactions.[36] It is one of several books taking on social and cultural issues by defining architectural and urban systems that were both adaptive and participatory. It was written when the early theories of cyberneticians Pask and Wiener finally had some real technological feasibility. As pointed out by Pask, the work was built upon John Frazer's (Episode 3) foundational concept that

FIGURE 5.2 Minimaforms office was one of many to expand the biological and ecological trajectories.

architecture should be a "living, evolving thing."[37] Going to the source of dynamic adaptability, Branko Kolarevic and Vera Parlać explored the definition of what is meant by "change" itself in architecture. They found the definitions were multiple, intertwined, and sometimes even contradictory.[38]

Again, operating with a broad and inclusive scope was the "call to action" put forth in response to a globally ominous ecological awareness in the book *XXL-XS: New Directions in Ecological Design*[39] by Mitchell Joachim and Michael Silver in 2016. Their extreme "toolbox approach" called for a total restructuring of the profession supported by numerous essays and contributions, all projecting far beyond the obvious, ranging from massive public works to the nano-scale, from terraforming and bio-manufacturing (Figure 5.3). They argue that the architecture profession, in general, has failed to take any leadership and failed to make use of the creative opportunities provided by thinking differently

Material Science and Material Exploration

The state of computational material research was well summarized in the 2013 book released by Michael Hensel, Achim Menges, and Michael Weinstock, *Emergent Technologies and Design: Towards a Biological Paradigm for Architecture*.[40] The book was based on work conducted with their students at the Architectural Association in London and covered numerous

FIGURE 5.3 Terreform ONE is an architecture, and urban design research group advancing the practice of socio-ecological design.

research strands in emergent technologies, including evolution in computation, material systems in computation, morphogenesis and performance, and material systems and sensor feedback. They defined the concept of emergence as the process by which properties "emerge" from within complex systems.[41] To engage in emergence, they argued, required an understanding of the behaviors of complex systems, including mathematical processes. These understandings and new digital tools produced new design strategies that were evolutionary, adaptive, and responsive.

This trajectory was spurred on by the wealth of explorations in biomimetics, which referred to the architectural application of developments in robotics and materials. Fundamentally, this meant nature was imaginative by necessity and had already solved many of the problems surrounding us. For Hensel, Menges, and Weinstock, animals, plants, and microbes were the consummate engineers. Nature had found what worked, what lasted, what was necessary and not necessary. This produced a holistic operational plan on what was most appropriate for this planet. Joseph Bar-Cohen put it well, "Nature has always inspired human achievements and has led to effective materials, structures, tools, mechanisms, processes, algorithms, methods, systems, and many other benefits."[42] Evolutionary systems describe the processes of such biologically inspired architecture that operates like an organism, directly analogous to the underlying design process of nature. The important thing here was that evolutionary systems repositioned the designer's role. As Gordon Pask stated 20 years earlier in his foreword to the book *An Evolutionary Architecture*,[43] "The role of the architect here, I think, is not so much to design a building or city as to catalyze them: to act that they may evolve."[44]

Many designers and academics were operating in this space, but one of the most notable pioneers in this area was Neri Oxman at MIT. Oxman started an interdisciplinary research group at MIT's Media Lab called "Material Ecology" and developed numerous notable projects focusing on digital morphogenesis. Her work operated at the intersection of multiple fields, but most notably at the time, it set new standards for interdisciplinary research.[45]

Similarly, Jenny Sabin, through her office and ties to her lab at Cornell, became one of the leading voices in transdisciplinary research across a wide range of scales and built projects (Figure 5.4). Her work grew to exemplify collaboration, combining biology, material science, and engineering into an architectural agenda. In 2017, her entry of *Lumen* won the MOMA PS1 competition with a knitted fabric of responsive tubular structures and a canopy of cellular components.

Also in 2016, Jan Knippers, the longtime Director at the Institute of Building Structures and Structural Design (ITKE) in Stuttgart, published *Biomimetic Research for Architecture and Building Construction*[46] along with Klaus Nickel and Thomas Speck. The book focused on Biological Design and Integrative Structures. The publication operated as an academic journal documenting comprehensive research with a fascinating collection of bio-inspired papers from numerous contributors working in the area at the time. The work, like that of Oxman's and Sabin's was transdisciplinary and similarly important, not only

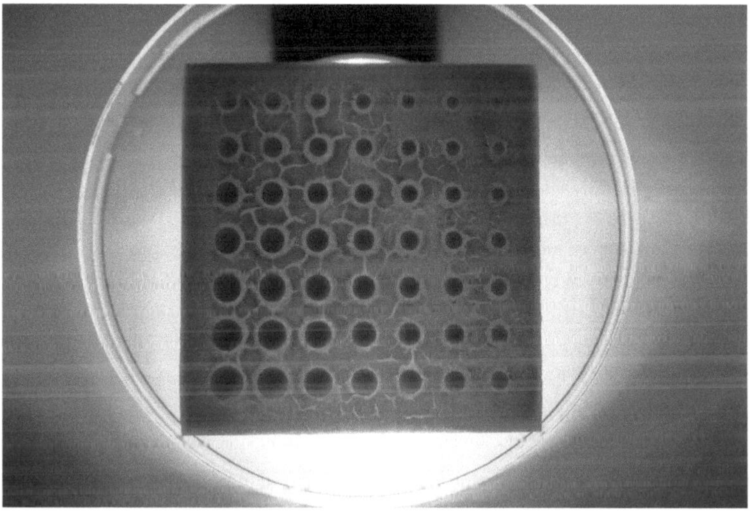

FIGURE 5.4 PolyBrick 3.0 by Jenny Sabin Studio, exemplifies combining biology, material science, and engineering into an architectural agenda.

in the technical achievements but also in demonstrating interdisciplinary collaboration and methodologies.

The field of 3D printing continued to develop with rigorous outcomes related to material performance, providing new opportunities for the future to quickly transform the built environment and gain traction as a serious research trajectory in materiality. Martin Bechthold, a longstanding thought leader in the field, argued that in the same way that new digital fabrication technologies catalyzed novel architectural design, material science catalyzed a new "bottom-up" approach to new material systems integration.[47]

While Bechthold's earlier work on innovative structural systems was important to a group exploring shell and tensile systems, his work in material systems, specifically ceramics, provided a critical foundation for this developing area. Much of the research led to a contemporary redefinition of architectural ceramics as enabled by material research, computation, and fabrication methods as outlined in the book *Ceramic Material Systems*,[48] which came out in 2015 by Bechthold with Anthony Kane and Nathan King.

In addition to ceramics, wood,[49] concrete,[50] and metals[51] are similarly included in the subsequent discussion of fabrication. Furthermore, almost every material became the topic of fascinating new and previously unimaginable potential applications in architecture, including plastics,[52] glass,[53] and fabrics. Michael Bell, a professor at Columbia University GSAPP, documented the contemporary state of materials in a series of books, each taking on a different topic with the state of current development and potential applications. Plastics were quickly becoming one of the most ubiquitous materials in construction and had the potential to reshape the roles of architects and engineers. At the time when wood, metals, and even glass were being implemented in new ways and taking on new characteristics, plastics, on the other hand, were a byproduct of chemical composition and were engineered from the start. Plastics emerged without a mandate or constraints, thus freer to an evolving definition of implementation and use. Bell also reconsidered glass within the context of recent engineering and structural achievements and did well to challenge assumptions about its aesthetic, structural, and spatial potential through a series of contemporary projects. John Klein and Chikara Inamura separately covered additive Manufacturing for Optically Transparent Glass, building on existing manufacturing traditions and introducing new dimensions of novelty across scales by producing unique structures with numerous potential applications in architectural design.[54] Catie Newell additionally pushed the boundaries of robotically fabricated glass research. In exploring the material through form, color, and transparency, she advanced methods using a UR robotic arm to fabricate polychromatic float glass for architectural applications. Notably, Sean Ahlquist would emerge to join Jenny Sabin's biomimetic work in textiles, to lead a unique area of research exploration in fabrics using industrial computer-numerically-controlled (CNC) knitting technology applied to sensorial architecture.[55]

Refining Territories in Digital Fabrication

In terms of rigor and depth, there were those such as Andrew Kudless, who, through his work at *Matsys*, continued to develop the emergent relationships between architecture, engineering, material science, and computation. The early work mentioned in Episode 4 was noted for innovation and craft, but also the illustrated steps for fabrication, which served as a foundation for many others. After numerous pavilions, walls, and objects that gradually scaled up to permanent pavilions, the completion of Confluence Park in San Antonio, TX demonstrated bridging the explorations into a permanent reality.

Adam Marcus and his office of *Variable Projects* similarly commenced a prolific phase of exploratory projects during this time, ranging from craft, materiality, ornament, and pattern. Fabrication underwent the most exhaustive exploratory phase in the last episode and established a growing taxonomy of work produced by a group of speculative practitioners and academics. The explorations were followed up by several pioneers who took on often unique perspectives within the context of this short episode riding on the innovation of the previous decade, including Jason Kelly Johnson and Nataly Gattegno with the office of FutureForms whose formal approach also ventured into responsive and interactive design. Jessica Rosenkrantz and Jesse Louis-Rosenberg took an approach to 3D printing that was a compelling inspiration to the architectural community. Their studio, *Nervous System*, combined many fields using digital fabrication to produce an archetype of design and manufacturing inspired by nature. One of their important contributions was making free, publicly accessible software for direct design-to-manufacturing as a means of mass customization and providing an alternative to mass manufacturing. Instead of creating hundreds, thousands, or millions of the same item, *Nervous System* understood it was creating something that may only appeal to one person (Figure 5.5). Still, the unique customization and personal alignment were the exact justification. Although mass customization had been in the parametric discussion since the beginning, Rosenkrantz and Louis-Rosenberg started small with clothing, jewelry, and products to facilitate the manufacturing aspect with a focus on producing.[56] Says Rosenkrantz, "In nature, there are dynamic processes that respond to their environment and they're different every single time, no two leaves are exactly the same."[57]

Similarly, the mass customization and industrial design intersection of 3D printing and digital fabrication technologies was the work of Behnaz Farahi. She, however, was specifically interested in the relationship to the human body and the emotive, social, and cultural issues it presented. In 2017, she edited an issue of *AD* entitled *3D Printed Body Architecture*.[58] Farahi, similar to some of those in the landscape ecology field, was interested in cultivating a deeper relationship "between the human body and the space around it through implementing emerging technologies."[59] The importance

FIGURE 5.5 The office of *Nervous System* enabled direct design-to-manufacturing as a vehicle to mass customization.

of her work reached beyond strictly technological sophistication or achievements, but rather, as she states, "…addresses critical issues such as feminism, emotion, bodily perception and social interaction."[60]

Skylar Tibbits also fostered a unique response to fabrication growing out of the meticulous assembly processes that proliferated in the pavilions of the last episode. He developed the concepts as the director of the Self-Assembly Lab at MIT, where he pioneered the movement in self-assembly, essentially programming physical materials to build themselves as a bottom-up process. Looking at self-assembly at various scales, Tibbits offered an alternative to the highly choreographed assemblies of the previous two decades. The work of the Self-Assembly Lab has pioneered many different methods whereby disordered parts become an ordered structure through local interaction.[61] Much of this pioneering work on methods such as programmable materials to pneumatics materials (Figure 5.6) is documented in his book *Self-Assembly Lab: Experiments in Programming Matter*,[62] released in 2016.

Many were responsible for advancing robotics in architecture at the time, but the longstanding work of the Gramazio and Kohler Research Group is of particular importance. In 2014, they published *The Robotic Touch: How Robots Change Architecture*[63] with Jan Willmann. Documenting 30 projects developed with robotic fabrication, they offered an unprecedented analysis of robotic fabrication's material and constructive aspects. *Towards a Robotic Architecture* (2018) by Mahesh Daas and Andrew J. Witt was the first to

FIGURE 5.6 The Self-Assembly Lab at MIT led by Skylar Tibbits, pioneered work in programmable materials.

provide a larger classification system, categorization, and taxonomy for robotics in architecture. The book was organized into four sections: *Framing Robotics* (concepts of production), *Robotectonics, Robotic Architecture* (a new language of architecture), and *Robofutures* to present a holistic understanding of the impacts of robots in architecture. In terms of robotic fabrication specifically, by the time of this episode, many schools of architecture had some form of robotic fabrication. The Rob/Arch conference would conduct important global events in 2014, 2016, and 2018. The books from each of these events were published in an ongoing series by Springer entitled *Robotic Fabrication in Architecture, Art and Design*,[64] promoting peer-reviewed papers from the conferences. The years of this episode would see a wide range of sub-topics, including dynamic material feedback, adaptive sensing and actuation, advanced construction, on-site and cooperative robotics, machine learning, human-machine interaction, programming interfaces, and new processes for large-scale automated construction (Figure 5.7).

Robotics at this time were being explored in architecture in various scales and applications. However, after years of experimentation with the adopted tools, Gramazio and Kohler admitted the real potential of robotic fabrication remained unexploited. In particular, they highlighted the greater potential of "their capability for serial production of non-standard elements as well as for varied construction processes."[65] Gramazio and Kohler were also deeply concerned with the possibilities of application at the larger architectural scale. In an important volume of *AD* also published in 2014, they attempted to reconcile these issues and reposition the technology as a game-changer for its potential for the construction industry.

FIGURE 5.7 The Rob/Arch conference continued to advance the global impacts of robots in architecture with Spatial Timber Assemblies at the ETH Zurich's Robotic Fabrication Laboratory.

While many chose to exclusively use robotics, many continued to pursue pluralistic approaches to digital fabrication research and advanced material system and structural system work. The work of Brandon Clifford (often with Wes McGee and the collaborative office of Matter Design) offered a compelling interpretation of fabrication related to bringing the lessons from ancient knowledge to contemporary practice. Clifford is most well-known for bringing megalithic sculptures to life to perform tasks through work that is very much tied to inherent issues of materiality and fabrication. Illustrated in their projects like "Patty & Jan," "Walking Assembly," and "Janus," one also sees the spectacle of architecture. Clifford suggested his interest is not so much defined as "thinking of architecture not as an end product, but as a performance from conception to completion."[66]

As the ICD Pavilions continued to pioneer new methodologies every year, integrating and progressing the discussion of robotic fabrication, a few constructed during this period specifically took materiality to new levels. Wood in particular, was examined for its inherent sustainability and was kick-started with the "HygroSkin – Meteorosensitive Pavilion." Here, Achim Menges and the research team explored climate-responsive architecture through the material properties of wood itself. Menges, along with Oliver Krieg and Tobias Schwinn, published *Advancing Wood Architecture: A Computational Approach*[67] in 2016, documenting the pioneering work in timber and robotic fabrication by four European research institutions. It was an important milestone as it also took on the issues articulated previously by Gramazio and Kohler through sharing in-depth technical information on several large-scale permanent buildings.

Divorced from any specific materiality, novel robotic fabrication and construction methods coupled with advancements in computational processes also led to a renaissance of shell structures. Philippe Block and Tom Van Mele generated numerous compelling research projects from within the Block Research Group at the ETH in Zurich. Many of these research projects and installations were outlined in the 2014 book *Shell Structures for Architecture: Form Finding and Optimization*[68] by Sigrid Adriaenssens, Philippe Block, Diederik Veenendaal, and Chris Williams, which included the techniques behind the analysis, form finding, optimization, and fabrication. The work offered another significant data point in the growing body of fabrication research formulated by combining external information and emerging computational tools. Thus far, examples have been biological systems, landscape and urban ecologies, and material science. In the case of Block and his colleagues, using "principles of traditional unreinforced masonry construction"[69] provided a foil to explore materials, sustainability, circular economies, and new methods for robotic fabrication.

Generative and Parametric Design

The "learn by doing" model of Processing[70] by Reas and Fry was released in a second, updated version in 2014 and was pivotal for designers in a broad range of fields. It was released almost at the same time as *Parametric Design for Architecture* (2013)[71] by Wassim Jabi, which was a fascinating book filled with coding examples for the advanced beginner wishing to sharpen their skills. The printed book, admittedly a challenging medium for code, did not cover visual programming, with the understanding that this could be found online. Rather, the book presented an approach to parametric design at a higher level, "Engaging the parametric and algorithmic processes," argued Jabi, "requires a fundamental mind shift…towards encoding design intent using systematic logic."[72]

Patrik Schumacher released his *Parametricism 2.0: Rethinking Architecture's Agenda for the 21st Century*[73] in 2016 as a follow-up to his 2011 *Autopoiesis*. Similar to the earlier release, Schumacher, through his collection of contributors, continued his unabashed case for parametric design as a global "ism." Schumacher argued that parametricism would soon be able to better address human factors like productivity, social interaction, culture, and well-being.[74] By extension, the data informing impacts related to the sun, gravity, and the wind would be expanded to include measurements of human factors, like how they move and interact in buildings. The data would also take into account historical and cultural factors. As with his contentious first book, Schumacher continued his presentation that the "style" or "movement" would eventually be embraced by all as the defining global style of our age. With this second edition, he expanded on his foundational thesis, and even if some found it difficult to reconcile his definition with his global ambitions, it was clear that parametricism was here to stay.

Although not as theoretically or formally as bold as what was classified as parametric in the discussion previously, BIM tools were also inherently parametric tools, and their impact on the profession was rapidly growing. Fostered by the impetus of building performance issues that were paramount in the Facades+ and Simulation for Architecture and Urban Design (SimAUD)[75] conferences, very high use of BIM was approaching 40% in Western countries and was growing every year.[76] It was important to recognize BIM's differences from a "dumb" 3D model, and at this time, many had transitioned from 2D CAD to 3D modeling but were not using BIM. BIM, and the collaborative processes of openBIM, was rather an information-driven approach with a parametrically integrated database of construction information. This ability to assess environmental impact was a significant development at this moment in time. "BIM has the potential to revolutionize the building industry, and yet not all architects and construction professionals fully understand what the benefits of BIM are or even the fundamental concepts behind it," says Karen Kensek in the book *Building Information Modeling,*[77] released in 2014. That same year, she also co-edited *Building Information Modeling: BIM in Current and Future Practice*[78] with Doug Noble, her colleague at USC, as a massively comprehensive overview of the topic. Sustainability and building performance were not new topics, but once connected to the functionality of BIM, these topics gained increasing attention in the academic and professional worlds. Even further, these topics gained focus through the quantifiable objectives of building performance simulation that are design and construction, as well as operation and control as comprehensively outlined by Pieter de Wilde in the comprehensive book *Building Performance Analysis,*[79] which came out in 2018. Building performance was becoming a major trajectory at that time, with many technical research topics pursued in academia and the building industry looking at multi-domain, dynamic, whole-building analysis (Figure 5.8). There were many

FIGURE 5.8 Sustainability and building performance become connected to the functionality of BIM.

applications, software, and plugins building off the earlier releases of Ecotect and Vasari, and there was a distinction to be made between simulation engines like EnergyPlus and various modeler applications/interfaces. Similar to Design Builder, which ran on the EnergyPlus Engine, Cove.tool was an important new Building Performance Simulation (BPS) tool released in 2017.[80] Geared toward the AECO industry, Cove.tool offered a variety of data-driven analysis tools, one of which was the analysis tool with inclusive analysis that also was heavily geared toward collaboration.

Parallel to building performance was the case made for another "ism" in "performalism" posited by Eran Neuman and Yasha Grobman in their 2013 book *Performalism: Form and Performance in Digital Architecture*.[81] Performalism oscillated between the functional performance and the image-based form. Performalism proposed that computer-based architecture transforms from function to performance in the architectural discourse. Although "performance," as Neuman and Grobman defined it, was broadly interpreted. Well outside the bounds of what is traditionally claimed as the previously described "building performance," all the examples they cite in the book profess a renewed interest in prioritizing performance in architecture, which was often explicitly tied to materiality and fabrication.

Outside of building performance, there was not a lot of new software or hardware released at this time relative to previous episodes. There were, however, several notable developments in VR and AR. The idea of Heilig's Sensorama version of virtual reality, as discussed in Episode 0, finally came into the public realm when the fairly obscure Oculus Rift was bought by the social media giant Facebook. In doing so, Oculus Rift rapidly gained momentum and catalyzed hundreds of companies to begin developing VR products and haptic interfaces. In architecture, a deeper understanding of AR and VR systems began to take place in much easier and cost-effective ways, enabling physical mock-ups and interactive scenarios. Also, professionals were now positioned to communicate among all the stakeholders on a project from different locations, sharing and interacting within the same virtual workspace simultaneously. Microsoft also released the HoloLens MR (Mixed Reality) headset in 2016 to provide a seamless mixed-reality experience. Users could interact with digital content in the context of the physical world around them, leading to more intuitive and immersive experiences. Several years later, in 2019, Trimble released the XR10 interface with the HoloLens intended specifically for the architecture and engineering community (Figure 5.9). The interface provided a platform for people to inhabit their designs naturally, either as a holographic scale model on a tabletop or through an immersive experience from within a digital building model. Ultimately the company released "Trimble Connect," a cloud-based collaboration platform designed to improve the coordination of constructible 3D models and their associated data.

FIGURE 5.9 Microsoft released the HoloLens MR (Mixed Reality) headset to provide a seamless mixed-reality experience.

The Growing Influence of the Profession

New forms of Collaboration and Interaction

This was a time when numerous academic programs also dove into the waters of collaboration on the premise that innovation hinged on putting new ideas into practice. Not unlike the pioneering IAAC or the partnership model of the Media Lab, new academic models of collaboration were also explored within the satellite IDEAS campus at UCLA, pairing studios with non-profit leaders to hold focused research studios. The studio goal was that of students "working directly with leaders in experimental architecture and technology."[82] Key to the success of the IDEAS campus was pairing each studio with a prominent studio director, including architects and thought leaders like Thom Mayne, Greg Lynn, and Frank Gehry.

An unprecedented partnership also occurred in 2014 when Autodesk partnered with David Benjamin's design studio "The Living." It was an interesting experiment to have a small boutique office collaborate with a large R&D department in a company like Autodesk. The idea was that the larger company would allow the small office to do what they were already doing more effectively through connections to an established ecosystem of researchers and research projects. Benjamin's office still worked on commissions for their clients, but from within the context of an environment of people working and thinking about similar and sometimes valuably dissimilar projects, they were also able to bring innovation and creative dialogue to a bigger corporate entity like Autodesk.

Also in 2013, Autodesk commenced the Pier 9 Workshop[83] under Carl Bass and Maurice Conti's leadership to offer additional support to promising researchers (Figure 5.10). In establishing a high-tech facility in San Francisco, the company wanted to showcase and demonstrate the expanded possibilities of making through hardware and software. It was established as an exploratory environment with production-level tools to foster innovation. The workshop was open to employees, but the crux of the initiative lay in the Artist in Residency Program it offered. It was, and still remains, a melting pot for art and technology, providing the tools for making "abstract technologies or concepts legible to members of the public."[84] Other large companies have since set up similar incubators like Trimble's ZeroSixty in 2018 to take advantage of the mutual benefit by fostering emerging firms taking their research projects to the next level.

At this time, computation had become deeply entrenched in the profession, and research had evolved to be legitimate and rigorous, with many offices setting up their in-house laboratories to explore cutting-edge research related to design practice. Professionals began to figure out how to utilize the technology effectively and monetize outcomes with the benefit of research being tied to actual projects. It was a time when the tools began to be used in rigorous and meaningful ways and affected all levels of design and building practices. Work in this sphere focused on data management issues in BIM, workflows, performance-based design, construction management, and

FIGURE 5.10 The Autodesk Workshop at Pier 9 was established as an exploratory environment with production-level tools to foster innovation.

methods, as well as materials and digital fabrication. The work pushing boundaries in architecture came out of many high-profile offices that often became innovators, pioneering demonstrations through built works. The early stories of Gehry, Foster, Grimshaw, and Zaha's offices were repeated now by the likes of SHoP Architects, Diller Scofidio + Renfro, KPF, SOM, HKS, AECOM, and many others. This period marks a flattening out of the knowledge gap between academia and the profession. Previously, the profession appropriated a great deal from academia, but now, many in the professional world began innovating in their own right, often surpassing that being developed in academia. This reflected a multigenerational tier of knowledge operating in some offices, like Foster or Gehry, or a fully digitally conversant practice like SHoP. It also resulted from firms investing in the hardware, software, training, and infrastructure necessary to cultivate their knowledge base that often set up highly innovative technology applications.

Within the offices, there are often the headliners of the offices that received most of the credit, but from a computation standpoint, there were emerging professionals who were the ones who brought the work to build reality. Dennis Sheldon is one such individual who was with Gehry Partners since the computational beginnings with Jim Glymph. Together they co-founded Gehry Technologies back in 2002 as a consulting office for many others in the profession, bridging the gap between internationally renowned designs and actual built architecture. This included the Alice Tully Hall at Lincoln Center for the Performing Arts in New York (Diller Scofidio + Renfro); the Beijing National ("Bird's Nest") Stadium (Herzog & de Meuron); the Louvre Abu Dhabi (Ateliers Jean Nouvel); KAUST Solar Tower in Jeddah, Saudi Arabia (HOK); Projecto Marina in Mexico City (Juan Pablo Serrano). Sheldon remained as Chief Technical Officer until 2014, when Trimble acquired the company. In 2020, he authored *The Disruptors: Technology-Driven Architect-Entrepreneurs* as a special issue of *AD*, exploring a range of technology-driven disruptions to the traditional practice in architecture. It signaled a time, as Sheldon puts it regarding technology-driven, architect-led entrepreneurship, "The identification of a new, unfilled opportunity in the industry, disclosed by advanced knowledge of practice and served by commercial ventured distinct from traditional modes of practice."[85]

Working alongside Sheldon in the early years of Gehry Technologies was Christiano Ceccato, who then left to work at ZHA in 2008. Working on complex and high-profile projects like Galaxy SOHO (2013), he implemented BIM protocols for cost control and management and has since spearheaded ZHA's entry into the aviation market, working on numerous international airports.

Another early Managing Director at Gehry Technologies/Gehry Partners who was previously at Morphosis was Rolando Mendoza, who then left to implement BIM strategies for Walt Disney Imagineering in Shanghai, China, then as Director of Virtual Design and Construction at Mortenson before migrating to be Design Technology Director at Gensler. Mendoza's series of moves illustrates what would become a growing practice of technology professionals being lured to different organizational structures, serving as an impetus to broader technological dissemination.

Another professional education pioneer emerging during this time was Nate Miller, who had been an associate partner at CASE (started by partners David Fano, Federico Negro, and Steve Sanderson) before launching "The Proving Ground" as an architectural technology consulting office solving computational problems including computational design, BIM workflows, sophisticated algorithms, and even methodologies for several high profile clients including HDR, RTKL, Snohetta, NBBJ, UNStudio, AECOM among others. The Proving Ground cultivated a following by making resources and plug-ins they developed readily accessible and holding numerous workshops at conferences like ACADIA, TEX-FAB, and even at professional offices like NBBJ. Similarly, Andy Payne was a computational designer working in the professional world who was interested in "design tooling" and developed. Firefly in 2013 with Firefly, mentioned in the previous episode. In 2015, while at Harvard, Payne worked with Panagiotis Michalatos to create Monolith,[86] one of the first voxel-based multimaterial 3D printing software. Michalatos had previously worked with AKT in London, providing computational solutions to a number of the firm's high-profile projects from 2006–2010. Lastly, it is worth mentioning the team of Mostapha Sadeghipour Roudsarii and Chris Mackey, who created Ladybug in 2012 and Honeybee in 2014 as plug-ins for Grasshopper. Now, as a full-time commercial service LLC, Ladybug Tools has grown to provide in-depth environmental building design capabilities to a wide range of architecture, engineering, and academic outlets.

It was also around this time in 2013 that Dynamo was developed by Ian Keough so that those using Revit could pursue computational design similarly to the way Grasshopper was being used in Rhino. It was brought to life through Matt Jezyk and Zach Kron, and Ian joined their group at Autodesk, where they merged the DesignScript, developed by Robert Aish, and Dynamo teams to create the DesignScript engine driving the Dynamo application. Dynamo was important because it was open-source, providing users clarity on how/why the software was operational and responding with additional commands for the software to become further customizable.

The SmartGeometry group and associated members continued to push boundaries in the practice-centered architectural computing world. Reflecting on the starting point of the organization and its founding members back in 2001 all the way to its current structure in 2013, Brady and Terri Peters edited a new book: *Inside SmartGeometry: Expanding the Architectural Possibilities of Computational Design*.[87] The book puts forth a retroactive manifesto documenting a mixture of diversified approaches ranging from software uses to fabrication techniques to interactive environments. Certainly, from earlier years, looking from an architecture practice standpoint, all the founding members of the SmartGeometry group and most of the workshop attendees were quite accomplished in the professional world, directly bridging the work of SmartGeometry into practice. J. Parrish became Architectural Director and Leader of Arup Sport and then worked at AECOM. Lars Hesselgren, who worked for years at Kohn Pedersen Fox (KPF) in London, became the Director of the Computational Design Research Group at PLP Architects. Hugh Whitehead founded the Specialist Modelling Group at Foster + Partners in 1998, which was responsible for many innovative buildings and consistently pioneered computational design methods as Director of Foster + Partners technology. Similarly to the lineage that came out of Gehry's office was that at Fosters + Partners. Xavier De Kestelier was a partner with the Specialist Modelling Group, working on numerous projects over a 17-year tenure exploring parametric design, digital fabrication, and additive manufacturing, and is notably responsible for his focus on research into space habitats fostering relationships with both NASA and the ESA (Figure 5.11). De Kestelier went on to become a director of SmartGeomerty. Also notable was the 20+ year career of Francis Aish (son of Robert Aish) who was a Partner and Head of Applied Research and Development. He was responsible for developing systems to model and solve complex, multi-disciplinary design problems and was involved in over 200 projects with the office. Lord Norman Foster, gave a keynote at the AAG 2018 Symposium alongside Francis Aish, representing more than half a century of persistent architectural innovation and providing a long-term perspective on the relationship between architecture and technology.

Central to the longevity of SmartGeometry was the computer scientist Robert Aish. As one of the original members and former SG Director, his dedicated focus has continued to guide computation toward design exploration rather than design management. Additional academics important

FIGURE 5.11 The Specialist Modelling Group at Norman Foster's office was one of many emerging in-house research laboratories.

to this period were Robert Woodbury (previously mentioned for his work in parametric design) and Axel Kilian, who was also involved in the very first workshops and has consistently been a pioneer in other emerging organizations including the Design Modelling Symposium and Advances in Architectural Geometry. The design thinking mantra of Aish was shared by Axel Kilian, who published numerous articles during this short episode on design thinking, material sensing and robotics, and architectural geometry.

Conclusion

The trajectories of development in architectural computation have always been incremental. In this episode, the narrowing consolidation of topics followed a preceding moment characterized by broader exploration and experimentation. After almost a decade of development/exploration and experimentation, the taxonomies began to refine themselves yet, at the same time, they opened up through new paradigms of interdisciplinary collaboration. Once the waters had calmed to an extent, there was a wealth of new theories of architecture in a global context finally viewed with enough distance to understand the foundations of the new technological world.

Notes

1 Carpo, M. (2013). *The Digital Turn in Architecture 1992–2012*. Chichester: John Wiley & Sons.
2 Carpo, M. (2017). *The Second Digital Turn: Design Beyond Intelligence*. London: MIT Press.
3 Ibid., p. 68.
4 Bratton, B. H. (2016). *The Stack: On Software and Sovereignty*. Cambridge, MA: MIT Press.
5 Ibid.
6 Bernstein, P. (2018). *Architecture | Design | Data: Practice Competency in the Era of Computation*. Basel: Birkhäuser.
7 Sheldon, D. (ed.) (2020). *The Disruptors: Technology-Driven Architect-Entrepreneurs*. London: Wiley.
8 Ibid.
9 Bernstein, P. (2018). *Architecture | Design | Data: Practice Competency in the Era of Computation*. Basel: Birkhäuser, p. 13.
10 Oxman, R. and Oxman, R. (eds.) (2014). *Theories of the Digital in Architecture*. Oxford: Routledge.
11 Ibid.
12 Ibid.
13 Gerber, D. J. and Ibanez, M. (2015). *Paradigms in Computing: Making, Machines, and Models for Design Agency in Architecture*. New York: eVolo Press.
14 Fox, M. (2009, September 30). "The End of Robotics in Architecture (As We Almost Got to Know It)." *UbiComp*. Available at: https://arl.human.cornell.edu/archibots/Fox_ARCHIBOTS09_2pp.pdf.
15 Blaine B. (2006). *Transmaterial: A Catalog of Materials That Redefine our Physical Environment*. New York: Princeton Architectural Press. See also Mori, T. (2002).

Immaterial/Ultramaterial: Architecture, Design, and Materials. Cambridge, MA: Harvard Design School George Braziller.
16 Ibid., p. xiv.
17 Sou Fujimoto (2013) and Bjarke Ingles (2016) provide examples of the later work directed toward larger issues beyond just material and fabrication methods.
18 Martens, B., Björk, B.-C., and Turk, Z. (2002). "Open, Self-organising Repository for Scientific Information Exchange – The SciX Project." *Proceedings of the 20th International Conference on Education and Research in Computer-Aided Architectural Design in Europe (eCAADe)*. doi:10.52842/conf.ecaade.2002.222
19 Cerovsek, T. and Martens, B. (2016). "CumInCAD 2.0: A Redesigned Scalable Cloud Deployment – Towards Higher Impact with Openness and Novel Features." *Proceedings of the 34th International Conference on Education and Research in Computer-Aided Architectural Design in Europe (eCAADe)*, Volume 1. doi:10.52842/conf.ecaade.2016.1.485
20 Ibid., p. 485.
21 Discussed in Episode 4 and more information available here: https://journals.sagepub.com/home/JAC
22 Brause, C., Ford, C., Kraus, C., Luhan, G., Murray, S., Newman, W. E., Olsen, C., Ripple, J., Schultz, A.-C., Uihlein, M., Wang, J., and Zarzycki, A. (2021). "Reflections on five years of TAD." *Technology|Architecture + Design, 5*(2), 119–120.
23 Robinson J. (2001). "The Form and Structure of Architectural Knowledge: From Practice to Discipline," in J. Robinson and A. Piotrowski (eds.), *The Discipline of Architecture*. Minneapolis: University of Minnesota Press, pp. 61–82.
24 *TAD Journal – Technology* (2019, March 12). Technology | Architecture + Design. See https://tadjournal.org/
25 "ATLAS timeline" (2017, July 20). The ATLAS Institute. See https://www.colorado.edu/atlas/about/atlas-timeline
26 See Al Gore's "An Inconvenient Truth as a Cultural Touchstone." Guggenheim, D. (Director) (2006, May 24). *An Inconvenient Truth* (J. Cassidy, Ed.) [Film]. Paramount Classics. As well as broader discourse surrounding the "Kyoto Protocol" (1997) and growing global activism "Global Day of Action" (2005) Student protests for institutional divestment regarding the use of fossil fuels (2011).
27 Menges, A. and Ahlquist, S. (2011). *Computational Design Thinking*. Chichester: John Wiley & Sons, pp. 8–11.
28 Ibid., p. 15.
29 Mostafavi, M. and Doherty, G. (2010 and 2016). *Ecological Urbanism*. Baden: Lars Müller Publishers.
30 Ibid.
31 Hagan, S. (2014). *Ecological Urbanism: The Nature of the City*. Oxford: Routledge, p. 13.
32 Reed, C. and Lister, N. (2014). *Projective Ecologies*. New York: Actar D, Inc.
33 Cantrell, B. E. and Holzman, J. (2015). *Responsive Landscapes: Strategies for Responsive Technologies in Landscape Architecture*. Oxford: Taylor & Francis.
34 Ibid., p. 5.
35 Spyropoulos, T. and Schumacher, P. (2013). *Adaptive Ecologies: Correlated Systems of Living*. Lodnon: Architectural Association.
36 Ibid.
37 Frazer, J. (1995). *An Evolutionary Architecture*. London: Architectural Association Publications, Themes VII, John Frazer and the Architectural Association, p. 6.
38 Kolarevic, B. and Parlać, V. (2015). *Building Dynamics: Exploring Architecture of Change*. Oxford: Taylor & Francis.
39 Joachim, M. and Silver, M. (2017). *XXL-XS: New Directions on Ecological Design*. Actar D, Inc.
40 Hensel, M., Menges, A., and Weinstock, M. (2013). *Emergent Technologies and Design: Towards a Biological Paradigm for Architecture*. Oxford: Taylor & Francis.

41 Ibid., p. 11.
42 Bar-Cohen, Yoseph. (2006). "Biomimetics – Using nature to inspire human innovation." *Bioinspiration & Biomimetics*, 1.
43 Frazer, J. (1995). *An Evolutionary Architecture,* London: Architectural Association Publications, Themes VII, John Frazer and the Architectural Association. p 7.
44 Pask, G. (Introduction) and Frazer, J. (1995). *An Evolutionary Architecture*. London: Architectural Association Publications, Themes VII, John Frazer and the Architectural Association.
45 Antonelli, P. (2020). *The Neri Oxman Material Ecology Catalogue*. New York: Museum of Modern Art.
46 Knippers, J., Nickel, K. G., and Speck, T. (2016). *Biomimetic Research for Architecture and Building Construction: Biological Design and Integrative Structures*. New York: Springer.
47 Bechthold, M. and Weaver, J. C. (2017). "Materials Science and Architecture." *Nature Reviews Materials, 2*(12). doi:10.1038/natrevmats.2017.82
48 Bechthold, M., Kane, A., and King, N. (2015). *Ceramic Material Systems: In Architecture and Interior Design*. Germany: Walter de Gruyter GmbH.
49 Wood, D. M., Correa, D., Krieg, O. D., and Menges, A. (2016). "Material Computation—4D Timber Construction: Towards Building-Scale Hygroscopic Actuated, Self-Constructing Timber Surfaces." *International Journal of Architectural Computing, 14*(1), 49–62. doi:10.1177/1478077115625522
50 Bell, M. and Buckley, C. (2010). *Solid States: Concrete in Transition*. Princeton, NJ: Princeton Architectural Press.
51 Bell, M. and Buckley, C. (2012) *Post-Ductility: Metals in Architecture and Engineering*. Princeton, NJ: Princeton Architectural Press.
52 Bell, M. and Buckley, C. (2014). *Permanent Change: Plastics in Architecture and Engineering*. Princeton, NJ: Princeton Architectural Press.
53 Bell, M. and Kim, J. (2009). *Engineered Transparency: The Technical, Visual, and Spatial Effects of Glass*. Princeton, NJ: Princeton Architectural Press.
54 Klein, J. (2015). *Additive Manufacturing of Optically Transparent Glass*. Massachusetts Institute of Technology, School of Architecture and Planning, Program in Media Arts and Sciences. See also Inamura, C. (2017). *Towards a New Transparency: High Fidelity Additive Manufacturing of Transparent Glass Structures Across Scales*. Cambridge, MA: MIT, School of Architecture and Planning, Program in Media Arts and Sciences.
55 Reichert, S., Menges, A., and Correa, D. (2015). "Meteorosensitive Architecture: Biomimetic Building Skins Based on Materially Embedded and Hygroscopically Enabled Responsiveness." *Computer-Aided Design, 60*, 50–69. doi:10.1016/j.cad.2014.02.010
56 See https://n-e-r-v-o-u-s.com/projects/software/
57 Lenander, J. (2015). "Future Couture: Nervous System's Kinematics Dress." MoMA, March 26, 2015. Available at: https://www.moma.org/explore/inside_out/2015/03/26/future-couture-nervous-systems-kinematics-dress/ [accessed January 18, 2024].
58 Leach, N. and Farahi, B. (eds.) (2018). *3D-Printed Body Architecture*. Chichester: John Wiley & Sons.
59 "Bio." Behnaz Farahi. See https://behnazfarahi.com/bio/ [accessed January 21, 2024].
60 Ibid.
61 Tibbits, S. (2013). "The Emergence of 4D Printing." [Video] In *TED Talks*. See https://www.ted.com/talks/skylar_tibbits_the_emergence_of_4d_printing?language=en
62 Tibbits, S. (2016). *Self-Assembly Lab: Experiments in Programming Matter*. Oxford: Taylor & Francis.
63 Gramazio, F., Kohler, M., and Willmann, J. (2014). *The Robotic Touch: How Robots Change Architecture*. Zurich: Park Books.

64 Reinhardt, D., Saunders, R., and Burry, J. (2016). *Robotic Fabrication in Architecture, Art and Design*. New York: Springer.
65 Gramazio, F. and Kohler, M. (2014). *Made by Robots: Challenging Architecture at a Larger Scale*. Chichester: John Wiley & Sons.
66 Matter Design. See https://www.matterdesignstudio.com/ [accessed December 12, 2023].
67 Menges, A., Tobias S., and Oliver D. K. (2016). *Advancing Wood Architecture: A Computational Approach*. Oxford: Routledge.
68 Adriaenssens, S., Block, P., Veenendaal, D., and Williams, C. (2014). *Shell Structures for Architecture: Form Finding and Optimization*. Oxford: Routledge.
69 "Prof. Dr. Philippe Block – Bio." Block Research Group. See https://block.arch.ethz.ch/brg/people/philippe-block [accessed December 14, 2023].
70 Reas, C. and Fry, B. (2014). *Processing: A Programming Handbook for Visual Designers and Artists*. London: MIT Press.
71 Jabi, W. (2013). *Parametric Design for Architecture*. London: Laurence King Publishing.
72 Ibid., p. 9.
73 Schumacher, P. (2016). *Parametricism 2.0: Rethinking Architecture's Agenda for the 21st Century*. United Kingdom: Wiley.
74 Ibid.
75 See https://www.simaud.org/
76 SmartMarket Report (2014). *The Business Value of BIM for Owners*. Columbus, OH: McGraw Hill Construction, pp. 1–64.
77 Kensek, K. M. (2014). *Building Information Modeling*. Oxford: Taylor & Francis.
78 Kensek, K. and Noble, D. (2014). *Building Information Modeling: BIM in Current and Future Practice*. Chichester: John Wiley & Sons.
79 de Wilde, Pieter. (2018). *Building Performance Analysis*. Chichester: John Wiley & Sons.
80 See https://cove.tools/products/analysis-tool
81 Grobman, Y. J. and Neuman, E. (2013). *Performalism: Form and Performance in Digital Architecture*. Oxford: Routledge.
82 *On the Ground: UCLA's new IDEAS campus*. (n.d.). Archinect. Seehttps://archinect.com/news/article/87928096/on-the-ground-ucla-s-new-ideas-campus.
83 See https://www.autodesk.com/technology-centers [accessed December 14, 2023].
84 "Pier 9 Artists in Residence Program." Sarah Brin, July 27, 2016. See https://sarahbrin.com/?p=730 [accessed December 14, 2023].
85 Sheldon, D. (2020). *The Disruptors: Technology-Driven Architect-Entrepreneurs*. Chichester: Wiley, p. 8.
86 Michalatos, P. and Payne, A. (2016). "Monolith: The Biomedical Paradigm and the Inner Complexity of Hierarchical Material Design." *Proceedings of the 34th International Conference on Education and Research in Computer Aided Architectural Design in Europe (eCAADe)*, Volume 1. doi:10.52842/conf.ecaade.2016.1.445
87 Peters, T. and Peters, B. (2013). *Inside SmartGeometry: Expanding the Architectural Possibilities of Computational Design*. Berlin: Wiley.

EPISODE 6

PARADIGMS (2019–2024)

Episode 6 is a story with a beginning still awaiting an ending. It is also somewhat of a new beginning altogether, and the potentially profound and far-reaching impacts of AI on architectural computing may likely dwarf anything that has been accomplished thus far. Unlike previous episodes, where specific markers delineated arcs to important periods, the present moment is defined more by open-ended developments and global events. Still, even in the impending shadow of AI, it is possible to see how computation in architecture progressed along several trajectories from 2019 to 2024. Although these trajectories were not equal in energy or influence, they established important contributions to existing foundations introduced in the previous episodes. What does stand out with a degree of profundity is the scale, complexity, and speed at which these aspects of our world present opportunities for response.

By 2019, pervasive computing started to saturate daily life. From wearables to automated tasks, the move of digital technologies to the background of life was well underway. So, too, was the implementation process into all phases of architectural operations. The hardware and software tools were no longer novel. From awareness to mastery, the spectrum of acceptance replaced previous luddite tendencies that painted a false dichotomy between analog and digital practices and pedagogies. We can attribute this to the fact that many of those who spent some or all of their career in an analog process were now largely no longer in the workforce. By contrast, we are transitioning into a moment where leadership, in general, is digitally capable, even digitally fluent, and it will not be too far off that the next generation of leadership is a fully digital native.[1]

Additionally, one advantageous outcome within the academic community was the continued refinement of research toward solving problems.

DOI: 10.4324/9781032671208-8

Previously, there were early growing pains of a relatively new field in computational design research, being self-focused and unable to build upon multiple decades or centuries of previous research work like other science and engineering fields. As academics and practitioners applied greater rigor throughout the field over the years, there was also a simultaneous awareness that research focus areas were expanding. By the late 2010s and early 2020s, research was underway to examine larger "wicked" problems. The Paris Accord in 2015 and the subsequent 17 SDGs (Sustainable Development Goals) provided a framework for many to recalibrate and focus their efforts. The inclusion of issues related to climate change, ecology, social justice, equity, poverty, and public health laid new groundwork and ways of engaging computational design research.

This period was also seismically shifted due to the global COVID-19 pandemic. Nothing more profoundly impacted personal and professional lives than the unprecedented issues surrounding COVID-19. Architecture was not exempt; consequently, computational tools and the digital environment evolved rapidly in response. From the places people worked and studied to how they worked and studied, the pandemic transformed life with such breadth and depth that returning to pre-pandemic operations was impossible. Yet the prior years of software and hardware development laid the groundwork for implementing the progressive applications that came to the fore during this time. Most prevalent was the necessary embrace of collaborative work environments, including Zoom, Microsoft Teams, Google Meet, and Webex, as well as Visual Collaboration Platforms such as Conceptboard, Miro, Mural, Stormboard, and Lucid Visual Collaboration Suite. Overnight, the profession learned to work collaboratively at a distance, leapfrogging past developments in this area. This period would also see continued advances in both scale and material exploration for additive manufacturing and critical developments for AR/VR/SR, impacting all aspects of the design to post-occupancy phases of the AECO industry. Digital Twinning became a strategic digital modeling trend, even though it has been available and used by some in the industry for over two decades.

The most significant and pervasive trajectory during this time has undoubtedly been Artificial Intelligence (AI). Like all these topics, AI is nascent in application and impact, yet it has been culturally latent and present for nearly seven decades. Over the past several years, the common perception is that AI has burst out into the open and become an inescapable aspect of everything we see and do, fueled by developments in Large Language Models (LLMs) and OpenAI's release of Chat GPT.[2] Much of this perceptual duality is found in the definitions of early Classic AI versus Deep Learning AI,[3] with the current fascination being the latter. Architecture has certainly been included in this wave of enthusiasm and exploration. More information, collaboration, integration, deeper analysis, and faster processing will produce a more robust decision-making process related to the environments created, whether built *or virtual*. While not the newest trajectory, AI promises to be the most far-reaching, potentially impacting all other trajectories.

Responsible Research Evolves

A decade earlier, many firms and researchers identified in previous episodes employed methodological plurality to explore new computational agendas. As these matured, gaining more "tools" or similar conceptual partnerships was insufficient. What became fruitful was to engage the complex problems more directly with a team of diverse experts leveraging computation as a common language or research tool. It is here that more succinct paradigms emerge. As mentioned in previous episodes, *IJAC* and CumInCAD[4] were two substantive advancements in computational design research. The first issue of *IJAC*, published in 2003, focused on VR, the Internet, and C++. Twenty years later, a more recent issue focuses on the *challenges of designing for human and planetary health*. In the last several years, no other topics have continued to direct computational research as much as the expansion of ecological, biological, and social systems. The seeds of these research areas were introduced in Episode 5 and continue with increased focus moving into this episode. There came about an evolving synergistic overlap in how these terms interact and an ongoing development of a framework to leverage digital technology and design thinking to solve increasingly complex problems. With the acknowledgment of research from groups formed over a decade earlier, like the Living Architecture Systems Group,[5] Future Cities Laboratory (FCL) Global,[6] and The Senseable City Lab at MIT,[7] many continued contributions during this time, furthering the push for integrated research fields.

Ecological, Biological, and Social Systems

At the start of the 2020s, the use of digital technology to integrate biological and material systems had pushed the trajectory into a greater level of interest for a growing audience. The growing cultural awareness of designers, architects, and researchers producing work in this area has increased. Early pioneers like Neri Oxman continued her case for biomorphic material synthesis in her "Material Ecology' exhibition at the Museum of Modern Art in 2020. As well as the previously mentioned fashion designer Iris van Herpen's growing international recognition for her ability to bring to life bio-inspired compositions from "dendrite drawings of neuroscientist Santiago Ramón y Cajal and the hydrozoa organisms" in her Spring '21 collection. From the 3D printed bio-sculpture "H.O.R.T.U.S. XL Astaxanthin.g" by ecoLogicStudio at the Pompidou (2019) to the more everyday object work of Biomedical Engineer and computational designer Nolan Kim, biomorphic and biophilic penetrated the broader context of our lives.

There also continued to be the next step in deepening academic research in this area. Dana Cupkova, at Carnegie Mellon University, would continue her work in ecological attunement, addressing the use of computational design and enhanced material strategies to confront a post-industrial, extreme urban environment.[8] Like others working in this space, her work continued to employ broader ecological systems thinking while confronting an environmental ethic.

Others, like Christina Cogdell, point out that when examining biological and morphologically derived concepts, one must be vigilant about terminology and conception appropriation. Her 2019 book *Toward a Living Architecture? Complexism and Biology in Generative Design*[9] builds a case based on contemporary biological sciences and seeks a more rigorous definition of sustainability while clarifying design concepts apart from the simple application of generative design methodology. The terminology, be it misappropriated, overused, or incorrectly applied, has flattened meaning. Some, like John Nastasi and his co-editors in the 2018 *AD* issue *SU+RE Sustainable + Resilient Design Systems*,[10] suggested re-energizing the mandate by clarifying the need for urgency through the lens of direct and even catastrophic human and environmental impact.

Continued development on digitally fabricated materials with sustainable outcomes has become a significant focus. Additionally, advanced materials research, especially when applied to sustainable building skins, has continued to expand from the nanoscale to the macroscale, creating entirely different strategies for environmental impact based on material science.[11] Across the spectrum, there was a broadening discourse about the materials we use to construct our built environment. Mycelium-based research rose to attention through David Benjamin's PS1 "Hy-Fi" installation in 2014 and, more recently, in his *Alive Pavilion* for the Venice Architecture Biennale in 2021. Benjamin's The Living demonstrates the effective use of organic materials with microbial properties to consider how a healthier and more sustainable built environment may not be far off (Figure 6.1). Implementing materials with lower carbon footprint, insulative properties, workforce selection, and economic benefits are driving material exploration innovation. From sugarcane[12] and coffee ground mixtures[13] in block construction to 3D printed products that facilitate non-human growth,[14] there is a rising consciousness about the sophistication of our material systems and how a broader life-cycle assessment could generate new outcomes.

The expanded focus on urban issues became a top priority for many researchers and design practices. With over half of the world's population currently living in metropolitan areas, which is expected to reach 70% by 2050,[15] there is an urgency to address many of the developing issues related to rapid growth. From civic infrastructure to social networks and affordable housing to surveillance systems, computational design technologies are helping researchers and designers navigate complex urban problems and evaluate possible opportunities.

FIGURE 6.1 The Alive Pavilion, created for the 2021 Venice Architecture Biennale, incorporates diverse microbial materials that respond to microclimates.

Responsibility and opportunity have driven discourse within the computational design field and connected this dialogue more broadly to a body of conceptual thinking. To that end, Graham Harman's writings on Heidegger,[16] specifically tools (equipment), and most recently, his latest publication on object-oriented ontology (OOO) theory and architecture have proven impactful.[17] Timothy Morton shares a similar space for his connection to (OOO) and his discussion of Hyperobjects.[18] Both contributed to a broader discourse of post-anthropocentric landscapes imbued with new ecological thinking. Not surprisingly, Donna Haraway's 1985 *Cyborg Manifesto*[19] has gained renewed interest as it aligns with post-humanist, post-anthropocentric ideas while also introducing thoughts on new materialism, ecofeminism, and a perspective of climate disaster resulting from forces she calls the *capitalocene*.[20]

As mentioned earlier, the complexity and scale of the issues related to climate change, social justice, and urban growth often mean categorizing those involved in a reductive manner. Identifying researchers and practitioners through overly simplified categories contradicts the systems design thinking employed by the most innovative players in this area. Those working in the eco-bio-social systems design space often find footing in the applications of objects, zones, and territories, leveraging transcalar approaches to address these issues. The point is made in the work of Kate Orff in the realm of regenerative landscape and social engagement with her work at the Center for Resilient Cities and Landscapes[21] and Neeraj Bhatia as he explores ecological and adaptive urbanism in his work with the Open Workshop and the Urban Works Agency.[22] The work of Kathy Velikov and Geoffry Thün (RVTR) also blends across these intersections as they engage with transcalar implementation into the "continually evolving ecologies: biotic, social, environmental, technological and cultural."[23]

Urban and Social Technology

In a context where everything is digital, simply being digitally driven was no longer a useful identifier for computational projects. The intersection of increasingly complex global problems with the capacity to analyze and model solutions for those problems placed the design disciplines in a valued position. The maturing computational design research around eco-bio-social design suggests opportunities that did not exist in the past. Many began to tackle the realm of research's urban-social-political dimensions, undertaking issues related to expressing or even exposing the systems that might otherwise go unnoticed. This work often focused on the technogenic, for instance, employing drone and photogrammetry technology, produces unprecedentedly large data sets requiring additional computational means to distill useful information. The work of Ersela Kripa and Stephen Mueller (Agency Architecture) on the US/Mexico border is an example of this approach, and their recent book *Fronts: Military Urbanisms and the Developing World* (2020)[24] examines the relationship between the security complex and the urban morphologies of the developing world. From Rafael Lozano-Hemmer's 1997 "Re:Positioning Fear, Relational Architecture 3"[25] installation, to the more recent "Teeter-totter Wall"[26] (2019) by Rael San Fratello, designers have continued critical explorations of broader socio-cultural issues to expand the dialogue. From a more global perspective, Jose Sanchez builds off his combinatorial work of the past decade (Episode 4) in his book *Architecture for the Commons, Participatory Systems in the Age of Platforms* (2020).[27] Here, Sanchez provides an in-depth look at the failings of certain digital theories and methods of the past four decades, coupled with political philosophies such as neoliberalism and "trickle-down economics." Sanchez, along with others like Gilles Retsin, Mollie Claypool, and the work of Daniel Koehler on Mereological Urbanism, calls for a new way of looking at production, manufacturing, economics, and the larger communities they aggregate into.[28]

There is a boldness for those working in this space. As Mitra Kanaani points out in her book *Ecological Design Thinking* (2022),[29] these researchers are simultaneously working as specialists and trans- and inter-disciplinarians, reaching beyond conventional boundaries. They exhibit dexterity in working through complex problems by implementing computational toolsets, producing some of the most compelling developments in this research area.

Advanced Structural and Material Integration

Advanced structural systems to digital heritage and even space exploration all presented promising areas for enhancing research moving toward application in the built environment. In these areas, the history of R&D is relatively well-defined. Many working in these areas are building off a strong foundation of pioneers. In the case of advanced structural systems, architectural engineering has offered some of the most innovative work. Many find structural inspiration in the work of Pier Luigi Nervi, Félix Candella, and Antoni Guadí and their use of non-Euclidean forms with the methodological procedures of ARUP, Buro Happold, Cecil Balmond, and Adams Kara Taylor. The most recent developments led to the deepening integration of new hybrid material systems, often incorporating carbon fiber for strength or an admixture substitute in concrete for strength and carbon footprint neutralization.[30] The work of Sawako Kaijima, in particular, integrates architectural, structural, and environmental knowledge to explore novel form-finding designs. Robotic fabrication also offered new opportunities for precision and additive fabrication production.[31] Current examples do not represent large-scale structures/infrastructure but connect to future opportunities. The recently completed 12 metre long pedestrian bridge in Amsterdam represents a new benchmark for 3D printed (additive manufacturing) construction (Figure 6.2). Developed by Joris Laarman Lab in

FIGURE 6.2 12m long 3D printed stainless steel bridge in Amsterdam. Design and fabrication by Joris Laarman Lab and MX3D, with structural and parametric services by ARUP.

collaboration with MX3D and ARUP, the bridge is fabricated from approximately 4.5 tons of stainless steel.

Current research publication interest in this field points toward the refinement of topology through evolutionary structural optimization (ESO) and bi-directional evolutionary structural optimization (BESO).[32] This method links material and fabrication efficiencies, given no pre-existing starting point for a structural determination – meaning only the material essential to structural integrity is robotically fabricated. NASA has also pursued this 3D printing technology with the help of AI for titanium scaffolding on their EXCITE Telescope (Figure 6.3). Providing superior strength at only one-third the weight. With the additional advantage of rapid production times, one-off manufacturing, and the ability to combine part assemblies into a single ensemble,[33] the AI-enabled additive manufacturing process has a key initiative for In-space Servicing, Assembly, and Manufacturing (ISAM) capabilities, which in turn is central to US planning on creating new space infrastructure.[34]

As Sylvia Lavin has pointed out, the limited programmatic function, economic proposition, and, at times, less than resolved detailing open pavilions up for critical evaluation in the academic setting.[35] However, in certain instances where the pavilion provides applied research testing, it is clear the evidence can be useful in advancing innovation in the broader field of architecture. As

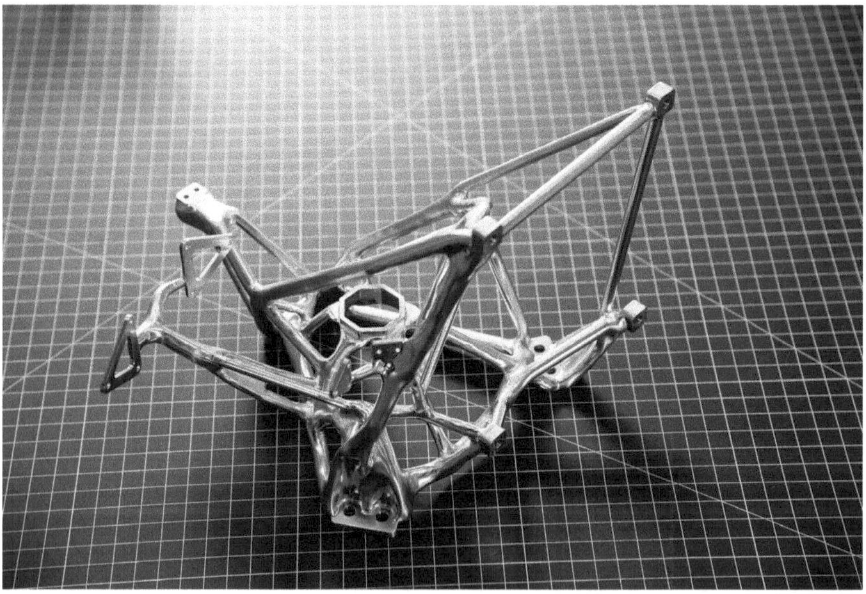

FIGURE 6.3 The AI-assisted 3D printed titanium scaffolding for the EXCITE telescope spectrometers was fabricated in 2023. The structure is designed to hold mirrors and instruments while also preserving laser pathways and room for hands to maneuver around for adjustment.

discussed in Episode 4, the ICD and ITKE pavilions represent an interesting test case for this type of applied research. Isolating methodology and materiality such that some would suggest the qualitative outcomes overshadow the quantitative outcomes. When looking at carbon fiber research, the ICD and ITKE Carbon Fiber Pavilions, there has been a growing body of data to expand a clearer understanding of the structural potential of this material when robotically woven. From 2013 through 2018, four installations utilized robotically constructed carbon fiber composite structures. This work examines *in situ* and off-site construction, weaving, assembly procedures, and morphological tectonic innovation issues. Most recently, the material research shifted in 2022 to flax fiber, a material that was "fully naturally renewable, biodegradable and regionally available."[36] The BUGA Fibre Pavilion[37] completed in 2019 (Figures 6.4 and 6.5) works from the preceding carbon fiber research and larger biomimetic research of the past decade. The pavilion spans 400 sq. meters and weighs five times less than a conventional steel structure due to material, component design, and fabrication methods. Additionally, the ICD/ITKE has completed two structures as a broader public demonstration of this research. In 2021, for the 17th International Architecture Exhibition – La Biennale di Venezia 2021, The Maison Fibre 2021[38] demonstrated a potential future material culture of de-materialization where, in the case of their pavilion, the two-story structure's overall weight was reduced 50-fold.

FIGURE 6.4 Robotic weaving took place at FibR GmbH where all components were produced. The structure is made from more than 100,000 meters of spatially arranged glass and carbon fibers.

FIGURE 6.5 The BUGA Fibre Pavilion, a robotically woven composite fabrication, was constructed off-site in 2019 and brought to the Bundesgartenschau grounds in Heilbronn. The completed structure covers 400 square meters and spans more than 23 meters.

While the pavilion can provide an applied research environment for testing materials and formal assemblies, there is a longstanding tradition of embedded complexity inherent in the production and configuration process of thousands of mass-customized parts. Skylar Tibbits offers a different perspective on this issue by leveraging what he calls material computation. For Tibbits, "material computation imagines embedding some of the more complex properties of today's digital forms of computing into material objects, such as modularity or reconfiguration (like the copy/paste function), or replication and error correction..."[39] He further elaborates that this can be achieved through morphological computation, which is the relationship between material, geometry, and computing.[40]

Digital Preservation

Digital Preservation has been a growing research field over the past two decades. A significant threshold was crossed in 2015 when the document concerning the *"Preservation of, and Access to, Documentary Heritage Including in Digital Form"*[41] was directly connected to the UNESCO Charter on Preservation of Digital Heritage from 2003.[42] While the majority of the significant advancements address the identification of cultural heritage associated with digital media, the broader extension of these efforts formalizes awareness of how digital technologies like LiDAR, photogrammetry, structured light scanning, and drone scanning are all now advancing documentation of cultural and historically significant structures and sites. CyARK[43] and the Virtual World Heritage Laboratory[44] at Indiana University are examples of leading expert organizations working globally to expand the knowledge and reach of this field. The increased formalized activity by these and others has transformed how spatial documentation hardware and software are being developed and funded. Like most forms of digital documentation, recent improvements to capturing detail (resolution) of structures and context have vastly improved. Still, experts in digital technology and the cultural heritage fields offer concerns about too strong a reliance on the technology, given it could flatten or even erase some tactile qualities that preserve these structures.[45] AR/VR technologies mitigate some of this concern by providing an immersive experience. Recent trends, especially in the EU, suggest that AR is being relied upon specifically to reconstruct sites and buildings, providing insights that would not otherwise be possible.[46] On April 15, 2019, the world watched as Notre Dame burned and subsequently accelerated public discourse regarding the more than "$4 trillion of at-risk assets around the globe," says Nicolas Mangon, VP of AEC Strategy & Marketing at Autodesk.[47] With natural disasters, war, and aging infrastructure, more transparent strategies for proactive cultural preservation have become central to governmental policies based on recognizing this growing urgency.[48]

Space Architecture

At the other end of the spectrum from preserving our cultural past, extraterrestrial architecture has gained momentum over the past few years within the architectural community, with governmental space agencies and major aerospace contractors spurring a renewed interest in near orbit and interplanetary exploration.[49] Several significant technological and material advancements have led to breakthroughs for new proposals for Project Olympus as a part of the Moon's Artemis mission.[50] Further out are the Mars missions, but simulated projects are already underway with the Crew Health and Performance Exploration Analog (CHAPEA)[51] project and the Mars Science City in the United Arab Emirates.[52] The continued work of Xavier De Kestelier, who brought his focus on research into space habitats done at Norman Foster's office with both NASA and the ESA to Hassel Studio. In the case of the Mars simulation projects and the Moon project, the design team of BIG-Bjarke Ingels Group and SEArch+[53] are working directly with ICON 3D Technology Company to utilize new advancements in large-format 3D printing technologies. For CHAPEA, the four-crew member team has lived in a 1700 sq ft 3D printed structure simulating Mars habitation. The mission will last 378 days and is followed by two more missions to gather additional data in anticipation of future habitation in Mars Science City and eventually Mars.[54] For its part, NASA has provided impetus and direction by holding several recent competitions[55] for 3D printed habitats, encouraging multi-disciplinary design and engineering teams to compete to advance the construction technology needed to create sustainable housing solutions in space.

Progressive Applications

Over the past several years, many digital tools and methods have followed a similar arc to the maturing research just covered. For example, work done in additive manufacturing, AR/VR, and digital twinning all benefited from previous foundational decades of innovation and development. Growing understanding and acceptance of foundational work repositions the learning curve and allows innovators to push into bolder developmental territories. Several decades ago, one could describe computational innovation in design applications as acts of creation, discovery, and appropriation. Current innovation is more nuanced and progresses through scale, speed, integration, and diffusion. Deepening research means scholars are building upon existing bodies of knowledge, working across disciplines to find interdisciplinary and cross-disciplinary opportunities. In this regard, there is a scaffolding to work from. In the past, this was much harder to identify if it existed. The speed at which communication, assimilation, and awareness transpires brings almost instant proliferation to discovery and advancement.

Additive Manufacturing

Additive manufacturing has widely transformed the aerospace, automotive, and medical industries and, to a lesser extent, has impacted the fashion and food industries.[56] Architecture has not been exempted, and as mentioned in Space Architecture, there is considerable interest in large-scale applications for off-planet printing of habitable structures. Large-format 3D printing advancements over the past decade have refined strength, admixtures, and rheology. Also, categorizing the application into large-scale components, large-format formwork, and monolithic on-site structures,[57] provides a more detailed opportunity to refine the research and development trajectories. Full-scale buildings no longer represent the challenge for onsite monolithic structures, and numerous have been completed to this date, passing the hurdles of logistics and code compliance. How big[58] and fast[59] becomes the next target for some working in this area. The 3D concrete printing industry is expected to grow from $210 million in 2022 to $9.095 billion by 2031, representing a 52% compounded annual growth rate.[60] Regulations, subsidies, and public policies will help to expedite market expansion in some parts of the world. For instance, in Dubai, 25% of construction is expected to be 3D printed concrete by 2030.[61]

Some companies and designers are moving into the mass production space. Entrepreneurial start-ups around the world are leading the growth, each finding a focus on one of the three categories of application methods and developing gantry and robotic arm printing technology.[62] ICON 3D Technology Company, mentioned in the Space Architecture section earlier, in partnership with Lennar Homes and the Bjarke Ingels Group (BIG), is working on an ambitious project of producing 100 3D printed concrete homes north of Austin, TX. The Wolf Ranch community, taking specific cues harkening back to the ambitions of the post-WWII tract homes, offers variety, speed, and durability as marketing features for future homeowners.[63] Similarly, other regions worldwide in the US, Europe, and Asia-Pacific are all seeing similar start-up companies with ambitious plans for multi-unit domestic projects and smaller cultural and community-focused projects slated for 2024 to 2030.[64]

Beyond scale and speed, developments in materials and material science for 3D printing offer further opportunities for advancement for architects, engineers, and those in the design profession. As Martin Bechtold[65] and others mentioned in previous episodes have pointed out, the interest in sustainability, material science, and smart materials now catalyzes design innovation. Specifically, that the creation and production of digital materials have accelerated this trajectory; 3D printing, from the nanoscale to the macro scale, sits at the center of this research and technological advancement. While other industry applications have advanced 3D printing for prototyping or product manufacturing[66] well ahead of architectural applications, architecture and design have recently built upon a growing foundation of success. Ron Rael and Virginia San Fratello's book *Printing Architecture*[67] (2018) identifies the opportunity for what materials can be 3D printed, which is completely wide open. In this book, Rael and San Fratello demonstrate projects from their firm, Emerging Objects,[68] printed from wood, salt, rubber, bioplastics, and even coffee (Figure 6.6).

Polymers, ceramics, and steel provide the most immediate and direct cross-over opportunities for 3D printed materials beyond concrete. On more minor scales, the ubiquity of PLA, PP, PSA, and ABA plastics covers a broad portion of the printed material portfolio and has almost supplanted traditional architectural model-making, becoming ubiquitous in the contemporary design studio. However, it is less likely that such styrene based materials will have a significant direct impact when moving to a larger scale due to strength and sustainability concerns. In the realm of plastics, shape memory polymers (SMPs) offer some of the most speculative but compelling research in the future.[69] Thermo-regulated polymers[70] and swellable polymers[71] provide a responsive material capable of dynamic and "programmable" or controlled outcomes for formal transformation. These materials have been explored at the furniture and interior surface scale. Low-modulus polymers offer a different trajectory. For this application, the 3D printed

FIGURE 6.6 3D Printed Cabin by Rael San Fratello of Emerging Objects in 2018. Planter Tile shapes and materials create a living wall of succulents. Several different materials were used, including shades of Portland cement, sawdust, and Chardonnay pomace.

polymer is developed as geometrically adaptive polymer foam, providing unique structural application opportunities introducing micro and mezzo dynamic capabilities.[72] For ceramic 3D printing, similar to concrete printing, equipment, rheology, and admixtures,[73] have provided advancement opportunities in full-scale printing. A compelling material choice due to accessibility, sustainability, and cost efficiency, researchers and designers are now pushing further into different design fronts. From mass-customized pottery[74] to artificial coral in the Maldives[75] to self-supporting monolithic structures (Figure 6.7), the use of ceramics in 3D printing is taking on a variety of new directions.

Enhancing more conventional applications of facade components, ceramic 3D printing can now leverage material science and geometric specificity to improve building performance. Thermal and acoustic performance are areas of interest in ceramic facade printing research and application.[76] Metals in 3D printing (additive manufacturing) have a long history for industrial design applications. Specifically in the aerospace, automotive, marine manufacturing, and medical fields, the R&D has an extensive foundation. When crossing into architecture, the research again builds upon appropriation. However, the principles of adoption build off many of the same principles. The opportunity to print lighter-weight structural members with equal or greater structural performance, the ability to utilize specialized

FIGURE 6.7 Image of Wasp 3D printing for MC A – Mario Cucinella Architects. The TECLA supporting structure is sourced from local soils and represents a broader area of research being done in the area of self-supporting full-scale 3D printed structures.

materials or multi-material printing, or the geometric and cost opportunities afforded by printing make this as compelling for architecture as other industrial design applications.[77] Tubular column printing and monolithic I-beam are now possible, with continued research to demonstrate the structural effectiveness of the optimization and material efficiency process.[78] The near future implementation possibilities across an entire project suggest that at a limited scope, this method could offer structural, material, and construction efficiencies not currently available through traditional methods. Beyond full member printing, component printing is presently under development. ARUP first developed optimized nodal printing of titanium steel in 2015[79] but has more recently been advanced by MX3D for the Takenaka Corporation in Japan. MX3D, mentioned earlier for their work on the fully 3D printed bridge in Amsterdam, has developed this latest metal joint using stainless steel via a Wire Arc Additive Manufacturing (WAAM) printing system, allowing for further structural reinforcement to take place via cast mortar filling the internal cavities of the wire printed node. In addition to homogenous 3D printing advancements, heterogenous 3D printing developments have also made substantial advances. Multi-Material Advanced Manufacturing (MMAM) is now a highly diverse and sophisticated material science and structural engineering research area. Multi nozzle or deposition extrusion now allows for various material performance outcomes.[80] Variable-density aggregate concrete, UV curable polymers, hygroscopic material printing, and functional gradient printing of multiple materials[81] all represent compelling new opportunities in recent years for the future of how 3D printing will continue to transform the built environment quickly.

The Development of Digital Twinning

NASA and the US Air Force first explored Digital Twinning to create real-time information flow for space exploration and aircraft.[82] Based on this early foundation discussed in Episode 3, digital twin models constructed through BIM software are applied to architecture, industrial design, and infrastructure, producing an enhanced decision-making framework. Beyond a simple three-dimensional model of the building or object, the exact digital representation provides details that start at the very earliest stages of preliminary design and planning through to occupancy, operations, and maintenance. In some cases, this can even extend to future use. To this end, digital twin models are dynamic and contribute real-time information to the AECO community, leveraging the ever-increasing capacity of Artificial Intelligence. The use of AI to have the physical building or object communicate with the digital model, creating real-time updates provides for problem-solving and evaluation capable of navigating around future problem scenarios.[83]

Specifically, digital twins now allow for simulation and, eventually, real-time calibration for climate control and thermal envelope regulation issues. Integration of weather patterns, building orientation, building airflow, and occupancy can all be fed into a much more sophisticated system of both current and future scenario building to increase the "intelligence" or optimization of the digital model, which in turn can provide information for the physical buildings or objects operation.[84] Beyond the single object or building, there is growing interest in creating digital twin systems that can model the interaction of elements within a given system. An example would be a neighborhood, a township, or even a city.[85] From a planning standpoint, the ability to create real-time data upstream in the planning stages or downstream in the post-occupancy phase would create entirely new opportunities for efficiency and resource usage. With the increased computational capacity, coupled with big data and the Internet of Things (IoT), the interconnectedness of complex systems is beginning to emerge as a real and vibrant possibility moving forward.[86]

Anticipated Impacts of Automation and Augmented/Virtual Reality

Besides the arrival of robotic fabrication and large-format extrusion printing, additional technologies continue to develop and provide anticipated impact on the design and construction fields moving forward. Construction robotics or construction automation are not new phenomena. Dating back to the early 1980s in Japan, construction companies began automating various tasks.[87] By the 1990s and early 2000s, demolition capabilities became much more advanced, allowing for elements of "breaking, crushing, shearing, digging, shoveling, grappling, surface removing and trenching of different materials." Demolition has even extended to the use of high-pressure water-jet propulsion performing "hydro-demolition" primarily on concrete, which has the advantage of leaving rebar intact after the operation is complete.[88] Current technologies take on a more diversified range of tasks and configurations. Biomorphic robots perform indoor site inspections using LiDAR, mentioned earlier in the Cultural Heritage section. Still, in many instances, the *agile-mobile-robot* can assess construction progress beyond the aforementioned historic preservation application (Figures 6.8 and 6.9).

Finally, single-task robotic installation represents another growing segment of the construction automation sector, from bricklaying and window installation to more complex prefabricated component configuration.[89] Much of this industry development is driven by a dual interest in promoting greater carbon-neutral construction methods and mediating inconsistency in labor practices.

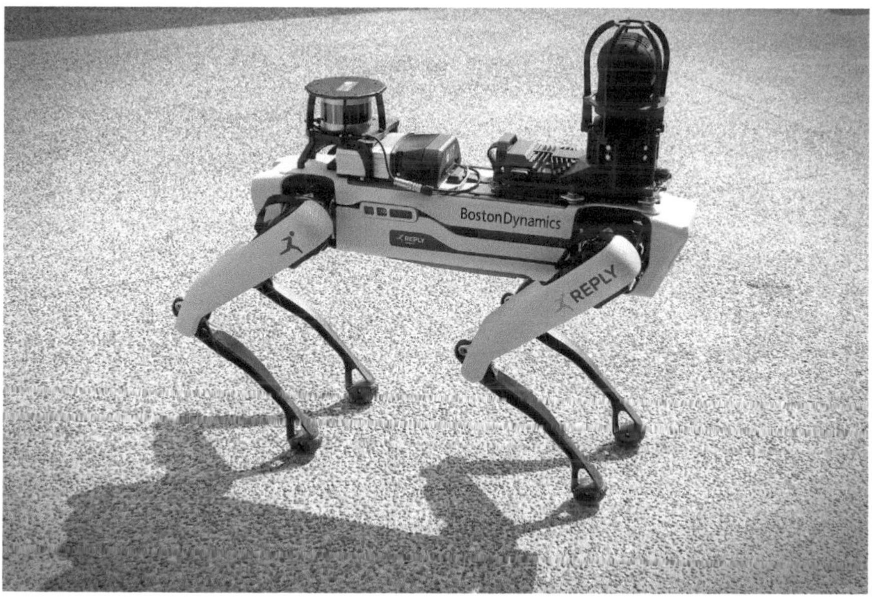

FIGURE 6.8 Boston Dynamics "Spot" platform with a Trimble X7 Scanner that uses LiDAR sensing up to 100 miles. Mobile robots can be used for predictive maintenance, operational routines, and navigating hazardous environments.

FIGURE 6.9 Demolition robots are becoming more common on construction sites. Increased capacity, safety, and access contribute to a growing need for alternative methods of robotic construction in the AEC industry.

Again, Augmented and Virtual reality (AR/VR) are not new developments and first came to general public awareness in the late 1980s, as mentioned in Episode 1. For the last 40 years, AR/VR technology has made significant advancements with the promise of synthesizing the digital and physical worlds. Although progress has not fully realized the cyberpunk future casting of William Gibson,[90] mentioned in Episode 2, technological advancements suggest the efforts to pursue digital-physical convergence are very active. Regardless of where one falls on the technophobia-technophilia spectrum, the incremental progression of AR/VR technology has allowed the AECO Industry to consider selective areas for implementation. Even with Meta Quest and, more recently, Apple's foray into the AR space with Vision Pro, the architecture and construction industries have primarily engaged the latest developments as an extension of preexisting tools. For architects and designers, immersive representation provides concept exploration and dynamic space engagement previously unavailable through conventional 2D images or animation. For contractors, planning, and simulation or on-site condition verification can now lead to greater efficiency and safety for workers, as demonstrated by Trimble's X-10 interface for the Hololens. These are not without merit and provide significant advancements based on efficiency, accuracy, and process refinement. However, moving forward, there will continue to be aspects of the use of

AR/VR that are moving the peripheral application more toward the center and simultaneously advancing some of the more speculative.

Starting in 2017, Fologram came to international prominence with their Steampunk installation for the 2019 Tallinn Architecture Biennale in Estonia.[91] Built out of steam-bent timber, the team of Gwyllim Jahn, Cameron Newnham, and Nick van den Berg created a live AR/MR link for Hololens that would seamlessly integrate with Rhino and Grasshopper. Since then, Fologram has extended its work with universities, educational organizations, and companies around the world to advance AR/MR use.[92] Again, returning to Gramazio and Kohler's work on non-standard application of brick-laying projects and research has developed through the arc of robotic installation.[93] However, their latest development in this research shows how to transform the brick-laying process through AR interaction. Replacing robots with low-skilled labor outfitted with augmented reality technology can extend the necessary choreography to assemble a non-standard wall. In this regard, the research trajectory can be traced from the earlier Gantenbein Winery completed in 2006 using robotically choreographed assembled wall sections to produce non-standard brick wall assemblies (Figures 6.10 and 6.11).

FIGURE 6.10 The augmented reality (AR) system developed by incon.ai and researchers at the ETH Zürich contributed to the construction of the Kitrvs Winery in Greece. Constructed out of 13,596 bricks using a custom-made dynamic optical guidance system.

FIGURE 6.11 The Kitrvs Winery in Greece was constructed in 2019 out of over 13,000 handmade bricks. The rotation and mortar joints are controlled through the coordination of the augmented reality interface.

More recently, speculation has been made that integrating digital infrastructure in AR/VR and autonomous robotic capabilities guided by AI could outline the framework for new urban and social infrastructure. For the 2019 Shenzhen Biennale of Urbanism/Architecture (UABB), Philip Yaun suggested this technology triptych could provide a new form of digital *eyes, hands*, and *brain* capable of collaborating with a physical and virtual society.[94] For Yaun, this unique synergy would provide a form of liberation and capacity for the individual to reconfigure a dynamic that has become increasingly homogenous. Technical advancement and capabilities regarding autonomous and AR/VR digital technologies will continue to evolve rapidly. However, these larger social, environmental, political, and theoretical questions regarding the future will underpin the critical questions of the next decade.

The New Accessibility of AI in Architecture and Design

This book ends on the beginning of the most significant recalibrations in the academic and professional field of architecture and design to have taken place since the computer first became mainstream nearly 30 years ago. It seems almost impossible to pick up any publication, listen to any podcast, or read any blog that doesn't currently attempt to assess the future role of AI. The pervasive nature of the conversation tends to suggest there is a novelty in the topic itself. Still, like most of the technology and concepts covered in this book, the incremental progression over time through advancements, research, breakthroughs, and sometimes even fortuitous events have led to our current cultural AI awakening. AI has been with us for over 70 years, first in concept, then in a technical lexicon with limited application, and now in ways poised to radically alter our lives.

A Brief History of AI

Dating back to the early 1940s, Warren McCulloch and Walter Pitts introduced the concept of *"artificial neurons"* based on a mathematical and biological framework. This early work shaped the preliminary formation of an *"artificial network,"* essential in establishing and utilizing computer processing to obtain information. Combining the concepts of artificial neurons and artificial networks provided the first model for an Artificial Neural Network (ANN). In 1950, Alan Turing added to the growing discourse with his seminal paper entitled "Computer Machinery and Intelligence."[95] Based on the earlier success, the Turing Machine raised critical questions about constructing and testing machine intelligence. By 1956, there was significant enough academic interest that a small group of researchers led by John McCarthy, Marvin Minsky, Nathaniel Rochester, and Claude Shannon gathered at Dartmouth University to discuss machine intelligence and coined the term "artificial intelligence."[96] After initial theoretical development, the 1950s and 1960s brought hardware advancements facilitating experiments that demonstrated "learning" machines and the first manifestation of an artificial neural network like Frank Rosenblatt's Perceptron used to classify images[97] (Figure 6.12).

The 1980s would see an upturn in research, enthusiasm, and advancement, primarily driven by increased computing power based on processing speeds. Periods of slower development and even more profound doubts about the field defined the interstitial decades of the 1970s, 1990s, and early 2000s. These decades are often referred to as the AI Winters. Even though research slowed, there were breakthroughs in creating new forms of Artificial Neural Networks (ANNs) that had largely gone unexplored since Rosenblatt's Perceptron binary classification dating back to 1957.[98]

While the subfield of Machine Learning (ML) gained traction and advancement in the late 1990s and early 2000s, the broader public's awareness was limited to events like chess matches between IBM's Deep Blue and the Grand Master Garry Kasparov (1997),[99] DARPA autonomous road challenge (2004),[100] or even NASA deploying the autonomous rovers Spirit[101] and Opportunity[102] on Mars (2004). Google would commercially test autonomous vehicles with its Waymo car in 2009,[103] laying the groundwork for broader assimilation as cultural and legal frameworks continued to soften. While these were the public-facing points of contact,

FIGURE 6.12 Frank Rosenblatt working on the "Perceptron." He developed the concept in 1958 as a type of neural network capable of learning and performing binary classification tasks. Rosenblatt described the machine as capable of having an original idea.

critical research advancements occurred during the same timeframe. Starting with ImageNet at Stanford University in 2009, researchers leveraged necessary steps in predictive accuracy through an assembled inventory of over 14 million categorized and labeled images.[104] The concept of Convolutional Neural Networks (CNNs) was introduced in the late 1980s to 1990s by Yann LeCun. CNN would later find traction and considerable interest in implementation almost a decade later, in the late 2000s. The CNN, or ConvNet as it would come to be known, was what ImageNet was built on for the Stanford project, and this technology provided the foundation to develop a system of image recognition based on hierarchical processing that ultimately became a primary building block for autonomous vehicle driving capabilities that are used today. In 2012, Andrew Ng and Jeff Dean made important contributions with their early research in *Large-Scale Unsupervised Learning*.[105] They would go on to help move these and other research advancements into the commercial space with their work in the Google Brain (now Google DeepMind). The research groundwork was also expanded in 2014 by Ian Goodfellow. His work to create a Generative Adversarial Network (GAN) established competing neural networks (generator and discriminator) such that more efficient image recognition and processing could take place.[106] In 2015, Geoffrey Hinton, Yann LeCun, and Yoshua Bengio published seminal work on artificial neural networks and the backpropagation algorithm, culminating over a decade of research.[107] By the mid-2010s, these advances and discoveries culminated in forming the foundation of the subset of machine learning called Deep Learning (DL). As a subset of ML, DL is characterized by an enhanced and increased number of relationships within datasets, capable of resolving complex problems. DL uses raw data to autonomously recognize patterns, such as image and speech applications, which have seen remarkable advancement in the past decade.

As the architect Neil Leach, among others, has pointed out, the current cultural fascination with AI is often synonymous with Machine Learning and, more specifically, with Deep Learning.[108] The DL breakthrough has transpired due to cloud-based services and computational processing power not available just a few years ago. Simultaneously, the amount of resources, researchers, and raw data filling the operational space makes this a field with enormous application opportunities.[109]

In another broadly recognized AI moment, AlphaGo, developed by Google's DeepMind, beat world champion Lee Sedol in 2016 (Figure 6.16). Similar to Deep Blue and Garry Kasparov in 1997, almost 20 years later, the advancements in ANN represented a different milestone. At face value, Go appears to be a more straightforward game than chess and, therefore, less complicated, with fewer calculations to consider. However, given the homogeneity of pieces and that play is initiated with an empty board, there are more permutations of moves, requiring intuition and reaction.[110]

Beyond winning the 5-game series, Move 37 in Match 2 represented a watershed moment where AlphaGo demonstrated what appeared to be an illogical move for professional Go players. This move proved to be the turning point in the Match and was a superior calculation for the long-term win. Move 37 was celebrated by AI enthusiasts and researchers as a moment where AlphaGo demonstrated something akin to creativity. Since this match, DeepMind has created several more robust iterations of Go-playing AI, each one with greater capacity for strategy, speed, and self-teaching capabilities.[111]

As mentioned earlier, Ian Goodfellow's breakthrough research on GANs in mid-2010 was a seismic moment in Unsupervised Deep Learning. GANs and transformer-based models, or more specifically, *Generative Pre trained Transformers* (GPT), have ushered in a renaissance of generative AI. Again, the origins go back much further into some of the earliest concepts of AI, but this past decade has welcomed deep learning into almost all corners of our lives.

These points have given vitality to the broader AI community and prompted some to call this new moment an AI Spring.[112] Others correctly raise accurate and valid questions about ethics, surveillance, power structures, and cultural preservation. These are essential questions deserving of consideration that are actively being debated even as we make remarkable advancements toward what were once seemingly out-of-reach concepts like singularity.[113]

Architecture + AI

Moving to the present, there is much speculation going on at the moment and no shortage of advocates, naysayers, researchers, pioneers, and even curious bystanders. While it would be tempting to establish a dichotomy between the efficiencies of the architectural practice and those engaged in broader theoretical speculations found within academic research, recent success in erasing these walls in favor of greater intellectual promiscuity should follow suit here. There is trepidation with the suggestions that Artificial Narrow Intelligence applications will replace those not using AI with those that are – or even just AI itself,[114] or as Matias del Campo suggests, that a *Post-Human Aesthetic* can now emerge in architecture through the collaborative interaction between the human imagination and AI deep learning capabilities.[115] Yet, what does this all mean for the future of Architecture? (Figure 6.13)

The answer to this question most likely lies somewhere between the professional practice framework, companies developing software driven by market forces, and computational development in deep learning areas of neural network structures and data sets. Phillip Bernstein's latest book, *Machine Learning: Architecture in the Age of Artificial Intelligence,*[116] looks at this issue through the lens of changing technology, the architect's agency in new innovative outcomes, the architect's role in project delivery, and the value of the architect's service. In his book *Architecture in the Age of Artificial Intelligence: An Introduction to AI for Architects,*[117] Neil Leach translates the ubiquity of AI touchpoints from theories to software applications. Leach's global research perspective on near-future applications yet with far-future implications offers a

FIGURE 6.13 AI-generated images from Matias del Campo, 2023, exploring the open dialogue between human creativity and machine intelligence.

malleable framework for designers and architects. There is certainly no shortage of voices or immediate evidence to contradict the groundswell of information championing AI's near and far-reaching impacts as a revolutionizing force in architecture as currently conceived.

The Extension of Architecture + AI Tools

As Bernstein points out, the evolution of design tools across the history of architecture is defined by increased levels of precision and, most recently, increased levels of automation.[118] The resultant outcome is a rapidly growing transformation of the design phases. Identifying currently used GAI in architecture and allied fields is elusive and potentially futile. The high degree of activity in this space, combined with how quickly the industry changes, suggests that many of the subsequently listed applications and companies might look very different in just a few years or even months. However, despite the potential for disruption and change in who is active in this market, there is an opportunity to understand the way AI impacts how architects work at this point in time. When reflecting on the previous technological impacts over the past several decades, from animation software to robotic fabrication, there is always an initial period of appropriation and exploration, noted in a similar obsession with initial AI visualization. The lessons of our architectural past have also taught us when equipped with new technology, some pioneering architects and designers will find a way to integrate it into new theories, methodologies, and outcomes. The upcoming experimentation with AI + architecture will generate entirely new bespoke tools and eventually lead to broader-based adoption, and increased market penetration will inevitably transform the framework of the AECO industry.

Early-stage project initiation often requires distilling large amounts of data into actionable information. The implementation of AI-enabled tools is highly suited for this purpose, especially for what might be considered lower-level thinking aspects like data collection, processing, classification, comparison, and even testing.[119] AI will assist in locating and developing scenarios that fulfill the objectives of a wide range of parameters.[120]

Image generation and massing configurations are readily available AI tools. Programs like Midjourney and DALL-E 2 provide easy onramps for quickly generating photorealistic images. Direct sketching, photo uploads, or text prompts allow for a starting point for continued refinements and adjustments.

Beyond the communication and visualization aspect of these software applications, though, important questions are inherent in the creative process. The more critical question is how more sophisticated programs like Stable Diffusion can productively be integrated into architectural workflows. AI can do extraordinary things beyond the capacity of the human mind. AI can solve incredibly complex problems, data mine and assimilate, and calculate on orders of magnitude almost beyond our comprehension, and as previously described, can self-evolve through deep learning. Yet, AI cannot invent its own rules, and at least for now, it cannot transcend its own programming beyond emulation to match that of the human imagination. So, where does the agency currently reside within a collaborative design methodology that implements deep learning procedures? As Matias del Campo, Alexandra Carlson, and Sandra Manniger have described,

> Borrowing from the conversations of Gottfried Semper about the nature of style it can be stated that style has turned into a posthuman quality, where artificial players contribute to the discussion by analyzing and proposing ideas for a cultural discussion with an ever-increasing speed. If robots can dream of gothic cathedrals, humans need to renegotiate their position in a contemporary design ecology.[121]

Direct interaction with renderings poses yet another form of visual generative AI. In the case of the recently released Adobe Firefly, image manipulation has remarkable capacity, given the data is taken from Wikimedia and Flickr, as well as millions of images and videos already in Adobe Stock. Additionally, Veras provides a direct plug-in for Revit, Rhino, and SketchUp using pre-existing models as the substrate for renderings. The graphic and text prompt interface offers a combined UI that allows easy assimilation into a workflow.

Much of the Generative AI discussed in this section operates at various scales. As such, architects and interior designers can often use similar digital tools for some of these functions. However, some specific AI geared toward front-end designers and back-end users are more specifically directed to Interior Design. In most cases, the majority of options offer similar functionality. Several Generative AI tools for stylizing rooms can produce photorealistic renderings. With varying degrees of sophistication, options, and interface capabilities, this can simply be an ideas generator or a full-fledged tool for design outcomes. The second category provides a way to generate 2D, 3D, and 360° virtual tours of interior spaces. The AI typically can provide additional features like furnishings and materials to assist with layout and design decisions.

2D orthographic drawing optimization is now possible based on criteria like space allocation, code, context, distances, and programmatic adjacencies. Increased sophistication in algorithms has provided for advancements in machine learning applications that can now refine multiple parameters when doing preliminary layouts, for instance.[122] Or general floor plan layout GANs garner substantial research[123] and market interest.[124]

Within the schematic design and design development phases, 3D modeling software integrating with Revit, Rhino, and other BIM software is now becoming more readily available and frequently utilized. Software like *ARCHITEChTURES, ARK AI, Hypar,* and *cove.tool* provides a range of options from massing and space planning to more specific optimization aspects like structural configuration, thermal including carbon footprint, and even code compliance. In the case of cove.tool, the application stretches across the broader industry with multiple functionalities and high interoperability capabilities.

Autodesk Forma (formally Spacemaker)[125] and XKool Technology target a broader market sector. In the case of Forma and XKool, the Generative AI is geared toward architects, urban designers, and developers. This scalar and operational trajectory provides a different data set but ultimately still keys off of vertical integration. As Neil Leach has pointed out, while Forma and XKool offer similar strategies for AI implementation, these companies will provide an interesting case study moving forward. Forma is part of the Boston-based Autodesk parent company, focused primarily on Western markets. The company is tied into a range of tools using AI and non-AI technologies, giving it a multi-layered approach to strategic integration for design and market penetration. By comparison, XKool Technologies is a Shenzhen-based company solely concentrating on deep learning and operating from the expansive data available within China, where there is larger availability and fewer regulations regarding access.[126]

Forma and XKool indicate strong Urban Design and Urban Planning advancement. In addition, there are additional tools for larger territories, multi-building complexes, ecological and infrastructural systems, information flow related to local zoning, investment scenario building, and feasibility studies. Software like Giraffe focuses on "urban analytics" pooling information from GIS information. Archistar, by comparison, has some areas of overlap but primarily targets the "property technology industry" in both the public, private, and governmental sectors. Still different, but within the urban space, is Delve, by Google's Sidewalk Lab. Delve combines features of both Archistar and Giraffe, where users can rapidly scenario-build for urban project optimization and value-based decision making. Additionally, a product like Digital Blue Foam offers designers a robust inventory of options from spatial analytics to Generative AI design solutions across multiple scales. Upstream online collaboration and downstream instant BIM coordination provide additional functionality.

Ultimately, the most critical aspect is not the tools or software but the spectrum of discourse around the tenets of professional operation and the data so critical to the functioning AI. Moving forward, the consideration for data creation, access, and ownership in the built and digital environment will drive not just a substantial aspect of the conversation regarding AI but the very nature of business itself. The platforms constructed for collaboration, regulation, and privatization will consume enormous energy in this discussion. The interoperability question becomes even more important within the industry as one thinks about curating data, zooming out from just the BIM model related to a project. In this regard, Phil Bernstein has suggested this is an opportunity for the AECO industry to redefine the sandbox and not just the "toys" of mutual interest.[127] Bernstein goes as far as to suggest that a "Global Built Asset Data Trust" is necessary to serve as a repository of data that can address some of the opportunities and concerns that will develop in the industry moving forward. It is conceivable that previous jurisdictional frameworks will no longer be suited for AI data frameworks in the AECO industry. There is no reason to think the regulatory structures in place for the built environment would independently need radical alteration, however, as more of the industry moves toward a virtual and GAI context, these questions will inevitably become more critical.

Professional and Academic Leadership

Leadership and vision within AI and ML for Architecture and the allied fields differ from implementing GAI tools for efficiency or speed. Many firms and researchers have been working in the AI space for some time to pioneer innovative approaches. To be effective, most of these firms and individuals must hypothesize about the near and far future according to their histories and practices, leveraging a deep knowledge of computational technology. From this position, a novel contribution is often made to the field, and the tapestry of leadership grows.

In the case of the Applied R&D (ARD) group at Foster + Partners, they articulate several application layers related to ML implementation, but their focus on creating and curating datasets is particularly interesting. The use of synthetic datasets has been successful in other industries, such as automotive and healthcare, so with ARD's own internal multi-objective optimization environment, ARD is working to create synthetic data for ML functionality. This controlled data can then be juxtaposed against a 50+ year history of collected data from the firm. In this instance, the challenge isn't in constructing the data via an algorithm but in classification and access.[128] For Foster + Partners, the firm's history and resources make this an intriguing exercise and potentially filled with valuable information for future applications.[129] For example, firms with longstanding histories, which are currently undertaking data mining of their archives, serve as important case studies given that strategic inclusion of historical data will be essential to ensure that recency bias is not a potential omission.

Patrik Schumacher's role as principal of Zaha Hadid Architects (ZHA) and an instructor at the AA DRL provides an opportunity to ask a broader question about how ML can expand into social behavior stemming from spatial configuration.[130] Extending beyond physical configuration, additional factors such as cultural, situational, and environmental protocols can also impact participation dynamics. For Schumacher, this approach to ML use reinforces his research on "agent-based parametric semiology."[131] By using ML in this way, Schumacher can test hypotheses and create synthetic data that could be leveraged with a digital twin to further assess the accuracy of the fundamental hypothesis of the research.[132] That is not to say that within practice, Schumacher is not advocating for AI to be an ideas generator within the firm. There is an open embrace for using DALL-E 2 and Midjourney for certain projects. He has suggested that up to 10–15% of the AI-generated output moves toward 3D development within the preliminary stages of project development.[133]

As established earlier, many important academic voices are currently contributing to the conversation. Through publication, symposium, and exhibitions. From Hernan Diaz Alonso and Casey Rehm's curated exhibition on AI at the FRAC (2019) entitled *The Architectural Beast*[134] to the more recent exhibition and symposium curated by Professors Kory Bieg, Daniel Kohler, and Clay Odem at the University of Texas (2023) entitled *Architecture after AI*,[135] there has been growing attention to the proliferation of work shaping the discourse. In a foreshadowing of what will indeed become more common in the near future, AIA New York held an event focusing on the *Future of Architectural Practice*,[136] featuring many of the academics and software companies already mentioned.

Matias del Campo and Sandra Manninger's theoretical work on GANs, style transfer, and the potential for 2D and 3D DL integration poses some of the most compelling work being done. Manninger, del Campo, Daniel Bologjan, and Immanuel Koh founded Neural Network Group,[137] which is "increasingly entangled in questions of agency, culture, and ethics in AI research." As a founding member, del Campo oversees the *Architecture and Artificial Intelligence Laboratory* at Taubman College of Architecture and Urban Planning at the University of Michigan. Daniel Kohler's work at UT Austin in urban design and AI-generated mereology provides a different scalar application of theoretical exploration. Specifically the research he and partner Rasa Navasaityte are doing on large-scale language image models (LLIs)[138] (Figure 6.14).

Continuing not Concluding

This episode was introduced as a pivotal moment, unfolding in many different directions, with no definitive landing point to summarize these past few years. To that end, Winston Churchill's 1942 quote seems appropriate, "Now this is not the end. It is not even the beginning of the end. But it is, perhaps, the end of the beginning." The certain *uncertainty* in Churchill's quote summarizes our current transitory moment since there is clear evidence of momentum, accomplishment, and inquiry setting valuable benchmarks for aggressively moving forward. In a few more years, it is very likely that as we start to realize the larger impacts of AI on achitecture and the allied fields the need to reconstitute beginnings, middles, and ends might be up for further consideration. Sam Altman, Founder and CEO of OpenAI, also offers a quote bookending Churchill, "AI will probably, most likely, lead to the end of the world, but in the

FIGURE 6.14 Large City House in Athens (left) and a *forensic landscape* of Astana (right) by Lab-eds (Daniel Koehler + Rasa Navasaityte). Research on large-scale-text-to-image (LLI) looks at data-centric building typologies to challenge classification systems. Synthetic datasets of 450,000 images into individual building segments, conducting a statistical analysis of compositional features across 5,600 cities.

meantime, there'll be great companies."[139] While there may have been a fair amount of irony in Altman's statement, it hasn't stopped many from recognizing that once we pass the threshold of specific human capabilities, our world has encountered a seismic, if not permanent, change (Figure 6.15).

We are only in the earliest days of Deep Learning, and while neural networks and unsupervised learning have led to the explosion in research, latent issues are gaining momentum, like reinforced learning and even entirely new questions waiting to be discovered.[140] There is much to explore, research, design, build, and observe regarding AI and the future of architecture.

Circling back to one of our early pioneers in computation, Don Greenberg reminds us of the value of self-awareness in developing the tools we choose to use or appropriate for design purposes, "I spent my life as a toolmaker. The architecture field is much to blame because they never put their creative input into what they want. That's why you're stuck with what you have now."[141] As straightforward as this may seem, there is an active debate about the latest developments of AI and ML related to future agency when working with increasingly sophisticated toolsets. If architects are to play a role in directing the technological development affecting design and the built environment, then we are once again faced with our question from earlier to ask what is *architectural about computation*, not the inverse. When

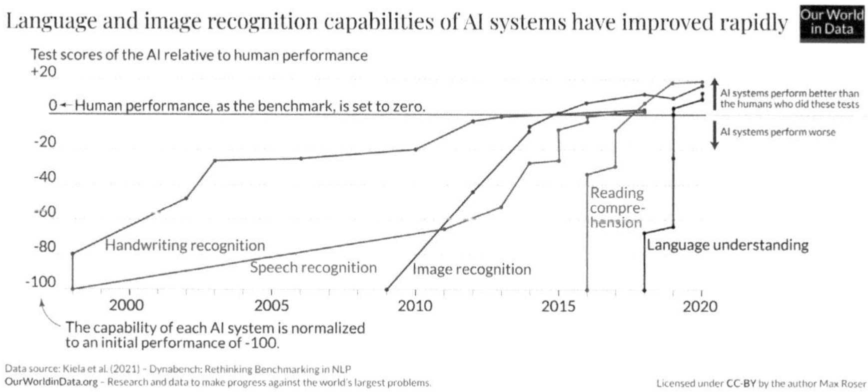

FIGURE 6.15 A 2023 Graph showing the development of AI systems for reading, writing, speaking, and image recognition. Over the past two decades, AI has advanced to the point it can now perform better image, language, and reading functions than the human brain.

technology evolves with the design, the tools facilitate the methodologies and outcomes and are not necessarily limited by their parameters.

Postscript

From Alberti to Babbage and from CAD/CAM to AI, the attempt to elucidate trajectories through the *evolution of computation in architecture* has been marked by the propagation of voices contributing to the larger field in a short period of time. It is neither a straight line nor a fractal tree, providing clarity and predictability in progression. It is not possible to separate the intertwining of early computer technology development from the application of computer technology within architecture. The early formulations of implementation provided a transitional period as we continued our zeal for exploration and application. As computational technology became synthesized into our modes of education and practice, the application started to fill a broad range of diverse issues. Most recently, the realization of ML/DL into a broader cultural fabric has, in essence, brought the development cycle full turn. Similar to the 1980s and 1990s, we are in the nascent days of understanding the broad implementation of AI in our lives and the specific implementation of architecture. There will inevitably be many more episodes to follow, filled with pioneers, physical and virtual advances, hardware and software, and most likely, things we have not yet even imagined.

Notes

1 Prensky, M. (2001). "Digital Natives, Digital Immigrants Part 1." *On the Horizon, 9* (5), 1–6. doi:10.1108/10748120110424816
2 See https://openai.com/
3 Leach, N. (2021). *Architecture in the Age of Artificial Intelligence: An Introduction to AI for Architects*. London: Bloomsbury Publishing.
4 Martens, B. (2004). "CAAD-Repositories for Scientific Information Exchange – An Overview on SciX-pilots Related to CAAD." *Proceedings of the 22nd International Conference on Education and Research in Computer-Aided Architectural Design in Europe (eCAADe)*. doi:10.52842/conf.ecaade.2004.262
5 See https://livingarchitecturesystems.com/people/ [accessed December 13, 2023].
6 See https://fcl.ethz.ch/ [accessed 13 December 13, 2023].
7 See https://senseable.mit.edu/ [accessed December 13, 2023].
8 Cupkova, D. (2022). "Architecture of Ecological Attunement," in R. Monacella and B. Keane (eds.), *Designing Landscape Architectural Education: Studio Ecologies for Unpredictable Futures*. Oxford: Taylor & Francis.
9 Cogdell, C. (2019). *Toward a Living Architecture? Complexism and Biology in Generative Design*. Minneapolis, MN: University of Minnesota Press.
10 Nastasi, J., May, E., and Snell, C. (eds.) (2018). *SU+RE: Sustainable + Resilient Design Systems*. Chichester: John Wiley & Sons, pp. 6–12
11 Wang, J., Shi, D., and Song, Y. (2022). *Advanced Materials in Smart Building Skins for Sustainability: From Nano to Macroscale*. Berlin: Springer Nature.
12 See https://uel.ac.uk/sugarcrete
13 Roychand, R., Kilmartin-Lynch, S., Saberian, M., Li, J., Zhang, G., and Li, C. Q. (2023). "Transforming Spent Coffee Grounds into a Valuable Resource for the Enhancement of Concrete Strength." *Journal of Cleaner Production, 419*, 138205. doi:10.1016/j.jclepro.2023.138205
14 Huaroc, C.B. (2024, January 21). "Interspecies Design: Developing Materials that Allow the Growth and Inhabitation of Non-human Species." *ArchDaily*, January 21. Available at: https://www.archdaily.com/1012323/interspecies-design-developing-materials-that-allow-the-growth-and-inhabitation-of-non-human-species?utm_medium=email&utm_source=AD%20EN&kth=4,096,871&mc_cid=0433b00bf7&mc_eid=d39b18a6f2
15 See https://www.worldbank.org/en/topic/urbandevelopment/overview# [accessed December 13, 2023].
16 Harman, G. (2011). *Tool-Being: Heidegger and the Metaphysics of Objects*. Chicago, IL: Open Court.
17 Harman, G. (2022). *Architecture and objects*. Minneapolis, MN: University of Minnesota Press.
18 Morton, T. (2013). *Hyperobjects: Philosophy and Ecology After the End of the World*. Minneapolis, MN: University of Minnesota Press. See also Morton, T. (2017). *Humankind: Solidarity with Non-human People*. Brooklyn, NY: Verso Books.
19 Haraway, D. (1985). "A Cyborg Manifesto: Science, Technology, and Socialist-Feminism in the Late Twentieth Century." *Socialist Review*.
20 Haraway, D. (2014). *Anthropocene, Capitalocene, Chthulucene: Staying with the Trouble*. See https://anthropocene.au.dk/conferences/arts-of-living-on-a-damaged-planet-may-2014 [accessed December 12, 2023].
21 The Center for Resilient Cities and Landscapes (CRCL) was established in 2018 at the Graduate School of Architecture Planning and Preservation, Columbia University. The CRCLCRCL is part of Columbia's Climate School and works across disciplines at Columbia by bridging design with science and policy to improve the adaptive capacity of people and places.
22 See https://www.urbanworks.cca.edu/about-1 [accessed December 13, 2023].
23 See https://www.rvtr.com/about [accessed December 13, 2023].

24 Kripa, E. and Mueller, S. (2020). *Fronts: Military Urbanisms and the Developing World*. San Francisco, CA: Applied Research & Design Publishing.

25 "Re:Positioning Fear." Rafael Lozano-Hemmer. See https://www.lozano-hemmer.com/repositioning_fear.php [accessed January 26, 2024].

26 See https://www.rael-sanfratello.com/made/teetertotter-wall

27 Sanchez, J. (2020). *Architecture for the Commons: Participatory Systems in the Age of Platforms*. Oxford: Routledge.

28 Retsin, G. (2019). *Discrete: Reappraising the Digital in Architecture*. Chichester: John Wiley & Sons.

29 Kanaani, M. (2022). *The Routledge Companion to Ecological Design Thinking: Healthful Ecotopian Visions for Architecture and Urbanism*. Oxford: Taylor & Francis.

30 See https://www.archdaily.com/969722/hilo-nest-research-building-takes-shape-in-switzerland [accessed December 12, 2023].

31 See https://www.arup.com/projects/mx3d-bridge [accessed December 14, 2023].

32 Bao, D. W., Yan, X., Snooks, R., and Xie, Y. M. (2020). "Bioinspired Generative Architectural Design Form-Finding and Advanced Robotic Fabrication Based on Structural Performance," in *Architectural Intelligence*. Singapore: Springer Nature Singapore, pp. 147–170. doi:10.1007/978-981-15-6568-7_10. See also Bao, D. W., Yan, X., and Xie, Y. M. (2022). "Encoding Topological Optimisation Logical Structure Rules into Multi-Agent System for Architectural Design and Robotic Fabrication." *International Journal of Architectural Computing, 20*(1), 7–17. doi:10.1177/14780771221082257

33 Hahn, J. (2023, March 6). "NASA uses AI to Design Hardware that is 'Three Times Better in Performance'." *Dezeen*, March 6. Available at: https://www.dezeen.com/2023/03/06/nasa-uses-ai-to-design-hardware-that-is-three-times-better-in-performance/

34 Hille, K. B. (2023, February 9). "NASA Turns to AI to Design Mission Hardware." NASA, February 9. Available at: https://www.nasa.gov/science-research/nasa-turns-to-ai-to-design-mission-hardware/

35 Lavin, S. (2012, October 1). "Vanishing Point: The Contemporary Pavilion." *Artforum*, October 1. Available at: https://www.artforum.com/features/vanishing-point-the-contemporary-pavilion-205927/

36 "livMatS Pavilion 2020–21." Universität Stuttgart – TIK. See https://www.itke.uni-stuttgart.de/research/icd-itke-research-pavilions/livMatS-pavilion-2020-21/ [accessed January 4, 2024].

37 "BUGA Fibre Pavilion 2019." Universität Stuttgart – TIK. See https://www.itke.uni-stuttgart.de/research/built-projects/buga-fibre-pavilion-2019/ [accessed January 4, 2024].

38 "Maison Fibre 2021." Universität Stuttgart – TIK. See https://www.itke.uni-stuttgart.de/research/built-projects/maison-fibre-2021/ [accessed January 9, 2024].

39 Tibbits, S. (2021). *Things Fall Together: A Guide to the New Materials Revolution*. Princeton, NJ: Princeton University Press, p. 21.

40 Ibid., p. 21.

41 See https://en.unesco.org/themes/information-preservation/digital-heritage [accessed December 14, 2023].

42 See https://unesdoc.unesco.org/ark:/48223/pf0000179529 [accessed December 14, 2023].

43 See https://www.cyark.org/ [accessed December 14, 2023].

44 See https://vwhl.luddy.indiana.edu/index.html [accessed December 14, 2023].

45 Nikonova, A. A. and Biryukova, M. "The Role of Digital Technologies in the Preservation of Cultural Heritage." *Muzeológia a Kultúrne Dedičstvo, 5*(1), 169–173. See also Boboc, R.G., Băutu, E., Gîrbacia, F., Popovici, N. and Popovici, D.M. (2022). "Augmented Reality in Cultural Heritage: An Overview of the Last Decade of Applications." *Applied Sciences, 12*(19), 9859. doi:10.3390/app12199859.

46 Boboc, Răzvan Gabriel, Elena Băutu, Florin Gîrbacia, Norina Popovici, and Dorin-Mircea Popovici. (2022). "Augmented Reality in Cultural Heritage: An Overview of the Last Decade of Applications." *Applied Sciences, 12*(19), 9859. doi:10.3390/app12199859.
47 Autodesk University (2020, March 13). "Digitizing History: Preserving and Recreating Heritage Sites with Digital Tools." Autodesk University. See https://medium.com/autodesk-university/digitizing-history-preserving-and-recreating-heritage-sites-with-digital-tools-abc200c5fa66
48 Telefónica (2023, May 14). "What Role can Technology Play in Historical Heritage Preservation?" *Telefónica*, May 14. Available at: https://www.telefonica.com/en/communication-room/blog/what-role-can-technology-play-in-historical-heritage-preservation/
49 See https://www.nasa.gov/moontomarsarchitecture/ [accessed December 14, 2023].
50 See https://www.nasa.gov/specials/artemis/ [accessed December 14, 2023].
51 See https://www.nasa.gov/humans-in-space/chapea/ [accessed December 14, 2023].
52 See https://big.dk/projects/mars-science-city-6213 [accessed December 14, 2023].
53 See https://www.spacexarch.com/ [accessed December 14, 2023].
54 "About CHAPEA." NASA. Available at: https://www.nasa.gov/humans-in-space/chapea/about-chapea/ [accessed December 14, 2023].
55 See https://www.nasa.gov/prizes-challenges-and-crowdsourcing/centennial-challenges/3d-printed-habitat-challenge/
56 Prashar, G., Vasudev, H., and Bhuddhi, D. (2023). "Additive Manufacturing: Expanding 3D Printing Horizon in Industry 4.0." *International Journal of Interactive Design Manufacturing, 17*, 2221–2235. doi:10.1007/s12008-022-00956-4
57 Xiao, J., Ji, G., Zhang, Y., Ma, G., Mechtcherine, V., Pan, J., Wang, L., Ding, T., Duan, Z., and Du, S. (2021). "Large-scale 3D Printing Concrete Technology: Current Status and Future Opportunities." *Cement and Concrete Composites, 122*, 104115. doi:10.1016/j.cemconcomp.2021.104115
58 See https://cobod.com/worlds-largest-3d-printed-building-in-florida [accessed December 18, 2023].
59 See https://resources.firstplanit.com/dubbed-germanys-city-of-science-heidelberg-will-soon-host-the-largest-3d-printed-building-in-europe/ [accessed December 18, 2023].
60 See https://finance.yahoo.com/news/3d-concrete-printing-market-size-131500566.html [accessed December 18, 2023].
61 Ma, G., Buswell, R., Leal da Silva, W. R., Wang, L., Xu, J., and Jones, S. Z. (2022). "Technology Readiness: A Global Snapshot of 3D Concrete Printing and the Frontiers for Development." *Cement and Concrete Research, 156*, 106774. doi:10.1016/j.cemconres.2022.106774
62 Examples of start-up companies: WinSun (China), XtreeE (France), Monolite UK (UK), ApisCor (Russia), CSP srl (Italy), CyBe Construction (Netherlands), and Sika (Switzerland). See Ahmed, G. H. (2023). "A Review of '3D concrete printing': Materials and Process Characterization, Economic Considerations and Environmental Sustainability." *Journal of Building Engineering, 66*, 105863. doi:10.1016/j.jobe.2023.105863.
63 See https://homes.iconbuild.com/wolf-ranch/ [accessed December 18, 2023]. See also https://www.wolfranchbyhillwood.com/news/latest-news/post/new-3d-printed-homes-coming-to-wolf-ranch-in-2023 [accessed December 18, 2023].
64 See https://www.skyquestt.com/report/3d-printed-houses-market#:~:text=Global%203D%2Dprinted%20Houses%20Market%20Insights,period%20(2023%2D2030) [accessed December 18, 2023].
65 Bechthold, M. and Weaver, J. C. (2017). "Materials Science and Architecture." *Nature Reviews Materials, 2*(12). doi:10.1038/natrevmats.2017.82

66 See the research, publications, and work of Dr. John Hart, Professor of Mechanical Engineering and Director of the Laboratory for Manufacturing and Productivity and Center for Additive and Digital Advanced Production Technologies (APT) at MIT for a further outline of prototyping, manufacturing, and product development outside of architecture. See https://professional.mit.edu/programs/faculty-profiles/john-hart

67 Rael, R. and Fratello, V. S. (2018). *Printing Architecture: Innovative Recipes for 3D Printing*. San Francisco, CA: Chronicle Books.

68 Emerging Objects. See https://emergingobjects.com/ [accessed December 20, 2023].

69 Ameen, A. A., Takhakh, A. M., and Abdal-hay, A. (2023). "An Overview of the Latest Research on the Impact of 3D Printing Parameters on Shape Memory Polymers." *European Polymer Journal, 194,* 112145. doi:10.1016/j.eurpolymj.2023.112145

70 Bechthold, M. and Weaver, J. C. (2017). "Materials Science and Architecture." *Nature Reviews Materials, 2*(12). doi:doi.org/10.1038/natrevmats.2017.82

71 Tibbits, S. and Cheung, K. (2012). "Programmable Materials for Architectural Assembly and Automation." *Assembly Automation, 32*(3), 216–225. doi:10.1108/01445151211244348

72 Bechthold, M. and Weaver, J. C. (2017). "Materials Science and Architecture." *Nature Reviews Materials, 2*(12). doi:10.1038/natrevmats.2017.82

73 del-Mazo-Barbara, L. and Ginebra, M.-P. (2021). "Rheological Characterisation of Ceramic Inks for 3D Direct Ink Writing: A Review." *Journal of the European Ceramic Society, 41*(16), 18–33. doi:10.1016/j.jeurceramsoc.2021.08.031

74 "3D Printing Clay" (2022, September 8). Parametric House. Available at: https://parametrichouse.com/3d-printing-clay/ [accessed December 18, 2023].

75 Boissonneault, T. (2018, August 17). "World's Largest 3D Printed Coral Reef Installed at Maldives Island Resort." *VoxelMatters*, August 17. Available at: https://www.voxelmatters.com/largest-3d-printed-coral-reef-maldives/

76 Bechthold, M., Kane, A., and King, J. (2015). *Ceramic Material Systems: In Architecture and Interior Design*. Basel: Birkhäuser

77 Buchanan, C. and Gardner, L. (2019). "Metal 3D Printing in Construction: A Review of Methods, Research, Applications, Opportunities and Challenges." *Engineering Structures, 180*, 332–348. doi:10.1016/j.engstruct.2018.11.045

78 Gardner, L. (2023). "Metal Additive Manufacturing in Structural Engineering – Review, Advances, Opportunities, and Outlook." *Structures, 47*, 2178–2193. doi:10.1016/j.istruc.2022.12.039

79 Galjaard, G., Hofman, S., Perry, N. and Ren, S. (2015). "Optimizing Structural Building Elements in Metal by using Additive Manufacturing." *Proceedings of the International Association for Shell and Spatial Structures (IASS) Symposium* 2015, Amsterdam Future Visions, August 17–20, 2015, Amsterdam, the Netherlands.

80 Pajonk, A., Prieto, A., Blum, U., and Knaack, U. (2022). "Multi-material Additive Manufacturing in Architecture and Construction: A Review." *Journal of Building Engineering, 45*, 103603. doi:10.1016/j.jobe.2021.103603

81 Craveiro, F., Nazarian, S., Bartolo, H., Bartolo, P. J., and Pinto Duarte, J. (2020). "An Automated System for 3D Printing Functionally Graded Concrete-based Materials." *Additive Manufacturing, 33*, 101146. doi:10.1016/j.addma.2020.101146

82 Glaessgen, E. and Stargel, D. (2012, April 23). "The Digital Twin Paradigm for Future NASA and U.S. Air Force vehicles." *53rd AIAA/ASME/ASCE/AHS/ASC Structures, Structural Dynamics and Materials Conference*. doi:10.2514/6.2012-1818

83 Arowoiya, V. A., Moehler, R. C., and Fang, Y. (2023). "Digital Twin Technology for Thermal Comfort and Energy Efficiency in Buildings: A State-of-the-Art and Future Directions." *Energy and Built Environment*, 5(5), 641–656. doi:10.1016/j.enbenv.2023.05.004

84 Souza, E. (2023, October 17). "How New Technologies Are Evolving to Embrace Sustainability in Architecture." *ArchDaily*, October 17. Available at: https://www.archdaily.com/991739/how-new-technologies-are-evolving-to-embrace-sustainability-in-architecture?ad_source=search&ad_medium=projects_tab&ad_source=search&ad_medium=search_result_all [accessed December 29, 2023].

85 Frearson, A. (2021, July 9). "Digital Twins Offer 'a compelling way of developing our cities' say Experts." Dezeen, July 9. Available at: https://www.dezeen.com/2021/07/09/digital-twins-develop-cities-digital-design-architecture/ [accessed December 29, 2023].

86 "What is a Digital Twin?" Markets and Markets. Available at: https://www.marketsandmarkets.com/Market-Reports/digital-twin-market-225269522.html [accessed December 29, 2023].

87 Iturralde, K., Pan, W., Linner, T., and Bock, T. (2022). "Automation and Robotic Technologies in the Construction Context: Research Experiences in Prefabricated Façade Modules," in *Rethinking Building Skins*. Amsterdam: Elsevier, pp. 475–493. doi:10.1016/b978-0-12-822477-9.00009-7

88 Casini, M. (2022). "Advanced Building Construction Methods," in *Construction 4.0*. Amsterdam: Elsevier, pp. 405–470. doi:10.1016/b978-0-12-821797-9.00006-4

89 Bock, T. and Linner, T. (2016). *Construction Robots: Elementary Technologies and Single-Task Construction Robots*. Cambridge: Cambridge University Press, pp. 50–77.

90 Hayward, P. (1993). "Situating Cyberspace: The Popularisation of Virtual Reality," in P. Hayward and T. Wollen (eds.), *Future Visions: New Technologies of the Screen*. Kiribati: BFI Publishing, pp. 180–204. See also Gibson, W. (1984). *Neuromancer*. London: Ace Books.

91 "Steampunk Pavilion." Fologram. Available at: https://docs.fologram.com/135ed9a4854149e38e7c89812cc7837e [accessed January 26, 2024].

92 "Examples." Fologram. See https://fologram.com/examples [accessed January 26, 2024].

93 "Projects." Gramazio Kohler Research. See https://gramaziokohler.arch.ethz.ch/web/e/projekte/371.html [accessed January 3, 2024].

94 Yuan, P. F. (2019, May 30). "Why Robotic Construction? / Philip F. Yuan for the Shenzhen Biennale (UABB) 2019." *ArchDaily*, May 30. Available at: https://www.archdaily.com/918077/why-robotic-construction-philip-f-yuan-for-the-shenzhen-biennale-uabb-2019?ad_source=search&ad_medium=projects_tab&ad_source=search&ad_medium=search_result_all

95 Turing, A. M. (1950). "I. Computing Machinery and Intelligence." *Mind, 59* (236), 433–460. doi:10.1093/mind/lix.236.433

96 "Artificial Intelligence (AI) Coined at Dartmouth." (n.d.). Dartmouth College. Available at: https://home.dartmouth.edu/about/artificial-intelligence-ai-coined-dartmouth [accessed January 4, 2024].

97 Chaillou, S. (2022). *Artificial Intelligence and Architecture: From Research to Practice*. Basel: Birkhäuser, pp. 16–17.

98 For more background on neural networks introduced from 1970–1990 see Goodfellow, I., Bengio, Y., and Courville, A. (2016). *Deep Learning*. Cambridge, MA: MIT Press. Available at: www.deeplearningbook.org

99 Chandrasekaran, R. (1997). "Kasparov Proves No Match for Computer." *Washington Post*, May 12. Available at: https://www.washingtonpost.com/wp-srv/tech/analysis/kasparov/kasparov.htm [accessed December 28, 2023].

100 "The Grand Challenge." DARPA. Available at: https://www.darpa.mil/about-us/timeline/-grand-challenge-for-autonomous-vehicles [accessed December 30, 2023].

101 "Spirit." NASA Science. See https://science.nasa.gov/mission/mer-spirit/ [accessed December 30, 2023].

102 "Opportunity." NASA Science. See https://science.nasa.gov/mission/mer-opportunity/ [accessed December 30, 2023].
103 DeBord, M. (2018, September 9). "Waymo Could be Worth as Much as $175 Billion — Here's a Brief History of the Google Car Project." *Business Insider*, September 9. Available at: https://www.businessinsider.com/google-car-project-history-2018-8
104 Deng, J., Dong, W., Socher, R., Li, L.-J., Li, K. and Fei-Fei, L. (2009, June). "ImageNet: A Large-scale Hierarchical Image Database." *2009 IEEE Conference on Computer Vision and Pattern Recognition*. doi:10.1109/cvpr.2009.5206848
105 Le, Q.V. (2013, May). "Building High-level Features using Large-scale Unsupervised Learning." *2013 IEEE International Conference on Acoustics, Speech, and Signal Processing*. doi:10.1109/icassp.2013.6639343
106 Giles, M. (2018, February 21). "The GANfather: The Man Who's Given Machines the Gift of Imagination." *MIT Technology Review*, February 21. Available at: https://www.technologyreview.com/2018/02/21/145289/the-ganfather-the-man-whos-given-machines-the-gift-of-imagination/
107 LeCun, Y., Bengio, Y., and Hinton, G. (2015). "Deep Learning." *Nature, 521* (7553), 436–444. doi:10.1038/nature14539
108 Leach, N. (2021). *Architecture in the Age of Artificial Intelligence: An Introduction to AI for Architects*. Bloomsbury Publishing, pp 17–18.
109 Ibid.
110 Borowiec, S. (2016, March 15). "AlphaGo Seals 4–1 Victory over Go Grandmaster Lee Sedol." *The Guardian*, March 15. Available at: https://www.theguardian.com/technology/2016/mar/15/googles-alphago-seals-4-1-victory-over-grandmaster-lee-sedol
111 Leach, N. (2021). *Architecture in the Age of Artificial Intelligence: An Introduction to AI for Architects*. London: Bloomsbury Publishing, pp. 55–56.
112 Manyika, J. and Bughin, J. (2019, October 14). "The Coming of AI Spring." McKinsey & Company, October 14. Available at: https://www.mckinsey.com/mgi/overview/in-the-news/the-coming-of-ai-spring
113 See Kurzweleil's prediction on singularity. Estimates now range from 2029 to 2045. More can also be found in Leach, N. (2021). *Architecture in the Age of Artificial Intelligence: An Introduction to AI for Architects*. London: Bloomsbury Publishing, pp. 165–166.
114 Ibid., p. 124. Maria Dantz in conversation with Neil Leach.
115 Gattupalli, A. (2022, December 10). "Post-Human Aesthetics in Architecture: In Conversation with Matias del Campo." *ArchDaily*, December 10. Available at: https://www.archdaily.com/989896/post-human-aesthetics-in-architecture-in-conversation-with-matias-del-campo. See also Progressive Architecture (2023). "AI Panel Talk – Matias del Campo and Daniel Koehler." *YouTube*. Available at: https://www.youtube.com/watch?v=iuwy5hm8duk. Here del Campo uses the term, not to suggest "after human" but to suggest a context where AI provides collaborative interaction via image production to formulate outcomes that is not otherwise possible without the use of imaginative prompting by humans.
116 Bernstein, P. (2022). *Machine Learning: Architecture in the Age of Artificial Intelligence*. Oxford: Routledge.
117 Leach, N. (2021). *Architecture in the Age of Artificial Intelligence: An Introduction to AI for Architects*. London: Bloomsbury Publishing.
118 Bernstein, P. (2022). *Machine Learning: Architecture in the Age of Artificial Intelligence*. Oxford: Routledge, pp. 10–11.
119 Ibid., pp. 47–48. Bernstein points out the AI assisted trajectory follows Anderson and Krathwohl's reworking of Bloom's Taxonomy. For more information on Anderson and Krathwohl's "Bloom's Digital Taxonomy" go to Revised Bloom's taxonomy, Iowa State University, Center for Excellence in Learning and

Teaching. Available at: https://www.celt.iastate.edu/instructional-strategies/effective-teaching-practices/revised-blooms-taxonomy [accessed January 8, 2024].

120 Bernstein, P., Greaves, M., McConnell, S., and Pearson, C. (2022). "Harnessing Artificial Intelligence to Design Healthy, Sustainable, and Equitable Places." *Computer, 55*(2), 67–71. doi:10.1109/mc.2021.3134422

121 del Campo, M., Carlson, A., and Manninger, S. (2020). "Towards Hallucinating Machines – Designing with Computational Vision." *International Journal of Architectural Computing, 19*(1), 88–103. doi:10.1177/1478077120963366

122 Zheng, H. and Ren, Y. (2020). "Architectural Layout Design Through Simulated Annealing Algorithm." *CAADRIA Proceedings*. doi:10.52842/conf.caadria.2020.1.275

123 Chaillou, S. (2020). "Space Layouts & GANs | GAN-Enabled Floor Plan Generation." *Towards Data Science*, January 13, 2020. Available at: https://towardsdatascience.com/space-layouts-gans-19861519a5e9

124 Finch 3D is a start-up from Oslo garnering widespread recognition for optimized and iterative floorplan layout tied to qualitative design impacts. See https://www.finch3d.com/

125 "Autodesk completes acquisition of Spacemaker, provider of AI and generative design-enabled urban design platform." Autodesk, Inc., November 24, 2020. See https://investors.autodesk.com/news-releases/news-release-details/autodesk-completes-acquisition-spacemaker-provider-ai-and [accessed January 3, 2024].

126 Leach, N. (2021). *Architecture in the Age of Artificial Intelligence: An Introduction to AI for Architects*. London: Bloomsbury Publishing, pp. 130–131.

127 Bernstein, P. (2022). *Machine Learning: Architecture in the Age of Artificial Intelligence*. Oxford: Routledge, pp. 124–130.

128 Chaillou, S. (2022). *Artificial Intelligence and Architecture: From Research to Practice*. Basel: Birkhäuser, pp. 136–145.

129 "Design, Technology, and the Team Between." Foster + Partners, July 3, 2023. Available at: https://www.fosterandpartners.com/insights/plus-journal/design-technology-and-the-team-between [accessed January 2, 2024].

130 Leach, N. (2021). *Architecture in the Age of Artificial Intelligence: An Introduction to AI for Architects*. London: Bloomsbury Publishing, pp. 108–110.

131 Schumacher, P. (2016). "Advancing Social Functionality via Agent-based Parametric Semiology." *Architectural Design, 86*(2), 108–113. doi:10.1002/ad.2031. See also Roibu, T. (2021, August 1). "Parametric Semiology: Creating Meaningful Architectural Spaces via Human Patterns of Behaviour." *Geometry Matters*, August 1. Available at: https://geometrymatters.com/parametric-semiology-creating-meaningful-architectural-spaces-via-human-patterns-of-behaviour/

132 Leach, N. (2021). *Architecture in the Age of Artificial Intelligence: An Introduction to AI for Architects*. London: Bloomsbury Publishing, p. 110.

133 Barker, N. (2023, April 26). "ZHA Developing 'most' Projects using AI-generated Images says Patrik Schumacher." *Dezeen*, April 26. Available at: https://www.dezeen.com/2023/04/26/zaha-hadid-architects-patrik-schumacher-ai-dalle-midjourney/

134 "The Architectural Beast, 2019." Frac Centre. See https://collections.frac-centre.fr/collection-art-architecture/diaz-alonso-hernan/the-architectural-beast-64.html?authID=200&ensembleID=2082 [accessed January 2, 2024].

135 "Architecture After AI." School of Architecture. See https://soa.utexas.edu/events/architecture-after-ai [accessed January 2, 2024].

136 Artificial Intelligence in Architecture (AI+A): Future of Architectural Practice – Calendar – AIA New York / Center for Architecture. (2023, November 28). https://calendar.aiany.org/2023/12/16/artificial-intelligence-in-architecture-aia-future-of-architectural-practice/

137 See AIARCHITECTS.ORG for additional detail and link to work.

138 Kohler, along with Rasa Navasaityte, co-founded Lab-eds in 2008 in addition to their academic positions. For additional information see https://lab-eds.org/. See

also Koehler, D. (2023). "More than Anything: Advocating for Synthetic Architectures within Large-scale Language-image Models." *International Journal of Architectural Computing, 21*(2), 242–255. doi:10.1177/14780771231170455

139 Galef, J. (2015, June 6). "Sam Altman Investing in 'AI Safety Research'." *Future of Life Institute*, June 6. Available at: https://futureoflife.org/ai/sam-altman-investing-in-ai-safety-research/?utm_source=Sailthru&utm_medium=email&utm_campaign=Future%20Perfect%205.24.23&utm_term=Future%20Perfect

140 Hao, K. (2019, January 25). "We Analyzed 16,625 Papers to Figure out Where AI is Headed Next." *MIT Technology Review*, January 25. Available at: https://www.technologyreview.com/2019/01/25/1436/we-analyzed-16625-papers-to-figure-out-where-ai-is-headed-next/

141 See https://medium.com/@Modelo/pioneers-in-computational-design-bb1c0f8a8234

LIST OF FIGURES

INDEX

Note: Page numbers in *italics* refer to figures.